Empire, Colonialism, and Famine

in the Nineteenth and Twentieth Centuries

Empire, Colonialism, and Famine

in the Nineteenth and Twentieth Centuries

edited by Bohdan Klid

KIYC CIUS

Canadian Institute of Ukrainian Studies Press
Edmonton 2022 Toronto

Canadian Institute of Ukrainian Studies Press
University of Alberta — University of Toronto
Edmonton, Alberta — Toronto, Ontario
Canada T6G 2H8 — Canada M5S 2C3

ISBN: 978-1-894865-66-1 (pbk.)

Library and Archives Canada Cataloguing in Publication

Title: Empire, colonialism, and famine in the nineteenth and twentieth centuries / edited by Bohdan Klid.
Names: Klid, Bohdan, editor.
Description: Essays based on two conferences organized by the Holodomor Research and Education Consortium held in Toronto in 2016 and in Kyiv in 2017. | Special issue of the East/West:
Journal of Ukrainian Studies. | Includes bibliographical references. | Some essays translated from the Ukrainian language.
Identifiers: Canadiana 20220181268 | ISBN 9781894865661 (softcover)
Subjects: LCSH: Famines—History—19th century—Congresses. | LCSH: Famines—History—20th century—Congresses. | LCSH: Imperialism—History—19th century—Congresses. | LCSH: Imperialism—History—20th century—Congresses. | LCGFT: Conference papers and proceedings.

Classification: LCC HV630 .E47 2022 | DDC 363.809/034—dc23

The Holodomor Research and Education Consortium (HREC) gratefully acknowledges the Temerty Foundation for its ongoing support of Holodomor studies, including the two conferences that inspired this volume.
The publication of this book has been generously supported by a subvention from the Ukrainian Studies Fund, Inc. A grant for this publication has also been provided by the Nestor Peczeniuk Memorial Endowment Fund at the Canadian Institute of Ukrainian Studies (CIUS), University of Alberta.

Printed in Canada

Table of Contents

Preface

The collection of essays in this volume stem from discussions between the late Mark von Hagen and Liudmyla Hrynevych on the imperial nature of Russian and Soviet rule in Ukraine and of Soviet Ukraine as a type of colony within the Soviet Union.[1] Mark, a historian whose research had focused on early Soviet military history, shifted his attention in the beginning of the 1990s to topics in Ukrainian history, and his interest in the Russian Empire and anti-imperial national movements in its colonial peripheries brought him to study the revolutionary period of 1917–1920 in Ukraine.[2] Familiar with Pavlo Khrystiuk's four-volume unfinished history,[3] Mark recognized that it contained sharp anti-colonial critiques of Russian imperial policies and Soviet Russia's policies and actions in Ukraine. After Ukraine had declared autonomy and then independence, the establishment of Bolshevik rule in Ukraine by force could be seen as an imperial conquest and the struggle of Ukrainians to establish and then regain their independence following occupation, as an anticolonial struggle.[4]

Liudmyla Hrynevych, one of Ukraine's leading scholars of the pre-famine and famine period of 1932–33, engaged in discussions with Mark on whether the policies and actions of the Kremlin leadership that caused and intensified famine conditions in Soviet Ukraine could be viewed within the context of an empire-colony relationship. Mark had by that time concluded

---

[1] During the course of editorial work on this volume, Liudmyla Hrynevych and I spoke often about her views, the literature on the Soviet Union as empire, and her conversations with Mark von Hagen.

[2] See Yaroslav Hrytsak's "Mark von Hagen: 'A Conscious Ukrainianist,'" *Ab Imperio*, 3 (2019): 233–42; and Andrii Portnov, "Mark von Hagen and Ukrainian Studies," Ibid.: 243–50.

[3] *Zamitky i materiialy do istorii ukrains'koi revoliutsii. 1917–1920 rr.* 4 volumes (Vienna: Ukrains'kyi sotsiolohichnyi instytut, 1921–22). Khrystiuk was a leading figure in the Ukrainian Social Revolutionary Party and held ministerial posts in Ukraine's newly independent governments of that turbulent period. Mark von Hagen's introduction to a forthcoming English translation of Khrystiuk's work was published recently in Ukrainian translation. See Mark von Hagen, "Peredmova do 'Zamitok I materiialiv do istorii ukrains'koi revoliutsii. 1917–1920 rr.' Pavla Khrystiuka," *Ukraina Moderna*, vol. 29 (2020): 70–121. See also Frank Sysyn's "Pavlo Khrystiuk i pereosmyslennia ioho robit u doslidzhenniakh Marka fon Hagena," Ibid.: 61-69.

[4] See his "Wartime Occupation and Peacetime Alien Rule: "Notes and Materials" toward a(n) (Anti-) (Post-) Colonial History of Ukraine," *Harvard Ukrainian Studies*, vol. 34, no. 1–4 (2015–2016): 153–94; and "Pavlo Khrystiuk's History and the Politics of Ukrainian Anti-Colonialism," in Iaroslav Mel'nyk, et al., ed., *Ukraina na istoriohrafichnii mapi mizhvoiennoi Ievropy: Materialy mizhnarodnoi naukovoi konferentsii (Miunkhen, Nimechchyna, 1-3 lypnia 2012 r.)[Ukraine on the Historiographic Map of Interwar Europe: Proceedings of the International Conference (Munich, Germany, 1-3 July, 2012)]* (Kyiv: Instytut Istorii Ukrainy NAN Ukrainy, 2014): 15–37.

that the Holodomor could be categorized as a type of colonial famine.[5] Liudmyla had similarly concluded that an empire-colony relationship explained in part the much lesser-known famine of 1928–29 and that this framework could be applied fruitfully to the study of the Holodomor.[6]

The discussions led to the organization of two conferences, organized by the Holodomor Research and Education Consortium, that examined the connection between empire building, imperial rule and famine, allowing the Ukrainian case to be compared with other instances of famines that had occurred in colonies or imperial states. The conferences took place in 2016 in Toronto (https://holodomor.ca/communism-and-hunger-the-ukrainian-chinese-kazakh-and-soviet-famines-in-comparative-perspective/) and in 2017 in Kyiv (https://www.holodomor-hrec.com/downloads/programe%20imperii%20all.indd.pdf). Papers based on the presentations are found in this volume.

Although Mark von Hagen attended the two conferences, his illness did not allow him to take part in the editorial work. The preparation of this volume required input, advice and assistance from several colleagues who merit acknowledgement and gratitude. Liudmyla Hrynevych took part in the planning and editorial work on the Ukrainian-language text co-written by Oleksandr Lysenko, Tetiana Zabolotna and Oleksandr Maievs'kyi. Mark Baker did most of the early editorial work and made suggestions on content. He also translated the article co-written by Lysenko, Zabolotna and Maievs'kyi. The essay by Liudmyla Hrynevych was translated by Andrew Sorokowski. Others who participated in the editorial work include Marta Baziuk, Oksana Vynnyk and the late Andrij Makuch. Journal editor Svitlana Krys oversaw final editorial preparation of the articles for a special issue of the online *East/West: Journal of Ukrainian Studies* (https://ewjus.com/index.php/ewjus/issue/view/19), which appeared in early 2021. I wish to thank her for her efforts and for permission to publish the essays as a book. I also wish to thank Oksana Vynnyk for preparing the index.

I am extremely grateful to all of my colleagues for their contributions, comments and advice in preparing this volume, and to the Temerty Foundation, which has generously supported the work of HREC since its inception.

Bohdan Klid

---

[5] "Wartime Occupation and Peacetime Alien Rule," 172–75.

[6] See her pioneering work *Holod 1928–1929 rr. u radians'kii Ukraini* (Kyiv: Instytut istorii Ukrainy NANU, 2013). Hrynevych treats the 1928-29 and 1932–33 famines in Ukraine as colonial famines in her essay in this volume.

Empire-Building, Imperial Policies, and Famine in Occupied Territories and Colonies

Bohdan Klid
University of Alberta

Abstract: The introductory article to the volume "Empire, Colonialism, and Famine in the Nineteenth and Twentieth Centuries" begins by pointing to some recent literature on famine theory, where stress has been made on responses of authorities to famine and on the political nature of modern famines. Literature on the connection between imperial policies, colonial rule, and famine is also briefly discussed. The Soviet Union is treated as an empire in the essay, and some of the literature on this question is also surveyed. The article then offers summaries of and highlights from essays in this volume that resulted from papers presented at two conferences on the theme "Empires and Famines in Comparative Historical Perspective," held in 2016 in Toronto and in 2017 in Kyiv. These include papers on famine and food policies during World War II in occupied Ukraine and Moldova. Essays on famines in Soviet Ukraine, British-ruled Ireland, and British-ruled Bengal, India, are summarized as well as an essay on Raphaël Lemkin's views on genocide and famine and an essay that looked at minorities in Mao's China during the 1958-62 famine. The essay concludes with the observation that the investigation of imperial policies, colonial rule, and famine should be pursued further, especially in the case of the Soviet Union where this line of research is just beginning.

Keywords: Soviet Union, famine, Ukraine, empire, imperialism, colonialism, genocide, India, Ireland, China.

Droughts and other natural disasters have led and can lead to serious food shortages. However, as Amartya Sen stressed in his ground-breaking study *Poverty and Famines*, declines in food availability need not result in starvation. When mass deaths occur, it nearly always involves decisions about distribution of food supplies and whether food is made accessible to those who need it.[1]

Sen in a later study argued that famines have not occurred in independent, democratic countries, suggesting a link between the existence of political liberties and civil rights and the absence of famine. Conversely, famines and mass starvation have occurred in countries where citizens

[1] In *Poverty and Famines,* Sen elaborates on the "entitlement approach" to understanding why famines occur. This work ushered in a new famine literature that has stressed the political nature of modern-era famines. For an overview of this literature, see Devereux, "Introduction"; and Edkins. In a recent study Alex de Waal concludes that modern famines are linked to political decisions or political failings.

lacked these rights (see *Development As Freedom* 151-52, 178-88).[2] It follows, therefore, that famines occurring in states where basic human rights are suppressed or absent can be seen as drawn-out forms of political violence that deprive people of the fundamental human right to life.[3]

Sen also pointed to a link between famine and colonial rule. Commenting on the Irish famines of the 1840s, he highlighted the "cultural alienation" in British-ruled Ireland, even though it was a part of the UK and had not been governed as a colony since 1800. Sen suggested that the political commitment to prevent starvation in England did not apply to Ireland. In the case of the 1943 Bengal famine in British-ruled India, which Sen himself survived, British convictions of cultural superiority dovetailed with an asymmetrical political power relationship (*Development As Freedom* 170-75).

In his path-breaking study, Mike Davis elaborates on the "political ecology of famine," making connections between British imperial rule—during which capitalist development was transforming the economies of its colonial realms—and the deaths of millions of non-European peasants from hunger in the process of incorporation into the British and world economy. Building on insights from Karl Polanyi's *The Great Transformation*, Davis addresses famines in India, China, and Africa, but also sees early parallels in the Irish famine of the 1840s, placing it in the context of Thomas Malthus's ideas, which were exploited to justify constraints to famine relief in India as well (9-10, 15-16, 32, 46, 306). The economist Stephen Devereux attributes some famines in the first part of the twentieth century to "synergies between drought and British/French colonial policies in West Africa, and German suppression of local uprisings in Tanzania" (*Famine in the Twentieth Century* 23). Alex de Waal, in his examination of the link between European colonialism and famines, uses the label "conquest famines," relying in part on Davis's study (53; see also 54, 67-73). Cormac Ó Gráda cautions, however, against an automatic linkage of colonialism and famine. In his view, the famines in nineteenth century British-ruled Ireland and India were attributable more to "the failure of the authorities of the day" than to colonial rule; he asserts that colonial authorities helped keep India free of famine in the early twentieth century up to the Bengal famine of 1943-44 (Ó Gráda 19-20).

Recent scholarship on famines has thus focused attention not only on the policies and actions of governments that lead to famines, but also on

---

[2] For a discussion of Sen's assertion that famines do not take place in democratic countries, see de Waal's chapter "Politics, War, Genocide," esp. pp. 94-99, in his *Mass Starvation*.

[3] The topics of right to food as a basic human right, the denial of food to people by states, and state policies that cause hunger, are discussed in Howard-Hassmann.

their responses or failures to respond adequately to famine conditions, including in overseas colonies or peripheral regions (internal colonies) of empires. Some governments have not only exhibited little will to prevent mass starvation but have sought to achieve political goals by manipulating food production and distribution of food supplies, sometimes as a weapon or means of controlling and/or exterminating social classes and disloyal groups.

Imperial famines include instances where imperial rule or colonial governance, featuring the vertical hierarchy of metropolis and colony, leads to the sacrifice of lives at the peripheries for the supposed greater good of the empire or to support an imperial or empire-building project. Such cases are most evident during times of war in the policies and treatment of peoples under military occupation. However, famines have also occurred in times of peace, as in the cases of the Soviet Union and, later China, when the imperial centre used its coercive powers to overturn and remake the social and economic order. In the case of the Soviet Union, the famines of the early 1930s were most severe and deadly in peripheral regions, such as Ukraine and Kazakhstan, which were populated largely by national minorities.

To explore the role of empires and colonial rule in famines, the Holodomor Research and Education Consortium at the Canadian Institute of Ukrainian Studies, University of Alberta, organized two conferences on the theme "Empire, Colonialism and Famine in Comparative Historical Perspective," in 2016 in Toronto and in 2017 in Kyiv. Several papers focused on famine and food policies during World War II, as empire-building, colonization, and colonial rule have often been triggered by, accompanied, or followed wars of conquest, where food policies tied to war efforts have led to famine. Notably, scholarship on Nazi Germany and its hunger policies in Eastern Europe, including the siege of Leningrad and the starvation of Soviet prisoners of war, and the centrality of Ukraine in securing food and as a territory for colonization, have been studied in the context of imperialism and empire-building (see, for instance, Mazower; Snyder, *Black Earth* and *Bloodlands*).[4] The connection between the quest for food security and empire-building during World War II was also the focus of the compelling study by Lizzie (Elizabeth) Collingham.

Three of the nine articles in this volume examine the food policies of Nazi Germany and its wartime ally Romania in occupied territories during World War II that are today part of Ukraine, Moldova, and Poland. While the

[4] Snyder emphasized the centrality of Ukraine and the enslavement of Ukrainians in Hitler's war plans in a speech before a gathering of Germany's Bundestag on 20 June 2017 ("Germany's Historical Responsibility for Ukraine"). See also the chapter "Nazi Colonialism and Ukraine," in Lower (32-41).

outbreak of diseases, food shortages, and even famine often are triggered during wars, these two occupying powers through their policies deliberately caused starvation in their occupied territories. The primary victims were the minority populations of Roma and Jews, most of whom were massacred during the Holocaust.[5]

In his essay, Kiril Feferman gives an overview of Nazi food policies toward Jews on Polish and Soviet territories occupied by German forces. He asserts that the policies reflected the approaches of both the ideologists, who were apt to support the quick elimination of Jews, and those who advocated a more pragmatic approach. While during World War II it quickly became clear that the Nazis aimed to destroy the Jews in German-occupied territories, the pragmatists hoped to utilize them for forced labour to aid the German war effort, which meant that Jews needed to be fed enough to enable them to work. In occupied Poland, Jews were forced into ghettos where they were subject to the vagaries of policies between pragmatists and ideologists. Overall, the rations allotted Polish Jews were roughly equal to the starvation-level rations allocated for POWs. The major goal of Jews then became to secure enough food to subsist. The search for food spawned widespread smuggling activities, carried out largely by children, which placed smugglers in danger of punishment, including execution. The struggle to obtain scarce food at elevated prices intensified competition, which led to denunciations to ghetto authorities or the Gestapo. (The topic of competition for survival is also discussed in Douglas Irvin-Erickson's essay in this volume.)

Paul Shapiro examines the treatment of Jews and Roma by Romanian authorities in occupied Bessarabia and Transnistria during World War II, and in particular, food policies toward these two minorities. Overall, there were similarities in food policies and in the treatment of Jews and Roma by Nazi German and Romanian authorities in occupied territories. It is widely known that agricultural products from German-occupied Ukraine were sent to Germany. Food products were also taken from territories occupied by Romanian troops such as Transnistria and sent to Romania, even while Romania, a subordinate ally of Nazi Germany, was sending its agricultural products to Nazi Germany. The treatment of Jews was especially inhumane, brutal, and deadly, and derived from the aim of the Romanian government to cleanse its territory of Jews to achieve ethnic purity.

With the advance of Romanian forces into Bessarabia—the province annexed from Romania one year earlier by the Soviet Union—massacres, killings, and executions of Jews began, which were similar to acts committed

[5] For a collection of essays on the Holocaust in Ukraine, see Brandon and Lower.

by German killing units upon entering Soviet Ukrainian territories. Similarly, Jews and Roma were deported and forced into ghettos and camps administered by authorities of both wartime allies. Many Jews and Roma were doomed to die of starvation or diseases related to malnutrition because the authorities who controlled food supplies established a hierarchy of consumption, where the needs of the people in Romania and in the occupied lands took precedence over those of Jews and Roma.

Shapiro describes the treatment of Jews and Roma, who were rounded up into ghettos and then forced to march to camps. Jews already suffered from hunger and disease in the transit camps and ghettos before they were compelled to leave Bessarabia for Transnistria in forced marches. When reaching Transnistria, Jews and Roma also faced food shortages and hunger, as Romanian authorities exported food from Transnistria to Romania and also prioritized feeding the local population. The policies of occupation authorities to isolate the Jews and Roma, prevent their access to local markets, punish those who tried to go there, and prevent local inhabitants from bringing food to them intensified famine conditions. As the goal of Romanian authorities was to eliminate and reduce the presence of Jews and Roma, starvation of the two groups constituted acceptable state policy. The result was that most Jews and Roma under Romanian occupation died in Bessarabia and Transnistria. According to Shapiro, about 280,000 to 380,000 Jews died, as did nearly half of the 25,000 Roma deported by Romanian authorities from Romania proper and Bessarabia east to Transnistria and Ukraine.

Finally, the article, co-authored by Oleksandr Lysenko, Oleksandr Maievs'kyi, and Tetiana Zabolotna,[6] demonstrates that the war created conditions for using famine as an instrument in achieving Nazi Germany's strategic goals in the eastern territories, one of which was to colonize Ukraine with German settlers.[7] The population under occupation, largely Ukrainians, was to be subjected eventually to either resettlement or elimination. German government policy makers at the highest levels who authorized excessive food procurements, primarily for consumption in Germany and in German-occupied western Europe, knew that these policies would create famine conditions in the east that could lead to the deaths of millions. German military leaders who took part in organizing and directing

[6] This essay is a translation of a previously published article in Ukrainian, which is–an expanded and revised version of a presentation made at the 2017 Kyiv conference by Oleksandr Lysenko.

[7] Timothy Snyder discusses Hitler's plans for colonizing Soviet Ukraine and food policies in occupied Reichskommissariat Ukraine in his monographs *Black Earth* and *Bloodlands*. Karel C. Berkhoff also devotes a chapter to the German policy of starvation in Ukraine's capital city (164-86).

food requisitioning and its export were also aware that these policies would cause hunger. Lysenko and others stress that Nazi food policies were aimed at attaining a reliable source of food supply for Germany and depopulating the eastern territories to allow for German colonization. These policies had a contradictory outcome, as Germany's need for food resources created shortages in the occupied territories, which sapped the morale and physical strength of its inhabitants, who were needed to produce the food. Eventually, Germany's food policies undermined its overall goals while causing enormous demographic losses among the inhabitants of the occupied territories.

Famine in German- and Romanian-occupied Ukraine during World War II was the direct result of the policies of occupation authorities. British India was not occupied by any of the Axis powers, but also was affected by famine. It was not, however, deliberately caused by British colonial authorities. Rather, Janam Mukherjee's essay argues that the outbreak of food shortages in Bengal in World War II stemmed basically from wartime conditions, while the failure to prevent mass starvation was linked more to policy failures in British-ruled India in 1943. When Great Britain declared war on Germany in September 1939, its colonial possessions were also drawn into the conflict. The British reverted to direct rule in India, as there was little or no support for the war effort among the Indian populace, and the main political force of the Indian subcontinent, the Indian National Congress, opposed it. The war, therefore, created conditions for the rise of authoritarian rule and provided justification for the confiscation and requisitioning of rice, which created chaos in the rice market and galloping inflation. Colonial officials failed to address adequately the critical food situation that ensued, which affected mostly the poor. Mukherjee notes that as the starvation of the poor was not a threat to the colonial regime or the war effort, it could be ignored by colonial officials.

In the second part of his paper Mukherjee looks at the political and economic effects of wartime developments in the colonial realm and the lingering effects of the famine in Bengal and, more widely, Indian society. Examining the political power relationships within the indigenous population, he notes that both Hindu and Muslim-led political forces referred to the famine and famine relief in their political power struggles. Although the Calcutta post-war riots of 1946 featured intense Hindu-Muslim violence that presaged events that would take place during the partition of the subcontinent, Mukherjee submits that these should not be seen as a direct consequence of the 1943 famine but viewed in a wider context of chronic, long-term, multi-generational poverty compounded by the war and the catastrophic famine.

State leaders, including of imperial states, have sought to minimize or deny culpability and suppress information related to famines they have induced, allowed to occur, or failed to alleviate. The decision of Winston Churchill's wartime British government not to send famine relief to India on "strategic grounds" helped seal the fates of 1.5 to 4 million people in Bengal—largely the poor—who died of famine and famine-related diseases in 1943. The authorities banned the first book to depict the tragedy, *Hungry Bengal*, in 1944, and five thousand copies were seized and destroyed (Collingham 141-54). An earlier determination to suppress information about a state-induced famine was Stalin's regime ban on mention of its man-made famines that led to some eight million deaths in the USSR in the early 1930s—almost four million in Soviet Ukraine alone—a taboo that remained in place until the late 1980s.

Imperial and colonial governments have justified and understated the horrific results of their policies. Soviet collectivization policies and the famines that accompanied, followed, or were linked to them can be understood as deriving from an imperial view that large parts of humanity are expendable in the building of a modern, industrial, militarily more powerful and greater imperial state and civilization. Soviet collectivization, which can be seen as constituting part of a great transformation of Soviet society of the 1930s, has been depicted as a war against the peasantry, resembling a military occupation conducted by militarized Communist Party members and reinforced and supported by Red Army soldiers and internal security service (OGPU) troops (Tarkhova; Romano and Tarkhova).[8]

The devastating famine that ravaged Soviet Ukraine in 1932-33, subsequently known as the Holodomor, has been studied and compared recently with other contemporary or nearly simultaneous famines that occurred in other parts of the Soviet Union, including in Soviet Kazakhstan, as well as with the 1958-62 famine in China, and with other state-induced famines in communist-ruled countries (see, for instance, Graziosi and Sysyn).[9] It seems that further study and comparison of the Holodomor (and

---

[8] See also Andrea Graziosi's *The Great Soviet Peasant War*, who argues that Bolshevik policies toward the peasantry amounted to the "Thirty Years War" of the twentieth century. This long essay, a revised version of a 1996 article, is published in his *Stalinism, Collectivization and the Great Famine*, pp. 5-64.

[9] For discussions on the Holodomor and the other Soviet famines that appeared in the wake of the publication of Anne Applebaum's *Red Famine*, see especially the comments by the two experts on the Kazakh famine, Niccolò Pianciola and Sarah Cameron. See also Rhoda E. Howard-Hassman's comparison of communist famines.

other Soviet famines, especially the Kazakh) with famines referred to as colonial or that took place in colonial-administered lands is needed.[10]

The Soviet state, established following the collapse of the tsarist-ruled Russian Empire in 1917, succeeded in reassembling most of its territories and nationalities, but its foundational, unifying principles were now based on communist ideology and the promotion of communist ideas, as well as on a contradictory anti-imperial platform that emphasized internationalism and promised to satisfy within one state the strivings of the non-Russian nations and peoples for autonomy and national cultural development. This multi-national state of formally sovereign national republics and lower-level national- or ethnic-based administrative units was structured as a federation, making it unique among empires, and not immediately or easily recognizable as one.

Unlike federal states, however, where subjects of the federation retain certain powers or share powers with the central government, in the Soviet Union, republic-level governments and branches of the Bolshevik party were subject to highly centralized control from the leadership of the Bolshevik Party (later Communist Party of the Soviet Union) based in the Kremlin, in Moscow, located in the Russian heartland. Centralization was facilitated when the Bolshevik party leadership began eliminating all opposition political parties and established a dictatorship soon after taking power. Although allowing for some autonomy in the 1920s, especially in national cultural development in the non-Russian republics, the units subordinate to the centre became subject to increasing centralization from the metropole that made the inequality of the centre-subcentre relationship even greater and more evident.[11]

In Ukraine, where important cultural and political figures were already being repressed or eliminated in the 1920s, repressions became wider in scope and intensity by the 1930s, when national communists were also targeted.[12] Nationality-based repressions and even ethnic cleansing were

---

[10] Niccolò Pianciola writes that "the more sources I read in archives in Kazakhstan and Russia, the more a strong central agency in the mass deaths of Kazakhs becomes apparent," pointing out that while Kazakhs were starving, meat from their livestock was being sent to Moscow, Leningrad, and other industrial centres, and livestock from Kazakh herds was being sent to collective farms outside Kazakhstan ("Ukraine and Kazakhstan" 442-43). See also his "Stalinskaia 'ierarkhiia potrebleniia.'"

[11] Valerii Vasyl'iev addresses the centre-subcentre political relationship between the central Soviet and Ukrainian leadership in *Politychne kerivnytstvo URSR i SRSR*.

[12] In the 1920s there were still significant numbers of both anti-communist intellectuals in Soviet Ukraine and supporters of national communism within the Ukrainian branch of the Bolshevik party, exemplified by such figures as Oleksandr Shums'kyi and Mykola Skrypnyk, who were critical of centralized control from Moscow. In 1928, the economist Mykhailo Volobuiev wrote that Ukraine had been a colony in imperial Russia and denounced the

being normalized by the middle of the 1930s (Martin 311-343). In the late 1920s and early 1930s, Stalin also succeeded in consolidating control over the Bolshevik party. Even more power was becoming concentrated in its small decision-making body, the politburo, controlled by Stalin. By the middle of the 1930s, Kremlin authorities were strongly promoting Russian imperial history, Russian culture and language use, and more generally, Russo-centric propaganda. Thus, the Soviet state, while still retaining its form as a federation, was becoming more closely associated with the core Russian nationality, elevating and promoting it (see Brandenberger; Barghoorn).

While the Soviet Union was generally viewed as an empire by scholars who treated the Soviet Union as a totalitarian state, in the last years of its existence and then following the collapse of the USSR a new literature on the USSR as empire appeared. Some of the scholars associated with this emerging trend deliberately distinguished themselves from the so-called totalitarian school (Motyl 3). This more recent historiography, in which the building of a new type of imperial, multi-national state was viewed by some of the scholars with a degree of favour—at least the Soviet state of the 1920s—warrants comparison with earlier treatments of the USSR as a totalitarian state.[13]

Soviet Ukraine was the most populous non-Russian republic in the USSR, known for its rich agricultural farmland and as its most important grain-producing region. Yet Ukraine suffered through several famines during the period it was part of the Soviet Union, three of them catastrophic: in 1921-23, 1928-29, 1932-33, and 1946-47.[14] It was also

---

Kremlin's economic policies in the Soviet era as continuing the colonial policies of the past. Mass arrests and a show trial of anti-communist intellectuals took place in 1929-30, while the national communists were purged and eliminated starting in 1932. On national communism in Ukraine, see Mace.

[13] For examples of the newer historiography, see Kivelson and Suny (especially the introductory chapter, "Thinking about Empire," which discusses the term "empire" and Russia's imperial forms); and Martin. Martin even coined the term "affirmative action empire" to denote an empire that promoted in the 1920s the national cultural development of its minorities. Hirsch, however, in her study, cautions against idealizing Soviet affirmative action policies of the 1920s, and sees not a retreat from but rather continuity in Soviet policies from the 1920s to the 1930s (see 9, incl. fn. 21). Of the more recent literature, Andreas Kappeler stresses imperial continuity, viewing the breakup of the Soviet Union as falling within the process of the breakup of European empires. For some examples of earlier literature see, for instance, Conquest's *The Last Empire: Nationality and the Soviet Future*, and his earlier *The Last Empire*. See also Kolarz's *Communism and Colonialism*, and his earlier *Russia and Her Colonies*; and Pipes.

[14] The famine of 1921-23 affected both Russian (the Volga region) and Ukrainian territories (the south). Grain from Ukraine was exported to Russia primarily to feed the hungry in Russia's Volga region, even though Ukraine was also suffering from famine (see Serbyn). Serbyn concluded that although Ukraine was formally a sovereign state, its Bolshevik

subject to famine-inducing policies under Nazi Germany's occupation. De Waal, commenting on Ukraine as an epicentre of major European famines in the twentieth century, noted that because of its soil fertility, Ukraine's grain served as "the foundation of land empires. That was its curse: the wheat fields were coveted by rulers from both east and west" (75).

However, famines that occurred in Ukraine under Soviet rule, in particular the devastating famine of 1932-33, have not been analyzed closely in the context of imperialism and colonial rule.[15] Such an approach is warranted. With the adoption of the first Five-Year Plan, central authorities in Moscow assumed greater control over Ukraine's economy during which the republic was treated as an economic colony to subsidize development in other parts of the Soviet Union. About one third of the capital formed in Ukraine during the period was exported, which constituted an unsustainably high 15% of national income. Much of this revenue came from Ukraine's agricultural sector (Krawchenko 116-17; Melnyk, *Soviet Capital Formation* 107-08; and his more recent "Ukraine Within the USSR" 122-24). Ukraine was also subjected to direct rule by the Kremlin beginning in late 1932-early 1933, which was the period when famine conditions were most intense. This occurred at the same time that the Kremlin was reinforcing its grain collection efforts to force the republic's producers to meet the country's assigned quota. Ukraine can thus be seen as being

government "behaved like agents of Moscow's colonial rule and exploitation of Ukraine" (183). The largely unknown 1928-29 famine is the topic of a recent study by Hrynevych who stresses that Soviet authorities were conducting grain requisitions in Ukraine during a period of severe food shortages and famine. The famine of 1932-1933 in Ukraine—known as the Holodomor—is the topic of many studies. For a recent treatment by an award-winning journalist, see Applebaum. For a summary work in English by a leading Ukrainian expert on the Holodomor, see Kulchytsky, *The Famine of 1932-1933*. For a treatment of the pan-Soviet famines of 1931-33, including the famine in Ukraine, see Davies and Wheatcroft. The 1946-47 famine has not been as thoroughly studied as the Soviet famines of 1931-33. Ganson concludes that the Soviet leadership could have prevented a mass famine but for political reasons did not do (114-15, 146). See also Ellman who posits that the excess deaths of an estimated one to 1.5 million people could have been prevented. Wheatcroft is less critical of the regime, arguing that the famine of 1946-47 conformed to other Soviet famines that followed droughts and sharp drops in grain production after years of food shortages (987 and 1004-05). The late Oleksandra Veselova was Ukraine's leading expert on this famine. She argued that the Soviet state was responsible for the famine through obligatory grain deliveries, depriving people of the means for survival (see "Famine in Ukraine" esp. 196, and "Henotsyd Holodomorom 1946-1947 rokiv v Ukraini"). Veselova points to the dependent, colonial status of Ukraine's government and its officials who obediently followed the centre's directives on grain collections during drought conditions and falling agricultural output. In Russian, the major study is by Zima, who faults the regime for its inhumane policy of holding grain in reserve during the famine.

[15] The diaspora historian Dmytro Solovei wrote a short study examining the 1921-22 and 1932-33 famines. Despite its title's suggestion, this long essay does not examine the question of Ukraine as a colony or the nature of colonial rule in Ukraine.

treated somewhat similarly to an overseas colony when colonial officials failed to carry out central directives effectively in ensuring the profitable exploitation of the colonies, or were regarded as untrustworthy, and even of being disloyal.[16] In addition to making key changes in the republic's top leadership, central authorities organized thoroughgoing purges of lower-ranking officials that led to the replacement of 70 percent of district-level Communist Party secretaries and more than half of all collective farm chairmen (Vasyl'iev 286-87).

Grain procurement quotas and agricultural polices imposed on Ukraine thus deserve careful study in the context of colonial-type exploitation (examined by Liudmyla Hrynevych in her essay focusing on the late 1920s), and in comparison with other regions of the USSR. The percentage of grain procured from Ukraine compared to all the other regions of the USSR, for instance, was raised from 29 percent in 1926-27 to 38.3 percent in 1927-28 (Slyn'ko 75). It should be noted that the percentage of grain procured by the centre from Ukraine's harvests was also very high, especially in 1931, when at least 41.3 percent of the harvest was taken. This was considerably higher than the average of 32 percent for all major regions of the USSR.[17] Russian historian N. A. Ivnitskii calculated that Ukraine's 1931 grain collection quota, including the milling fee, constituted 50 percent of the biological harvest estimate. He concluded that this created a "catastrophic situation for Ukraine" (Ivnitskii 128-29). Another Russian historian, Sergei Nefedov, estimated that 58 percent of the grain harvested at collective farms in Ukraine was taken to meet the 1931 quota (Ellman and Nefedov 1059).

In her essay, Liudmyla Hrynevych proposes that application of theoretical models of dependency and imperialism can explain important

---

[16] Vasyl'iev discusses in detail the institution of direct rule, the figures installed or sent to Ukraine to carry out the Kremlin's directives, and the subordination to the Kremlin of Ukraine's leadership in the context of the relations between Ukrainian leaders and Kremlin authorities during the unfolding famine crisis (252-91; 283-84).

[17] Other major grain-producing regions of the USSR had large percentages of their harvests procured, but nor as large as Ukraine's. These include the northern Caucasus (34.2%), Lower Volga (41%), Central Volga (38.6%), and Kazakh ASSR (39.5%) (Kondrashin 144-45). Ukrainian scholars have pointed to Ukraine's heavy grain quotas in comparison with other regions of the USSR. See, for instance, Kulchytsky's discussion of the 1930 and 1931 grain quotas, and the politics and consequences, especially peasant disturbances, linked to these (*The Famine of 1932-1933* 41-48, esp. 47-48). See also the chart showing the amount of grain taken from Ukraine and other grain-producing regions of the USSR from the 1930 and 1931 harvests, and the grain quotas established for 1932 (Kul'chyts'kyi, *Stalins'kyi "sokrushitel'nyi" udar 1932–1933* 209-10). Kulchytsky emphasizes that the amount of grain taken from Ukraine's 1930 harvest exceeded the total taken from all of the USSR's other major grain-producing regions combined. This had never occurred earlier—neither before the revolution nor during the NEP years.

aspects of Communist Party leader Joseph Stalin's faminogenic[18] policies in the Soviet Union. While Stalin's "revolution from above" in the late 1920s-early 1930s resulted in food shortages throughout and deadly famines in various regions of the USSR, Hrynevych maintains that the imposition of this "communist experiment" was intensified in Ukraine and other territories of the USSR by the top-down relations of the centre (the Kremlin, in Moscow) to the peripheral regions like Ukraine (with its capital then in Kharkiv). This top-down relationship featured the use of political domination and control over economic resources in ways that were injurious to the peripheral regions, especially Ukraine. These factors, Hrynevych suggests, led to mass deaths through famine.

In buttressing her thesis, Hrynevych points to decisions of the Kremlin leadership in the late 1920s, in conjunction with the adoption of the first Five-Year Plan. These choices intensified Ukraine's specialization as a granary of the USSR, placing unrealistic expectations on future grain production goals. Ukraine was saddled with the task of supplying grain-deficit regions and cities of the USSR as well as produce for export. Hrynevych stresses the importance of the decision in 1928 to dissolve the Ukraine-based trust Ukrkhlib (Ukrainian Bread) and its takeover by Soiuzkhleb (Union Bread) based in Moscow, a move that gave the centre full control over grain collections, exports, and distribution. The economic planning decisions made in the metropole led to the charge in 1928 by the young Ukrainian economist Mykhailo Volobuiev that the centre was continuing the exploitative colonial practices of the past when Ukraine had been a colony of the Russian Empire.

Hrynevych then examines grain collection and distribution policies and actions taken by or authorized by Kremlin authorities and their administrators in Ukraine on the eve of and during the little-known 1928-29 famine in Ukraine. With drought conditions pointing toward a failing harvest, the Kremlin sent its envoy Anastas Mikoian to Ukraine, who insisted that the republic rely on its own resources to feed its population. Hrynevych argues that the aid authorized by the Kremlin after famine struck should be seen as a typically imperial practice given that the exploitation of the republic continued as the Kremlin cut Ukraine's budget during the crisis. The centre also insisted that Ukraine continue making payments to the state grain fund until early 1929, and grain continued to be procured from the republic despite the harvest failure. Hrynevych suggests

[18] David Marcus coined the term "faminogenic" to describe state policies and activities that create famine conditions or that support their creation, and proposed establishing four levels of criminal responsibility for states that cause famines or fail to respond promptly and effectively in alleviating food shortages and famine conditions (245n9).

that the food aid given Ukraine in 1933 during the peak of the 1932-33 famine should be seen in the same way, as the assistance represented only a partial return of grain that had been requisitioned earlier.

The Ukrainian famine of 1932-33 (Holodomor) has been compared to the Irish Great Famine (Gorta Mór) of the 1840s (see Noack et al., *Holodomor and Gorta Mór*; Curran et al.).[19] A comparison of the histories of the Irish and Ukrainian peoples shows parallels in the modern period. Both were subordinate political units of imperial states that suffered through horrific famines prior to achieving independence. Although Ireland and Ukraine were integrated into imperial political structures, with Ukraine having, formally, attributes of statehood as a republic, the two units were dependent on decisions made in the metropole. Moreover, mass starvation and the deaths of millions occurred in regions where the overwhelming majority of the population was ethnically different from those living in or near the imperial centre.

In both countries the famines have been enshrined in their national narratives and feature in national identity formation and the politics of collective memory.[20] The editors of a collection of essays on the Irish and Ukrainians famines stressed "the centrality of [the] two famines for the development of modern Ireland and modern Ukraine" while noting that historians of empire have tended not to pay much attention to the historical parallels (Noack et al., "Introduction" 1).

Michael Hechter in his essay does compare the two famines in the context of internal colonialism and alien rule. In the 1970s, he authored a seminal study on the extension of control over the Celtic fringe, which was culturally distinct from the core territories of Great Britain, and discussed how this influenced regional economic development of the Celtic lands (Hechter, *Internal Colonialism*). Applying views developed in this book and in his latest study (*Alien Rule*), Hechter notes in his article that both Ukraine and Ireland were dependent peripheral regions in imperial states that were subjected to alien rule. While integrated politically into metropolitan state structures, the experiences of Ukraine and Ireland also mirrored in part those of European overseas colonies. For many Western European countries, Hechter observes, state building entailed internal colonialism, where the lack of political sovereignty of internal colonies placed limits on their economic welfare and threatened their cultural integrity.

In comparing the Irish and Ukrainian famines, Hechter notes the policy in both the UK and the USSR of continued export of agricultural goods. As

---

[19] The volume edited by Curran et al. also examines the Finnish famine of the 1860s.

[20] For an example of similar cultural engagement with famine memory in Ireland and Ukraine, see Holt and Mahoney.

native leaders would be more likely to respond to grievances from subjects close to home, Hechter posits that had Ireland and Ukraine been self-governing, their political leaders may have taken decisive steps to relieve the suffering. Rather than viewing the two famines as outcomes exclusively tied to ideology, Hechter proposes they also be seen as by-products of alien rule, as foreign rulers are less likely to be concerned about the well-being of different peoples in peripheral regions; moreover, the relationship between the core and peripheries tends to be rather exploitative. According to Hechter, the main goal of establishing control over alien territory through conquest—which requires the expenditure of both human and material resources on the part of the conquering power—is to gain profit for the core regime.

The difficulties in determining whether the Irish Great Famine can be seen as colonial are discussed in the essay by Peter Gray. While acknowledging that Ireland had a long-standing colonial relationship with England and later Great Britain, Gray points to ambiguities in this relationship caused by the creation of a "hybrid entity," following the Act of Union of 1800. This act, while integrating Ireland into imperial state structures also retained structural legacies from the period of direct colonial subordination.

Gray also surveys historical literature of various schools that examined socio-economic structures existing in 1845; the trigger mechanisms for the famine; and factors that determined the state's response to the famine. He concludes that identifying a clearly colonial dimension is difficult beyond the structural factor of the acute levels of potato dependency. Government policy, he notes, did not differ toward Scotland at the time where there also was a potato famine. However, the situation in Ireland differed from that in Scotland because of the continuing colonial legacy, in which the basic social structures inherited from the earlier period of direct colonial rule remained. Gray concludes that the continued use of military force by the British as state policy against Irish nationalists and as a means to quell outbreaks of social violence should be seen as a colonial-type practice.

The Soviet famines of 1931-33 occurred in a communist state with sizeable national minorities. In his essay on the famine of 1958-1962 in China, Lucien Bianco makes comparisons to the famines in the Soviet Union of the early 1930s.[21] He stresses that although the Chinese famine is notable as the most murderous in human history in absolute numbers, proportionately fewer died in China than during the famines in Soviet-ruled Kazakhstan and Ukraine. For the entire Soviet Union, however, the

[21] Bianco discusses in more detail similarities and differences between the Soviet and Chinese famines in a previously published article. See also Graziosi "Stalin's and Mao's Famines."

proportion of famine deaths was somewhat less than in China. Similarities include rapid urbanization due to policies of accelerated industrialization, which in both countries was financed largely at the cost of the rural economies and peasantry. One of the direct causes of famine in both countries were ruthless and excessive grain requisitions that continued even while famine raged.

Bianco points out that in contrast to the Soviet Union where national minorities constituted the majority of victims, death rates were lower among minorities in China. Minority regions in the northern and western peripheries of China were not important grain-producing regions and were not well integrated or connected to transportation infrastructure, so their mandatory deliveries of grain to the state were much lower or non-existent. In provinces where both Han Chinese and Tibetans lived, both ethnic groups suffered alike during the famine. In China, Han peasants constituted the overwhelming majority of famine victims, while peripheral provinces containing ethnic minorities suffered less. Comparing the Soviet and Chinese famines, Bianco notes that while about five percent of Chinese famine deaths constituted ethnic minorities, this figure was about 80 percent in the Soviet Union.

The study of genocide and the destruction of ethnic, religious, and social communities, and nations owes much to Raphaël Lemkin. In his pioneering study *Axis Rule in Occupied Europe,* Lemkin viewed the mass killings under Nazi Germany in World War II as linked to a colonial project. It was in this study that Lemkin coined the term "genocide" and elaborated on its meaning. In his article, Douglas Irvin-Erickson emphasizes that Lemkin did not limit his understanding of genocide to instances of mass killing but more broadly to include the destruction of heterogeneous communities for the purpose of creating homogeneous ones. Irvin-Erickson notes that as a young jurist Lemkin paid close attention to the development of Soviet law. In supporting the creation of a communist society, Soviet law authorized and legitimized the arrest, suppression, oppression, and killing of people who had a social consciousness deemed to be criminal. State violence and coercion was sanctioned to destroy and transform bourgeois groups and national minorities into Soviet citizens. Genocide under Soviet auspices was thus legitimized through laws, some of which called for the removal of national minorities from society under slogans of social protection. The goal was to create, destroy, and reorganize social relationships by managing identity formation in support of the Soviet revolutionary project and state.

Applying his understanding of genocide to the mass killings and repressions in Ukraine, Lemkin saw the famine of 1932-33 as the most brutal act within a wider pattern of the destruction of a nation. In notes prepared for a planned study of the history of genocide, Lemkin outlined his views on the Ukrainian genocide, considering the famine as a component of a four-pronged attack against the Ukrainian people. The others parts were severe repressions against the intelligentsia, destruction of the national church, and a long-term policy aimed at the dispersion and emigration of Ukrainians from Ukraine, and the immigration of Russians into the republic, the ultimate goal being a weakening of the cohesiveness of the Ukrainian nation. According to Irvin-Erickson, Lemkin viewed famine and hunger as tools for committing genocide—as violence targeting large numbers of individuals that placed them in competition with one another in a struggle for survival, turning famine victims into enemies of one another. Lemkin noted that famine and hunger thus destroyed social bonds of trust and solidarity, inflicting permanent damage to an individual's sense of belonging and trust in a society. In line with Lemkin's views, as pointed by Irvin-Erickson, the Ukrainian peasantry was sacrificed to promote uniformity. As the patterns of economic organization of most of those identifying as Ukrainian were antithetical to the plans of the Soviet state, they were targets. The goal of the Soviet state was to create Soviet national unity by the complete destruction of all cultures and all ideas save one—Soviet.

In chapters 8 and 9 of *Axis Rule in Occupied Europe*, Lemkin wrote about regulations and anti-Jewish laws that introduced restrictions, including food rationing based on racial criteria. These racially-motivated preferences privileged German nationals, who were to be provided with 100 percent of their caloric needs, while other ethnic and national groups were to receive less: Greeks were to receive 30 percent, while Jews, who were at the bottom of the food rationing hierarchy, 20 percent. Irvin-Erickson asserts that Lemkin saw this discrimination in access to food as an element in a larger pattern of endangering undesired national groups. Laws were passed prohibiting Jews from leaving ghettos for food, with infractions punishable by execution. Jewish Councils, or *Judenrat*, were to function as tools to shatter the bonds of social cohesion, as Jewish victims were forced into competition with one another for survival. Irvin-Erickson's article highlights Lemkin's conclusion that ghetto life showed that techniques of genocide could be economic and political levers that deprive people of basics like food and shelter. As friends, neighbours, and family members were forced to compete for food, thinking in more general and national terms became impossible. Irvin-Erickson concludes that to Lemkin, this constituted the destruction of group life and the shattering of social bonds, as enforced starvation proved to be effective in destroying the national pattern of a targeted group.

The essays in this volume collectively demonstrate that famines which have occurred in colonies and former colonies, or in peripheral regions (internal colonies) of empires, especially where the economies are largely rural-based, can be fruitfully studied within the context of imperial policies and colonial rule. Starvation as state policy was practised in Ukraine, Moldova, and Poland under Nazi German and Romanian occupation during World War II, which was directly linked to their expansionist and empire-building efforts. The catastrophic famines in British-ruled Ireland and India took place in an overseas colony (India) or former colony (Ireland). India, however, was a distant colony containing racially different peoples, while Ireland was closer to the imperial centre and inhabited largely by Celts, who were of the same race and culturally closer to the English. In the cases of Ireland and Ukraine, neither were ruled like an overseas colony during their famines. Rather, both were treated more like internal colonies (peripheral regions of empires) that were in the process of being integrated into imperial political structures, which were controlled largely by representatives of the core nationalities. Ukrainians, thus, found themselves in a somewhat similar cultural relationship to the Russians as the Irish to the English. Both Ukraine and Ireland suffered catastrophic famines as peripheral regions (internal colonies)—inhabited largely by minority nationalities—of imperial states. In the case of the Chinese famine, however, no link seems to exist between the policies of the imperial centre and famine in peripheral regions where ethnic minorities were concentrated. The Chinese famine, instead, was most intense in the grain-producing regions inhabited largely by Han Chinese, who constituted the core nationality of the Chinese state.

Recent scholarly literature has established the political nature of modern famines, if not always in their causes then certainly in the reactions and responses of state authorities to food shortages and the onset of famine conditions. The cases of Ukraine and Ireland, as well as Bengal, demonstrate some similarities in that the responses of the imperial authorities were woefully inadequate to mitigate the worst of the suffering and deaths from starvation. In the case of Ukraine, however, the authorities caused the famine through their policies. Moreover, they intensified famine conditions, causing additional suffering and deaths, by authorizing searches and the confiscation of food found in the homes of the peasantry, even from already-starving peasant households. Overall, the famines that occurred in overseas colonies or peripheral regions (internal colonies) of empires suggest that the investigation of links between imperial policies, colonial rule, and famine merit further study, especially in the case of the Soviet Union and its internal colonies.

Works Cited

Applebaum, Anne. *Red Famine: Stalin's War on Ukraine*. Doubleday, 2017.

Barghoorn, Frederick C. *Soviet Russian Nationalism.* Oxford UP, 1956.

Berkhoff, Karel C. "Famine in Kiev." *Harvest of Despair: Life and Death in Ukraine under Nazi Rule*, The Belknap Press, 2004, pp. 164-86.

Bianco, Lucien. "Comparing the Soviet and Chinese Famines: Their Perpetrators, Actors and Victims." *Communism and Hunger: The Ukrainian, Kazakh and Soviet Famines in Comparative Perspective*, edited by Andrea Graziosi and Frank E. Sysyn, Canadian Institute of Ukrainian Studies P, 2016, pp. 59-82.

Brandenberger, David. *National Bolshevism: Stalinist Mass Culture and the Formation of Modern Russian National Identity, 1931-1956.* Harvard UP, 2002.

Brandon, Ray, and Wendy Lower, editors. *The Shoah in Ukraine: History, Testimony, Memorialization*. Indiana UP, 2008.

Cameron, Sarah. "Questioning the Distinctiveness of the Ukrainian Famine." *Contemporary European History*, vol. 27, no. 3, 2018, pp. 460-64. DOI: 10.1017/S0960777318000346

Collingham, Lizzie. *The Taste of War: World War II and the Battle for Food.* The Penguin Press, 2012.

Conquest, Robert, editor. *The Last Empire.* Ampersand Books, 1962.

---. *The Last Empire: Nationality and the Soviet Future.* Hoover Institution Press, 1986.

Curran, Declan, et al., editors. *Famines in European Economic History: The Last Great European Famines Reconsidered.* Routledge, 2015.

Davies, R. W., and Stephen G. Wheatcroft. *The Years of Hunger: Soviet Agriculture, 1931-1933.* Palgrave Macmillan, 2004.

Davis, Mike. *Late Victorian Holocausts: El Niño Famines and the Making of the Third World*. Verso, 2001.

Devereux, Stephen. *Famine in the Twentieth Century. IDS Working Papers*, vol. 105, 2000, https://www.ids.ac.uk/download.php?file=files/dmfile/wp105.pdf. Accessed 8 Mar. 2021.

---. "Introduction: From 'Old Famines' to 'New Famines.'" *The New Famines: Why Famines Persist in an Era of Globalization*, edited by Stephen Devereux, Routledge, 2007, pp. 1-26.

De Waal, Alex. *Mass Starvation: The History and Future of Famine.* Polity Press, 2018.

Edkins, Jenny. "The Criminalization of Mass Starvations: From Natural Disaster to Crime against Humanity." *The New Famines: Why Famines Persist in an Era of Globalization*, edited by Stephen Devereux, Routledge, 2007, pp. 50-65.

Ellman, Michael. "The 1947 Soviet Famine and the Entitlement Approach to Famines." *Cambridge Journal of Economics*, vol. 24, no. 5, 2000, pp. 603-30. DOI: 10.1093/CJE/24.5.603

Ellman, Michael, and Sergei Nefedov. "The Soviet Famine of 1931-1934: Genocide, a Result of Poor Harvests, or the Outcome of a Conflict between the State and the Peasants?" *Europe-Asia Studies*, vol. 71, no. 6, 2019, pp. 1048-65. DOI: 10.1080/09668136.2019.1617464

Ganson, Nicholas. *The Soviet Famine of 1946-47 in Global and Historical Perspective*. Palgrave Macmillan, 2009.

Graziosi, Andrea. *The Great Soviet Peasant War: Bolsheviks and Peasants, 1917-1933*. Ukrainian Research Institute of Harvard University, 1997.

---. "Stalin's and Mao's Famines: Similarities and Differences." *Communism and Hunger: The Ukrainian, Kazakh and Soviet Famines in Comparative Perspective*, edited by Andrea Graziosi and Frank E. Sysyn, Canadian Institute of Ukrainian Studies P, 2016, pp. 83-101.

---. *Stalinism, Collectivization and the Great Famine*. Ukrainian Studies Fund, 2009.

Graziosi, Andrea, and Frank E. Sysyn, editors. *Communism and Hunger: The Ukrainian, Kazakh and Soviet Famines in Comparative Perspective*. Canadian Institute of Ukrainian Studies P, 2016.

Hechter, Michael. *Alien Rule*. Cambridge UP, 2013.

---. *Internal Colonialism: The Celtic Fringe in British National Development. U of California P, 1975.*

Hirsch, Francine. *Empire of Nations: Ethnographic Knowledge and the Making of the Soviet Union*. Cornell UP, 2005.

Holt, Emily, and Grace Mahoney. "Rupture and Call: Famine Encounters from Contemporary Irish and Ukrainian Women in the Arts." *East/West: Journal of Ukrainian Studies*, vol. 7, no. 2, 2020, pp. 69-97. DOI: 10.21226/ewjus612

Howard-Hassmann, Rhoda E. *State Food Crimes*. Cambridge UP, 2016.

Hrynevych, Liudmyla. *Holod 1928-1929 rr. u radians'kii Ukraini*. Instytut istorii Ukrainy, 2013.

Ivnitskii, N. A. *Golod 1932-1933 godov v SSSR: Ukraina, Kazakhstan, severnyi Kavkaz, Povolzh'e, zapadnaia Sibir', Ural*. Sobranie, 2009.

Kappeler, Andreas. *The Russian Empire: A Multiethnic History*. Longman, 2001.

Kivelson, Valerie A., and Ronald Grigor Suny. *Russia's Empires*. Oxford UP, 2017.

Kolarz, Walter. *Communism and Colonialism*. St. Martin's Press, 1964.

---. *Russia and Her Colonies*. 3rd edition, G. Philip, 1953.

Kondrashin, Viktor. *Golod 1932-1933 godov: tragediia rosiiskoi derevni*. ROSSPEN, 2018.

Krawchenko, Bohdan. *Social Change and National Consciousness in Twentieth-Century Ukraine*. Canadian Institute of Ukrainian Studies P / St. Antony's College, 1987.

Kulchytsky, Stanislav. *The Famine of 1932-1933 in Ukraine: An Anatomy of the Holodomor.* Canadian Institute of Ukrainian Studies P, 2018.

--- (Stanislav Kul'chyts'kyi). *Stalins'kyi "sokrushitel'nyi" udar 1932-1933.* Kyiv, Tempora, 2013.

Lemkin, Raphael (Raphaël Lemkin). *Axis Rule in Occupied Europe: Laws of Occupation, Analysis of Government, Proposals for Redress.* Carnegie Endowment for International Peace, 1944.

Lower, Wendy. *Nazi Empire-Building and the Holocaust in Ukraine.* U of North Carolina P, 2005.

Mace, James E. *Communism and the Dilemmas of National Liberation: National Communism in Soviet Ukraine 1918-1933.* Harvard Ukrainian Research Institute, 1983.

Marcus, David. "Famine Crimes in International Law." *The American Journal of International Law*, vol. 97, no. 2, April 2003, pp. 245-81. DOI: 10.2307/3100102

Martin, Terry. *The Affirmative Action Empire: Nations and Nationalism in the Soviet Union, 1923-1939*. Cornell UP, 2001.

Mazower, Mark. *Hitler's Empire: How the Nazis Ruled Europe.* Penguin Books, 2008.

Melnyk, Z. Lew (Zinowij Lew Melnyk). "Ukraine within the USSR: An Economic Perspective, 1928/29-1932 and 1959-1980." *Nationalities Papers*, vol. 35, no. 1, 2007, pp. 121-69. DOI: 10.1080/00905990601129438

---. *Soviet Capital Formation. Ukraine, 1928/29-1932*. Ukrainian Free UP, 1965.

Motyl, Alexander J. *Imperial Ends: The Decay, Collapse, and Revival of Empires.* Columbia UP, 2001.

Noack, Christian, et al., editors. *Holodomor and Gorta Mór: Histories, Memories, and Representations of Famine in Ukraine and Ireland.* Anthem Press, 2012.

---. "Introduction. Holodomor and Gorta Mór: Histories, Memories and Representations of Famine in Ukraine and Ireland." *Holodomor and Gorta Mór: Histories, Memories and Representations of Famine in Ukraine and Ireland*, edited by Christian Noack et al., Anthem Press, 2012.

Ó Gráda, Cormac. *Famine: A Short History.* Princeton UP, 2009.

Pianciola, Niccolò. "Stalinskaia 'ierarkhiia potrebleniia' i velikii golod 1931-1933 gg. v Kazakhstane." *Ab Imperio*, vol. 2, 2018, pp. 80-116.

---. "Ukraine and Kazakhstan: Comparing the Famines." *Contemporary European History*, vol. 27, no. 3, 2018, pp. 440-44.

Pipes, Richard. *The Formation of the Soviet Union, Communism and Nationalism, 1917-1923.* Harvard UP, 1954.

Polanyi, Karl. *The Great Transformation: The Political and Economic Origins of Our Time.* Beacon Press, 2001 (©1944).

Romano, Andrea, and Nonna Tarkhova. *L'Armata Rossa e la collettivizzazione delle campagne nell'URSS, 1928-1933: raccolta di documenti dai Fondi dell'Archivio militare di Stato Russo.* Instituto universitario orientale, 1996.

Sen, Amartya. *Development As Freedom.* Alfred A. Knopf, 2001.

---. *Poverty and Famines: An Essay on Entitlement and Deprivation.* Clarendon Press, 1981.

Serbyn, Roman. "The Origin of the Ukrainian Famine of 1921-23 in the Light of Recent Research." *Famine-Genocide in Ukraine, 1932-1933: Western Archives, Testimonies and New Research*, edited by Wsevolod W. Isajiw, Ukrainian Canadian Research and Documentation Centre, 2003, pp. 165-83.

Slyn'ko, I. I. *Sotsialistychna perebudova i tekhnichna rekonstruktsiia sil's'koho hospodarstva Ukrainy (1927-1932 rr.).* Vyd. Akademii nauk Ukr. SSR, 1961.

Snyder, Timothy. *Black Earth: The Holocaust as History and Warning.* Tim Duggan Books, 2015.

---. *Bloodlands: Europe between Hitler and Stalin.* Basic Books, 2010.

---. "Germany's Historical Responsibility for Ukraine." *Marieluise Beck. Mitglied des Deutschen Bundestags.* 20 June 2017, https://marieluisebeck.de/artikel/20-06-2017/timothy-snyder-germanys-historical-responsibility-ukraine. Accessed 20 Feb. 2020.[22]

Solovei, Dmytro. *Holod u systemi koloniial'noho panuvannia TsK KPSS v Ukraini (do 40-litn'oho iuvileiiu KP(b)U i 25-oi richnytsi holodu 1932-1933 rr. v Ukraini.* Institute for the Study of the USSR, 1959.

Tarkhova, Nonna. *Krasnaia Armiia i stalinskaia kollektivizatsiia, 1928-1933 gg.* ROSSPEN, 2010.

Vasyl'iev, Valerii. *Politychne kerivnytstvo URSR i SRSR: dynamika vidnosyn tsentr-subtsentr vlady (1917-1938).* Instytut istorii Ukrainy, 2014.

Veselova, Oleksandra. "Famine in Ukraine after the Second World War." *Harvard Ukrainian Studies*, vol. 30, nos. 1-4, 2008, pp. 183-98.

---. "Henotsyd Holodomorom 1946-1947 rokiv v Ukraini." *Problemy istorii Ukrainy: Fakty, sudzhennia, poshuky. Mizhvidomchyi zbirnyk naukovykh prats'*, vol. 7, 2003, pp. 384-405.

[22] The text of the talk, titled "Germans must remember the truth about Ukraine—for their own sake," can also be read here: https://www.eurozine.com/germans-must-remember-the-truth-about-ukraine-for-their-own-sake/. Accessed 22 Feb. 2021.

Wheatcroft, Stephen. "The Soviet Famine of 1946-1947, the Weather and Human Agency in Historical Perspective." *Europe-Asia Studies*, vol. 64, no. 6, 1XZ, Aug. 2012, pp. 987-1005. DOI: 10.1080/09668136.2012.691725

Zima, F. V. *Golod v SSSR 1946-1947: proiskhozhdenie i posledstviia.* Rossiiskaia akademiia nauk / Institut rossiiskoi istorii, 1996.

Famine As an Instrument of Nazi Occupation Policy in Ukraine, 1941-44[1]

Oleksandr Lysenko
Institute of the History of Ukraine, National Academy of Sciences of Ukraine

Tetiana Zabolotna
Institute of the History of Ukraine, National Academy of Sciences of Ukraine

Oleksandr Maievs'kyi
Institute of the History of Ukraine, National Academy of Sciences of Ukraine

Translated from Ukrainian by Mark Baker

Abstract: The article examines a range of questions tied to Nazi Germany's socio-economic policies in occupied Ukraine during World War II. In line with implementing the General Plan "Ost," the top leadership of the Third Reich intended to cleanse the "eastern territories" of its "superfluous" population for German colonization. As contained in the "Principles of Economic Policy in the East," these directives provided for the physical extermination of tens of millions of people in various ways, as well as the deportation of part of the indigenous population to remote areas. Ukraine's economic exploitation was built in such a way that it doomed the local urban and rural societies to a miserable, half-starved existence. The systematic seizure of food for the needs of the Wehrmacht, the Reich, and its allies made the death of the inhabitants of the occupied lands only a matter of time. The instrumentalization of terror by famine was manifested, on the one hand, by the creation of special structures that requisitioned food resources, and on the other by establishing norms of food supplies that were below the minimal needs for existence. As well, the strict regulation of trade set limits to the sources of food products that could be brought to the cities. This caused mass starvation. The deaths and the diseases that followed created hundreds of thousands of victims among Ukrainians.

Keywords: Ukraine, World War II, Nazi occupation policy, famine, survival strategies, morbidity.

---

[1] This is a condensed version of the original Ukrainian-language article, authored by Oleksandr Lysenko, Tetiana Zabolotna, and Oleksandr Maievs'kyi, that appeared in the journal *Viis'kovo-istorychnyi merydian,* vol. 4 (18), 2017, pp. 61-92. It is republished here in translation with permission. Bibliographic references have been reformatted according to MLA, as per *EWJUS*'s style guidelines.

In the numerous memoirs of ordinary participants and contemporaries of World War II, memories of famine are among the most difficult experiences described. The war created conditions that allowed for the use of famine as an instrument through which the Wehrmacht and its allies could achieve strategic goals of the eastern campaign. While significant differences of opinion existed among the leaders of the Third Reich on how best to manage the "eastern territories" they planned to conquer, their views concerning the concept of developing "*Lebensraum*" basically concurred. This vision was most clearly outlined by Adolf Hitler, who stated,

> We have an obligation to depopulate to the same degree to which we are obliged to worry about the German population. We must develop a technique of depopulation. You ask, what does it mean to depopulate? Do I intend to eliminate whole peoples? Yes, exactly, everything is leading to this. Nature is harsh; thus, we are obliged to be the same. (Rauschning 129-30).

In the process of realizing the sinister general plan "Ost," the Nazi leaders intended to resettle and eliminate 31 million inhabitants of Poland and the western regions of the USSR, where 65 percent of the Ukrainians, 75 percent of the Belarusians, and 80-85 percent of the Poles lived. There were proposals to increase to 51 million those from the native population to be removed in order to quicken the tempo of colonization from thirty to ten years.

On 17 October 1941, during a meeting with Reich Minister of Armaments and Munitions Fritz Todt and Gauleiter Fritz Sauckel, the Führer stressed the necessity of determining the responsibilities of the Reich Minister for the Occupied Eastern Territories, Alfred Rosenberg. Rosenberg's task "would be to push the Slavs, gathered on reservations, as quickly as possible to such a state where they would either abandon their fatherland or die" (Kosyk 537).

Commenting on his "Principles of Economic Policy in the East" (2 May 1941), Hermann Göring noted, "without a doubt, tens of millions of people will perish from hunger when we take all that we need" (*Istoriia Ukrains'koi RSR* 136). The Reich Marshal considered the food problem easy to overcome with the help of cabbage and turnips. Whoever refused to work would be deprived of all food, and the stubborn ones would be shot on the spot.

"The Directives on Economic Policy for Organizing the Economy in the East," included the following instructions:

> The isolation of the black-earth regions will ensure for us in any circumstances the availability of more or less significant surpluses in those regions. As a result—the cessation of supply for the whole forest zone,

> including large industrial centres (Moscow and Petersburg) . . . . the German administration in this region must make every effort to mitigate the consequences of famine, which undoubtedly will break out and accelerate the process of naturalization. It is necessary to strive for the more intensive agricultural development of these regions, for example, by expanding sown areas of potatoes and other important, useful, high-yielding crops. But famine ultimately cannot be avoided. Several tens of millions of people in this territory will become superfluous and die or will be forced to resettle to Siberia. Attempts to save this population from starvation by sending surpluses from the Black Earth zone could be made only at the cost of the deterioration of the European food supply. They could undermine the capacity of Germany to sustain itself in the war and weaken the blockade strength of Germany and Europe. (Sukharev 435)

Pre-war Germany experienced a substantial shortage of agricultural products, and domestic production did not cover the food requirements of the population. In wartime conditions, the situation was further complicated as previously established trade connections with other states were severed; also, agriculture lost large numbers of workers to mobilization while receiving fewer machines and work tools. The leadership of the Third Reich sought to make up for the deficit in food products at the expense of the occupied, dependent, and "neutral" countries of Western Europe and the newly occupied territories of eastern Europe. Ukraine, with its agricultural potential, was given a leading role. Nazi officials planned to export to Germany from the south and southwestern Soviet Union (that is, Ukraine) all food products and raw materials that they considered "in excess amounts." For the local producers of these products and raw materials, they planned to leave less than the minimum necessary to sustain this population. The Nazis established the following hierarchy for the distribution of food products: "1) for the active army; 2) for the rest of the troops on hostile territory; 3) for troops located in Germany; 4) for the German civilian population; and, in the last instance, for the population of the occupied countries" (Perekhrest 173). Ukraine was also viewed as a market for manufactured goods of western European industry that were to be paid for in agricultural products and raw materials.

An analysis of the directives and orders of the Reich ministries, in particular, of Herbert Backe's Ministry for Food and Agriculture (1942-45), shows that in the occupied eastern territories the organization of a massive famine was foreseen, one that would lead to maximal destruction of the urban and village populations of the region and open up limitless possibilities for German colonization of Ukrainian lands.

The preconditions for famine had been created well in advance. The systematic evacuation measures of the Soviet authorities, implemented in line with a "scorched earth" strategy, had led to the removal of reserves of food products and raw materials, forage for livestock, and the livestock themselves from territory threatened with German occupation. All that could not be evacuated to the eastern regions was ordered destroyed or ruined by burning, soaking with water, gasoline, etc. Any reserves of food products (cellars, stores, bases) that remained after the Red Army's retreat were taken by the local population, which anticipated the onset of difficult times. The savviest managed to accumulate significant stores of valuables. However, the majority were unable to create reserves for a "rainy day."

Already in the summer of 1941, difficulties with food supplies were evident, even in areas near the front and under Soviet administrative control. For example, on 15 August 1941, the People's Commissar of Internal Affairs of the UkrSSR, V. Serhiienko, reported to the leader of the NKVD, Lavrentii Beria, and the secretary of the Central Committee of the Communist Party (B) of Ukraine, Nikita Khrushchev, that the food supply situation for inhabitants of Kyiv was in a clearly unsatisfactory state. According to preliminary estimates, the city had available fats and sugar for only two days. The situation with delivery of meat and vegetables to the city was particularly bad. Over the previous five days, no meat at all had been delivered to trade organizations. The actions of the director of a nearby state farm (State Farm No. 8), Tikhonov, had negatively affected the vegetable supply for Kyivites: he had ordered the destruction of a whole store of vegetables—trampled and flooded with water from the irrigation system. Stocks of flour for the capital barely reached ten tons, and deliveries from the periphery had become irregular. Eating establishments had not received produce for five days and their stocks were rapidly vanishing. The author of the report stated that there were two main causes of the extremely unsatisfactory situation: a sharp reduction in the delivery of food products and the desertion of many leaders of the trade network, the communal eateries, and delivery systems (altogether 250 persons). Those fleeing often took state monetary resources with them.[2]

From the first days of the occupation, the "new" authorities introduced their own order and legal norms. The initial measures were aimed at subduing the local population and ensuring a comfortable stay for the functionaries of the occupying authorities and officers and soldiers of the Wehrmacht. Representatives of the German occupation organs demanded the return of anything the population had "illegally" appropriated. Severe punishments were to be applied for violations, as announced in periodicals of Kirovohrad (now Kropyvnytskyi), Dnipropetrovsk (now Dnipro), and

[2] Haluzevyi derzhavnyi arkhiv Sluzhby bezpeky Ukrainy (hereafter HDA SBU), fond 16, opys 34 (1951), sprava 2, arkush 82-88.

Zaporizhzhia ("Vid mis'koi upravy"; "Obov''iazkova postanova;" "Rozporiadzhennia").

While confiscating looted goods, the authorities would quite frequently take personal food stocks as well. Severe limits on food reserves were established; anything that exceeded them was subject to requisition. For example, on 16 December 1941, the command of the German army in Crimea issued an order to the population of Simferopol that surpluses of food products were to be taken to the city government's warehouses (the territory of Crimea until 1954 was part of the Russian Soviet Federative Socialist Republic [RSFSR]). A representative of the authorities explained these measures as necessary to address the hunger, which threatened the population that had no food reserves ("K prikazu o sdache" 2). Subsequently, the military commandant of Simferopol issued a demand that before the end of 1941 all citizens surrender product surpluses in excess of forty kilos of grain or flour, two kilos of fat, and two kilos of sugar per person (Pashchenia 83). In Artem district, people were allowed to keep fifty kilos of grain and thirty-five kilos of flour per family member ("Ob''iavlenie" 2). That these limitation orders were issued throughout the whole period of occupation suggests the population was sabotaging the authorities' explicit decisions. No doubt with their earlier experience of famine in 1932-33 in mind, the population, especially the peasants, strove by any means to hide food products. However, the threat of punishment forced the population under occupation to act carefully. Whoever did not manage to keep some food, would soon experience hunger. The situation was even worse in the cities where the absence of foodstuffs in trade networks meant that people were not able to stock up. However, even in the countryside the situation became more difficult in connection with requisitioning introduced by the occupying organs. For the needs of the German armed forces, they seized cattle, horses, pigs, poultry, and animal products from the village inhabitants (Marchenko 11).

German military and civilian leaders were well aware that such measures would induce famine. The Commander of the Eleventh Army, Erich von Manstein, in an order from 20 November 1941, emphasized the necessity of exporting the maximum amount of agricultural products to the homeland, while foreseeing that in the cities a significant portion of the local population would go hungry (*Nuremberg* 641). The German administration gave certain privileges (especially in the provisioning of food) to Russian Cossacks on occupied territories of the RSFSR. Cossacks that served in the occupation structures and armed forces received tax benefits and were given additional grants of lands and draught animals (Kadyrov 190). Support of the population in occupied Belarus had its own specifics. The "General political-economic directives for the economic organization 'East,'" issued 23 May 1941, stated that Belarus, which was part of the "forest zone," was to provide "significant meat deliveries."[3] At the same time, the territory of Belarus was to be treated separately from the black earth zone, where there were "surplus products." The foreseen deficit of food products in Belarus, however, did not mean that the products would be supplied from the black-earth districts or from Germany itself. Thus, even here the program of supplying the population of the Reich and the Wehrmacht doomed millions of local inhabitants to hunger (Novikov 51-52).

From other documents, it becomes clear that the Nazis' food supply policy was oriented toward solving a pre-war task: a) obtaining reliable sources of food supplies for Germany; and b) depopulating the future "*Lebensraum*." A report by the inspector of armaments in Ukraine (2 December 1941) included a list of actions necessary to ensure the Reich an uninterrupted supply of food. The decisive measure was the reduction of the internal consumption of the "natives" to a bare minimum through the following steps: a) the elimination of surplus eaters—Jews, inhabitants of large cities; b) a maximal reduction of the food ration norms of the local population; c) reduction of the food supplied to the rural population (Sorokin 179).

The occupying authorities had no single system for supplying food products to the civilian inhabitants of the occupied territories. In any event, the complex food supply situation negatively influenced the attitude of the local population toward the Nazi occupants, raising the threat of the emergence and/or activization of a passive or active resistance movement. Given this "mine of slow-motion activity," the occupation organs developed plans, and local military and civilian authorities addressed this problem, depending on the specific situation. However, measures were largely in the form of propaganda rather than improvements in food security. The local press played a special role in propaganda. Newspapers included pieces informing readers about the organization of special communal dining outlets and on procedures for issuing food ration coupons and the provisioning of products to certain entitled categories of the population (orphans, invalids, pensioners, families of those repressed by the Soviet regime).

The local administration's active measures in this sphere were announced in the press. For example, as early as 7 October 1941, the Kyiv press published an image of the bread ration card that building administrations and building owners were to issue to each family ("Oholoshennia" 4). However, there was no mention of what the norms of

---

[3] See "Wirtschaftspolitische Richtlinien für die Wirtschaftsorganisation Ost von 23.5.41., erarbeinet von der Gruppe Landwirtschaft" in Ferchl 65-66.

provision through the cards would be, or that bread would not be distributed for weeks. We know from the diary of a Kyivite, I. Khoroshunova, that she first used ration cards to obtain bread on 10 October 1941 (the Germans had arrived in Kyiv on 19 September). The initial norm was 200 grams per person, regardless of whether or not she worked. "Eleven streets are assigned to each store. So the queues begin from early morning. And many go without bread. And the bread for that day disappears" (Khoroshunova; entry from 11 Oct. 1941). Herring was offered for sale twice, sold in allotments of a half-kilo per person. "Get Stalin's [herring], while it is still available, for we won't get a taste of Hitler's [herring] for some time to come," Kyivites sadly joked (Vrons'ka 281). By mid-October 1941 the reserves of bread had been exhausted. Khoroshunova commented: "A real famine has begun here. There is no bread . . . . It's been impossible to buy anything. All the stores are closed. And now at the markets peasants exchange produce for completely new things only." Further, she noted, "It turns out that one hundred grams of bread is a huge portion. They last gave us bread, two hundred grams each, on the thirtieth [of October 1941]. They promised [more bread] on the fifth [of November], but they did not give it" (Khoroshunova; entries from 17 Oct. and 8 Nov. 1941). The next time Kyivites received this critical product was on 16 and 30 November. In December, bread was also distributed only twice, and this concluded the deliveries for 1941 (Vrons'ka 281). Thus, the rations provided were miserly, and depended on the region, the time of year, and the category of ration card. While in Sumy region and in "Transnistria" the daily ration for working people was 200 grams of bread daily, and in Kirovohrad—400 grams, dependents were not entitled to receive anything; in Kyiv, however, this category of the population could count on receiving 200 grams of bread per week, that is, about 29 grams per day (Tarnavs'kyi 301).

Taking into account German occupation laws on food supply and the limited resources available, local governments strove to improve the situation of city dwellers by establishing norms of food supply. Thus, the Kyiv city administration in April 1942 issued the instruction "On the procedure for issuing food ration cards to the population of Kyiv and with them implementing control over the distribution of food products." According to this document, food ration cards were to be issued to

> a) working men; b) unemployed men; c) dependents of the mentioned persons—women and boys up to age 16; d) invalids and pensioners; e) pupils and students who were studying at the time of issue of the cards; f) female housekeepers and dependent women, regardless of age; g) families of individuals repressed or deported by the Bolsheviks from Kyiv; h) women and children of POWs; i) artisans and private traders with licences

> at the time of registration; j) individuals of the free professions (doctors, lawyers, and others); k) workers and employees who work outside Kyiv and come to the city on business or vacation for more than two weeks; l) families of the sick or those staying for in-patient treatment; m) individuals evacuated from other locations whose periods of stay in Kyiv are determined to be more than two weeks; and n) children staying permanently in homes for children.[4]

Four categories of consumers were established for the ration cards: the first included invalids, pensioners, private traders, and members of the free professions; to the second belonged dependents of working people and the families of those who had left to work in Germany; to the third belonged those working full time at enterprises and institutions; and to the fourth belonged Volksdeutsch and workers in demanding jobs (at facilities producing weapons, on railroads, in mineral mining, and so on).[5]

The situation with bread supplies stabilized more or less only in the second half of 1942, once the harvest came in: the average weekly bread ration, even for dependents, rose to 1,500 grams. This increase, however, coincided with a significant decrease in the quality of bread, which was confirmed by the spike in the number of people who became sick from eating products with various inedible admixtures.[6] The hungry inhabitants of the large Ukrainian urbanized centres were forced to add to their diets unsuitable items: oilcake, bran, frozen potatoes, beets, potato skins, meat from dead horses, pets, and even casein glue, as was recorded in Kramatorsk and Kharkiv.

Socially unprotected categories (children, the disabled, the elderly) constantly suffered from hunger. The local authorities organized cafeterias, where a small portion of the needy could suppress the feeling of hunger for several hours with a thin soup, sometimes with a slice of bread. The average cost of lunch in these special public eateries was 1.1-1.7 rubles. Of course, the number of lunches at that subsidized price was limited because the cafeterias did not receive expected funds from the administrations. District departments referred to the fact that they did not have the necessary funds and could cover only part of the expenses.

The local authorities were not successful in addressing the food shortages. They did not, after all, have their own food reserves. The only remaining option was to haul in food products from the villages. However, the absence of means of transportation and fuel hindered this simplest way

---

[4] Tsentral'nyi derzhavnyi arkhiv vyshchykh orhaniv Ukrainy (hereafter: TsDAVO), f. 3676, op. 4, spr. 475, ark. 460.

[5] Derzhavnyi arkhiv Kyivs'koi oblasti (hereafter: DAKO), f. R-2356, op. 5, spr. 13, ark. 62, 63.

[6] TsDAVO, f. 3676, op. 4, spr. 475, ark 43.

to solve the food problem, and the newly established co-operatives and consumer associations gradually transformed into conduits for enriching their founders.

Townspeople, attempting to solve the difficult food problem themselves, hiked to nearby and distant villages to exchange industrial goods for food. Throughout the Nazi occupation, street markets were important sources, although the occupation authorities restricted food imports, introduced "firm prices," fought the "bagmen," and even banned the street market trade, which left many people during the winters of 1941-42 and 1942-43 on the verge of death by starvation. The shortage of food products and the spread of the "black market" caused speculation, inflation, and a surge in prices at the markets. In Kharkiv during the summer of 1942, one kilo of bread cost 150 rubles, while the officially set price was 1.7 rubles; one egg cost 8 rubles (officially, 0.80 rub.); one litre of milk—20 rubles (1.2 rub.), one litre of sunflower oil—280 rubles (14.5 rubles), butter—600 rubles, one kilogram of backfat—1,000 rubles, one kilogram of wheat bread—50 rubles, rye—35 rubles, one kilo of sugar—500 rubles (Pashchenia 86).

The low purchasing power of the local population was determined by extremely low wages in comparison with prices. In the territory of the Reichskomissariat Ukraine, a worker earned 400 rubles per month, an accountant—500 rubles, a typist—400 rubles, managers of various levels—from 900 to 1,500 rubles. In the summer of 1942, the salary of the average white-collar employee was 700-800 rubles, at a time when one kilo of backfat cost 750 rubles. By March 1943, one kilo of this product could be bought for six thousand rubles, while salaries remained the same (Spudka 13).

Neither the personal efforts of the urban population nor the actions of the local occupation authorities could prevent the onset of starvation. In early March 1942, Joseph Goebbels noted in his diary: "The situation with food supply in the occupied eastern regions is extremely difficult. There, thousands and tens of thousands of people are dying from hunger, which does not interest anyone at all" (Miuller 132).

Nazi policies that induced the famine also led to the eating of corpses and cannibalism. According to Oleksandr Symonov, a professor of fine arts from Kharkiv, the Germans hanged those accused of cannibalism with a sign on their chests: "I was hanged for selling human meat" (Skorobahatov 278). According to some sources, in the summer of 1942, at the street market in "Kinna Ploshcha" (Equestrian Square) in Kharkiv, a man was hanged for selling a liver and lungs of people who had died of hunger (Skorobahatov 278). In Kyiv, there were rumours that in the Podil neighbourhood a group had been uncovered that was killing people and selling their meat. There were other cases of killing for this purpose. All the same, the official press reported only one act of cannibalism, when a fifty-year-old man named Korniienko ate a sixteen-year-old girl. As a result, Korniienko was publicly hanged on 27 January 1943 in the centre of Kyiv (Berkhoff 181).

Nazi policies and practices also led to mass diseases associated with systematic malnutrition—hypertrophy, dystrophy, rickets, nephritis, scurvy, tuberculosis, measles, scarlet fever, diphtheria, whooping cough—and death from these diseases. From the arrival of the German troops in Kyiv (19 September 1941) to 1 April 1942, about eight thousand of the city's inhabitants died of hunger, cold, and illnesses caused by them (Malakov). According to data from the Kharkiv city administration, as presented by A. Skorobahatov, in 1942 (more exactly, from the second half of December 1941 to the first half of December 1942), 13,139 people of Kharkiv starved to death, accounting for 58.4 percent of all deaths in that period. Even this unprecedented high percentage of deaths from hunger was likely higher still: according to the head of the department of Kharkiv's city administration, Professor Ie. Ie. Dobrovol's'kyi, some doctors filled out the "doctor's reports" about the death of citizens incorrectly, avoiding the diagnosis of "death from hunger," replacing it with other causes, such as "edema from insufficient protein," "paralysis of the heart," "child frailty," and others (Skorobahatov 279). Thus, as in Soviet times, the truth was concealed; the "new" authorities avoided the disclosure of information about the terrible consequences of its rule for the local population, giving preference to self-congratulatory, optimistic newspaper articles with a perceptible, propagandistic "spirit." Timothy Snyder, speaking about the commonalities of the two totalitarian regimes, asserts, "in light of the scarcities, particularly of food supplies, both regimes integrated mass murder with economic planning" (16).

The food supply situation in the occupied settlements of Ukraine remained difficult throughout the entire stay of the German authorities and troops in the captured territories and for long after. The actions of local authorities in this area as reported in the newspapers seemed rather effective and active, but, in fact, they mostly had a declarative character. In fact, the population was compelled to save itself from death by starvation. And the delivery norms anticipated by the local authorities, based on the food ration cards, were so paltry as to look more like mockery than help.

The course taken to organize an artificial famine was a component of German agrarian policy. As planned, large cities were not sufficiently provided with food. People starved who did not have work or social connections with the village, especially in the winter. This was primarily the case in Kyiv, the Donbas, the Crimea, and northeastern Ukraine. The Kharkiv region was declared a zone of "total requisitioning" (in German: "*Kahlfraßzone*," literally where "absolutely everything is eaten"), in which the Wehrmacht divisions obtained food at their own discretion. The consequences were disastrous for the local population (Pol'), who were offered trips to Germany, where the Ostarbeiter would supposedly be ensured a pleasant living situation and nourishment ("Pratsia v Nimechchyni").

Although the policy of forced removal of working people from the occupied territories to contribute to the Third Reich economy was framed in terms of their rational use and preservation, in practice it was often otherwise. Already during the transportation stage, Ostarbeiters were subjected to starvation. Paraskeviia Kyslenko, a resident of the town of Ladan (Pryluky district), recalled that she was first taken away with others from her village in a closed train car to Kyiv; there they stayed in a camp; they were then sent to Magdeburg in closed train cars. During this exhausting trip, they were given food only once. Vasyl' Nalyvaika, a resident of the village of Andriivka (Mykhailo-Kotsiubynskyi district), recalled: "We travelled in a closed train car under guard. They gave us nothing to eat." A native of the village of Ivankivtsi, Ol'ha Berezhna, who was taken to Germany as a sixteen-year-old because her father was a party member, wrote, "We travelled for a month; there was nothing to eat; they only gave us boiling water" (Nesterenko 155). Kateryna Kashka from Chernihiv region recalled the following:

> They brought us to a concentration camp. Each morning they gave us bread with sawdust (only 100 grams per day) and margarine (5 grams each). And for lunch there was some sort of brew made from moldy biscuits—it would hang down from the ladle, when it was poured onto the plates. No matter how hungry I was, I could not swallow even a spoonful! Well, I thought, I'll die, what can you do? . . . For two weeks we were kept in that camp. Then, they took us to the bathhouse, but people were so exhausted that some did not make it there. All were emaciated, skinny, like living skeletons. (Nesterenko 157).

The press of the occupation authorities gave the opposite impression. Indeed, it was reported in these newspapers that the future workers of the Third Reich were provided with food in transit, and there were descriptions of the pleasant living conditions in Germany. And the trip abroad was generally viewed as a chance to change one's life for the better: to see the world, to gain a profession, to experience life in a cultured environment, and so on. Especially persuasive for the population were letters from the Ostarbeiters published in the periodicals.[7]

---

[7] *Holos Volyni*, 21 Feb. 1942, p. 2; *Nove ukrains'ke slovo*, 26 April 1942, p. 3; *Volyn'*, 14 May 1942, p. 2; *Volyn'*, 17 May 1942, p. 2; *Volyn'*, 21 May 1942, p. 2; *Nove ukrains'ke slovo*, 13 June 1942, p. 4; *Uriadovi Dunaievets'ki visti*, 14 June 1942, p. 3; *Nove ukrains'ke slovo*, 19 July 1942,

A rather common practice for distracting the local population from the problems of daily life was the publication of articles on the Famine of 1932-33 ("Ugroza goloda v SSSR;" "Do statystyky holodu"). One of these publications included vivid statistical data that underscored Soviet crimes ("Do statystyky holodu"). Such articles were intended to increase the hatred of the local population toward Soviet rule and to divert people's attention from the problems of the present to the horrific times of the past. In addition, the occupation press contained reports on the difficult food situation in the Soviet Union.[8]

Thus, the Nazi leaders and the occupation administration created a contradictory situation, which they were not able to overcome. The first dichotomy was that while the Reich truly needed a healthy workforce, economizing had a detrimental effect on the working capabilities of the inhabitants of the occupied territories, prisoners of war, and Ukrainian Ostarbeiters. The second dichotomy was between Germany's growing needs for agricultural raw materials and products, on the one hand, and the reduction of these resources in the occupied lands, on the other. The methods chosen by the Nazi authorities to conquer and subjugate Ukraine determined the collapse of Berlin's occupation policy and caused enormous demographic losses among the inhabitants in the occupied territories and their descendants.

Works Cited

Berkhoff, Karel C. *Harvest of Despair: Life and Death in Ukraine under Nazi Rule*. Harvard UP, 2004.

"Do statystyky holodu." *Donetskii vestnik*, 11 Dec. 1942, p. 4.

"Do statystyky holodu v Ukraini." *Nova Ukraina*, 11 May 1943, p. 3.

---

p. 4; *Vasyl'kivs'ki visti*, 26 July 1942, p. 3; *Dniprova khvylia*, 26 Sept. 1942, p. 3; *Olevs'ki visti*, 4 Oct. 1942, p. 4; *Volyn'*, 12 Nov. 1942, p. 3; *Volyn'*, 15 Aug. 1943, p. 4; *Volyn'*, 19 Aug. 1943, p. 4; *Volyn'*, 26 Aug. 1943, p. 4; *Ukrains'kyi holos* (Proskuriv), 16 Sept. 1943, p. 4; *Olevs'ki visti*, 15 Aug. 1943, p. 4; and others.

[8] "Prodovol'che postachannia naselennia SSSR pid chas viiny," *Nove ukrains'ke slovo*, no. 234 (249), 8 Oct. 1942, p. 3; "Golod v Kuibysheve," *Donetskii vestnik*, 24 Feb. 1943, p. 2; "Tsar'-golod v SSSR," *Molva*, 30 Sept. 1943, p. 1; "Predstoit zima poval'nogo goloda," *Nash put'* (Kherson), 8 Aug. 1943, p. 3; "Holod u bil'shovykiv," *Dnipropetrovs'ka hazeta*, 9 Feb. 1943, p. 2; "Golod nastupaet," *Poslednie novosti*, 26 Jan. 1942, p. 1; "SSSR nakanune goloda," *Golos pravdy*, 4 Feb. 1944, p. 6.

Ferchl, Irene Philipp. *Verbrechen der Wehrmacht: Dimensionen des Vernichtungskrieges 1941-1944: Ausstellungskatalog.* Hamburger Institut für Sozialforschung, Hamburger Edition, 2002.

Istoriia Ukrains'koi RSR u 8 t. 10 kn. Vol. 7, Naukova Dumka, 1977.

Kadyrov, B. G. "Nemetsko-fashistskaia okkupatsiia sovetskikh territorii v 1941-1943 gg." *Aktual'nye problemy ekonomiki i prava,* no. 2, 2007, pp. 188-92.

Khoroshunova, Irina A. "Pervyi god voiny." *Al'manakh "Iehupets',"* no. 9, Aug. 2013, pp. 45-46, 51, https://gordonua.com/specprojects/khoroshunova2.html. Accessed 22 Jan. 2019.

Kosyk, Volodymyr. *Ukraina i Nimechchyna u Druhii svitovii viini.* Naukove tovarystvo imeni T. Shevchenka u L'vovi, 1993.

"K prikazu o sdache izlishkov produktov." *Golos Kryma,* 21 Dec. 1941, p. 2.

Malakov, D. "Nezabutnie mynule Kyieva—u fotoal'bomi 'Kyiv 1939-1945.'" *Dzerkalo tyzhnia,* 4-10 Feb. 2006, https://dt.ua/SOCIETY/nezabutne_minule_kieva__u_fotoalbomi_kiyiv_19391945.html. Accessed 13 Dec. 2018.

Marchenko, V. A. *Rozsekrecheni dokumenty period natsysts'koi okupatsii Sums'koi oblasti 1941-1943 rokiv (Ohliad dokumentiv).* Derzhavnyi arkhiv Sums'koi oblasti, 2003.

Miuller, N. *Vermakht i okkupatsii (1941-1944). O roli Vermakhta i ego rukovodiashchikh organov v osushchestvlenii okkupatsionnogo rezhima na sovetskoi territorii.* Voenizdat, 1974.

Nesterenko, L. "Ostarbaitery Chernihivshchyny: verbuvannia, umovy pratsi na chuzhyni ta zhyttia pislia povernennia." *Ukrains'ka Druha svitova: Materialy mizhnarodnoi naukovoi konferentsii do 70-i richnytsi peremohy nad natsyzmom u Druhii svitovii viini (5 travnia 2015 r., m. Kyiv),* K. I. S., 2015, pp. 153-61.

Novikov, S. E. "Germanskaia okkupatsionnaia politika na okupirovannoi territorii Belarusi (1941-1944)." *Rossiiskie i slavianskie issledovaniia: nauch. sb.,* no. 2, Belorusskii gosudarstvennyi universitet, 2007, pp. 51-63.

Nuremberg Trial Proceedings. Vol. 20, William S. Hein, 1947, http://avalon.law.yale.edu/imt/08-10-46.asp. Accessed 8 Feb. 2021.

"Ob''iavlenie." *Bakhmutskii vestnik,* 25 Feb. 1942, p. 2.

"Obov''iazkova postanova Dnipropetrovs'koi mis'koi upravy." *Dnipropetrovs'ka hazeta,* 1 Nov. 1941, p. 2.

"Oholoshennia." *Ukrains'ke slovo,* 7 Oct. 1941, p. 4.

Pashchenia, V. N. "'Novyi poriadok' na okkupirovannoi territorii Krymskoi ASSR v 1941-1944 gg. i tatarskii vopros." *Kul'tura narodov Prichernomor'ia,* no. 79, 2006, pp. 82-88.

Perekhrest, O. H. "Sil's'kohospodars'kyi potentsial Ukrainy v heostratehichnykh ta voiennykh planakh natsysts'koi Nimechchyny." *Storinky voiennoi istorii Ukrainy*, vol. 13, 2010, pp. 170-74.

Pol', Diter (Dieter Pohl). "Nimets'ka okupatsiina polityka Ukrainy 1941-1944 u konteksti podii Druhoi svitovoi viiny." *Histor!ans,* 19 June 2015, http://www.historians.in.ua/index.php/en/doslidzhennya/1547-diter-pol-nimetska-okupatsiia-ukrainy-1941-1944-u-konteksti-podii-druhoi-svitovoi-viiny. Accessed 13 Dec. 2018.

"Pratsia v Nimechchyni." *Kam"ians'ki visti*, 1 June 1943, p. 1.

Rauschning, Hermann. *Gespräche mit Hitler*. Europa Verlag, 1940.

"Rozporiadzhennia." *Nove Zaporizhzhia*, no. 12, 21 Dec. 1941, p. 3.

Skorobahatov, A. V. *Kharkiv u chasy nimets'koi okupatsii (1941-1944)*. Prapor, 2004.

Snaider, Timoti (Timothy Snyder). "Znekhtuvana diisnist' Holokostu." *Krytyka*, no. 9-10 (143-144), Sept.-Oct. 2009, pp. 14-16. Translation of Timothy Snyder, "Holocaust: The Ignored Reality," *New York Review of Books*, vol. 56, no. 12, 2009. https://www.nybooks.com/articles/2009/07/16/holocaust-the-ignored-reality/. Accessed 8 Feb. 2021.

Sorokin, G. M., et al. "Nemetsko-fashistskaia sistema ogrableniia i ekonomicheskoi ekspluatatsii okkupirovannykh territorii SSSR." *Nemetsko-fashistskii okkupatsionnyi rezhim (1941-1944): Sbornik statei*, edited by E. A. Boltin, Politizdat, 1965, pp. 151-186.

Spudka, I. M. "Nimets'ka okupatsiina polityka u sotsiokul'turnii sferi v reikhskomisariati 'Ukraina.'" 2007. Zaporiz'kyi natsional'nyi universytet, PhD dissertation (Avtoreferat dys. na zdobuttia nauk. stupenia kand. ist. nauk).

Sukharev, A. Ia, editor. *Niurnbergskii protsess: Sbornik materialov*. Iuridicheskaia Literatura, vol. 1, 1978. 8 vols.

Tarnavs'kyi, I. S. *Polityka Tret'oho Reikhu ta ioho soiuznykiv na okupovanykh ukrains'kykh zemliakh v roky Druhoi svitovoi viiny*. TOV "VPP 'Promin',"2012.

"Ugroza goloda v SSSR." *Odesskaia gazeta*, 23 July 1942, p. 2.

"Vid mis'koi upravy." *Ukrains'kyi holos*, 15 Oct. 1941, p. 4.

Vrons'ka, T. V., et al., editors. *Kyiv u dni natsysts'koi navaly: Za dokumentamy radians'kykh spetssluzhb*. Instytut istorii Ukrainy, 2003.

Dying Hungry: Nazi Ideology and the Pragmatism behind Starvation in Implementing the Final Solution

Kiril Feferman
Ariel University

Abstract: German theories and policies regarding the relationship between food and Jewish citizens of eastern Europe served as an important foundation of the Nazis' *Judenpolitik* during the Holocaust (1933-45). The mass starvation of Jews in German-dominated Europe was the result of a carefully calculated policy to make the Jews pay for a long list of misfortunes they had allegedly inflicted on the Germans. This policy evolved from a highly restrictive and discriminatory approach toward German Jews, which unfolded against a backdrop of harsh food policies applied to the local non-Jewish population.

Keywords: food, malnutrition, starvation, Holocaust, war.

INTRODUCTION

Weaponizing food supplies to achieve political and military goals is a relatively widespread phenomenon in human history, and, along with Hitler's racist ideology, explains German food policies toward Jews during World War II (Oberschall and Seidman; De Waal 94-112). The Nazis' position was that there was no room for Jewish existence in the German-dominated world and this goal must be achieved as quickly as possible (Browning 374-423). Food was in short supply in the German Reich even prior to the German invasion of the Soviet Union in 1941, and the longer the war dragged on, the more acute the food problem became.

These were the considerations put forth by some of the economic experts who participated in a high-level gathering in Berlin on 2 May 1941. The meeting included General Georg Thomas, Wehrmacht supreme "economic" officer, and was convened to determine food policy for the occupied Soviet territories (Kay 697). Pragmatic considerations might have been to feed some of the Jews in order to extend the Jewish forced labour in the German war machine.

However, the pragmatists were not the only actors determining the contours of German food policies toward the Jews. Notable among them were some "old fighters" in the Nazi movement, who contended that the

Jews would have to be starved precisely because of how they had behaved toward the German population during World War I, which, they claimed, ultimately brought about the German collapse (Cory 128-30).[1]
Nazi Germany's food policies reflected approaches advocated by German ideologists and pragmatists. This article outlines the Nazis' views on the food factor vis-à-vis Jews prior to the Nazi seizure of power in Germany in January 1933, before the onset of World War II, during the war on the territory of the German Reich, and in the Polish and Soviet territories under German control. Special emphasis is placed on the impact of German food policies on Jewish society.

Nazi Views on Jews and the Food Situation in Germany

Prior to their ascent to power, Nazi ideologists, including Hitler, had declared that there was a relationship between the food situation and the Jewish question. Their stance can be traced back to the noticeable deterioration in the food situation in Kaiser Germany during World War I (see, for example, Davis, especially 170-216; and Allen). From the Nazi perspective, this development did not come about spontaneously, or as a result of poor planning, or from the Allies' blockade as is often assumed in scholarship (Braun 25-26). The Nazis suspected that German Jews were actively involved in and benefitting from the food deficit and the flourishing black market. The Nazis posited that it was the growing dissatisfaction of ordinary German civilians with wartime hardships, including food deficits, that eventually brought about the collapse of the German home front and the humiliating defeat of the country in World War I (Götz 30).

The Nazis drew several lessons from this "Great War." First, a proper food procurement system was recognized as a factor of paramount importance to the resilience of the home front and to secure victory in the war overall. Second, all means were justifiable to avoid the erosion of civilian morale that would follow from a deterioration in the availability of food. Third, other peoples would have to pay for the well-being of Germans. Among the other peoples, Jews were singled out to suffer particularly from Nazi food policies, in keeping with Nazi racial doctrine. Nazi fanatics contended that Jews bore the principal responsibility for the German defeat in World War I and hence should be punished by starvation, as the Jews were accused of employing starvation against the German civilian population. Thus, an agreement was reached between Nazi pragmatists and

---

[1] The most prominent was Herbert Backe, who in 1942 became the Staatssekretär for the Ministry for Food, and in 1944, for the Ministry of Agriculture.

Nazi fanatics, who had differing approaches to food policy concerning the Jews.

Nazi Germany

When the Nazis rose to power in 1933, the aforementioned theoretical considerations became translated into policy. The new Nazi government had to tackle a grave food crisis that brought people to the point of hunger, and a vow to eliminate hunger was one of its most important promises. The Nazi food policy frequently overlapped with their promise to rid the German nation of Jews (Weinreb 50); however, their propaganda described the current hunger as a weapon wielded by the Jews (Weinreb 52). A study published in 1937 by Richard Darré, German Minister of Food and Agriculture, considered the elimination of German Jews against the background of the country's autarchic food policies (Weinreb 58). A serious phase of discrimination in food policy was reached as the German state ramped up for war in August 1939, when rationing was introduced throughout the German Reich. Predictably, the policy was predicated on Nazi racial-biological ideology that presumed a racial pecking order.

As a result, German Jews were confronted with increasing discrimination in food rations in various forms, some depending on local decision-makers, others centrally orchestrated. This included *inter alia* higher prices, lower rations, and restrictions on the hours that Jews were allowed to shop in food stores (Kaplan 150-51). A corollary of this policy was a growing popular enmity toward Jews shopping amidst Germans (Kaplan 33-34). Nonetheless, unlike in Eastern Europe, there is no record of starvation among German Jews during World War II because the overall level of food provisions delivered to the population in Germany was considerably higher than elsewhere in Europe, especially in eastern Europe. In addition, in conducting its Jewish policies in the Reich, the German government avoided creating situations that would risk alienating the local population. This included avoiding the starvation of the Jews in Germany (see, for example, Cesarani 149).

Occupied Poland

The situation was markedly worse for the Jews in German-occupied Poland, where they were rounded up and incarcerated in ghettos. German policies toward Jews evolved as a result of constant interactions and disputes in the German administration between those eager to capitalize on Jewish labour and those willing to facilitate the total extraction of Jewish wealth through the leverage of deliberate starvation (Browning 113). Thus, the German policies in occupied Poland reflected old disagreements between the ideologists and the pragmatists.

German orders for occupied Poland stipulated that, in terms of calories, each Jew was entitled to roughly what a prisoner of war could expect, which was half of what was allocated to Poles. As a result, even the most privileged Jews in the community, whether incarcerated in ghettos or in civilian camps, were doomed to starvation (Janczewska; see also Roland 99-104). Every free Jew had now the same aim of every prisoner of Nazi camps: to procure food. This was difficult all over German-dominated Europe, as food was becoming increasingly scarce (Obenaus). However, the situation in German-controlled Poland was considerably worse than elsewhere, except for the occupied Soviet territories (excluding the former Baltic states) (Kroener et al. 376-77).

The growing danger of starvation led to appalling inequality in Jewish society in the ghettos and camps. *Judenrat* officials were entitled to 1,665 calories per day, which was high compared to the entitlement of other ghetto inhabitants, but still considerably below the survival level of 2,400 calories. Those working during the day needed 3,000 calories to maintain their health. These privileged Jews were uniquely placed to abuse their positions and to extort bribes from other Jews. The tiny stratum of wealthy Jews also fared well in the ghettos. Consequently, a small minority of Jews experienced a certain degree of feast amidst famine. This feast continued until the beginning of the large-scale deportations from the ghettos to death camps in occupied Poland that started in the summer of 1942.

Jewish refugees from other locations within Poland were at the bottom of the nutrition, or to be more precise, malnutrition ladder;[2] they were entitled to 807 calories per day. Farther below were the unemployed, who received still less. To survive, people in these categories needed to supplement their rations; otherwise, they were on a fast track to starvation, and frequently became the first Jews to perish in the ghettos.

Theoretically, work was the only way for a Jew imprisoned in a ghetto or a camp to survive. Work not only protected Jews from deportation, it entitled them to higher food rations (Gruner). Yet, on closer examination, it turns out that Jews lawfully employed received only 1,220 calories per day, that is, far below the minimum needed for survival. Privileged categories of the Jewish population, such as Jewish police and very skilled workers, were entitled to increased rations (and there were free meals for children), but even the privileged needed more than their rations to ensure their survival and that of their families. In order to survive, everyone in the ghetto, except perhaps the wealthiest and the highest stratum of the *Judenrat* bureaucrats, needed to augment their rations somehow.

[2] Every region was assigned one ghetto, and Jews from all over the region were assembled there.

The most widespread method of accessing more food was to become involved in food smuggling. This entailed breaking the law and was fraught with mortal danger, as the guards (either Polish or German) shot freely at those caught smuggling. If food smugglers were fortunate enough to avoid the guards, they could be seized by Jewish policemen who could turn them over to local or German police, or in the best case, content themselves with extorting a bribe.

Despite these risks, the food conditions were so appalling that increasing numbers of Jews in the ghettos saw smuggling as their only chance of survival. The natural outcome of the Jewish demand for food and the supply offered by the local population, primarily peasants, was the development of a black market (Kochanowski). Jews thus sold or exchanged their personal belongings in this illegal market for food at prices that reflected the inadequate food supply in the General Government. Pressure on the food supply was augmented by the arbitrary requisitioning of troops and private purchases by members of the occupying power (Kroener et al. 378-79).

Official German opposition to the black market served to further increase the price of produce, as locals assessed and factored in the risks involved in selling foodstuffs to Jews. Finally, prices, or the exchange rate, for food depended on availability (unavailability in the ghettos). Consequently, Jews had to pay increasingly exorbitant prices for food, while those able to produce food, primarily peasants, benefitted.

Because of their small size, children carried out most of the food smuggling; they were able to penetrate through small openings in the walls surrounding the ghettos. Thus, Jewish child smugglers began to provide food for themselves, and eventually for their families. The new role of children as providers for their families should be contrasted with the inability of their parents to provide not only for themselves but also for their children—a development unprecedented in Jewish history, and perhaps in world history. As a result of a reversal of the natural order, the family as a solid institution and a cornerstone of society dissolved or collapsed in the ghettos.

Another widespread method of obtaining extra food was by denouncing other ghetto inhabitants, whether to the ghetto authorities or to the Gestapo. However, the price received for a denunciation was low.

Finally, the incessant search for more food led to a sharp decline in moral values among ghetto and camp prisoners. Youth crime increased dramatically. Theft and prostitution, especially among the adolescents, gained currency. Moreover, ghetto inhabitants frequently refused to report to the authorities the deaths of household members in a timely fashion in order to continue receiving food rations meant for the deceased person, essentially a desecration of the dead.

Although smuggling grew significantly, it failed to solve the food problem for many ghetto inhabitants. A sharp deterioration in the food situation was noticeable everywhere in the ghettos and camps, and its most visible manifestations were a rapid increase in the mortality rate and public indifference to corpses lying in the streets. On 17 May 1941, a German Foreign Ministry representative attached to the Fourth Army reported the situation in the Warsaw ghetto: "the incidence of death from starvation increased massively. Weakened, emaciated to skeletons, women, men, and children are lying about the pavements with distorted faces" (Kroener et al. 379). The problem of malnutrition haunted everyone. Judging by contemporary accounts, all people could think about was the ache in their stomachs and where they might find something to eat (Goldenberg 166-69).

Outside of the ghettos, in cases where Jews were rescued, their rescuers had to provide food for the Jews in their shelters. The inability or reluctance of a potential rescuer to procure food was tantamount to a death sentence for these Jews (Michlic).

Occupied Soviet Territories

Territories that Nazi Germany occupied in the course of its invasion of the Soviet Union were administered as colonies, which meant they received even harsher treatment than other areas under German control (Lower 18-29). The policy was grounded in the need to mobilize maximum resources to provide the fighting forces and the homeland with urgently needed raw materials and foodstuffs. Given the expected exacerbation of shortages in the Reich in the autumn of 1941, the Wehrmacht intended to occupy the Soviet wheat-producing regions and maintain operations largely by living off the land (Müller, "From Economic Alliance" 140-41). This policy was reiterated on several occasions by the highest civil and military authorities of the Reich (Müller, "From Economic Alliance" 174-75).

To achieve these goals, the urban populations of the western Soviet Union and Ukraine were to be starved, including, first and foremost, the Jews (Kay). The destruction of the Jews was regarded by Nazi pragmatists as necessary to rid the territories under German control of "surplus mouths." These notions were succinctly expressed in a report sent on 2 December 1941 by Professor P. H. Seraphim, a logistics expert in Ukraine, to General Thomas from the Wehrmacht Economic Department:

> The creaming-off of agricultural surpluses from the Ukraine as food supplies for the Reich is only conceivable if trade in the Ukraine is pushed down to a minimum. Efforts to achieve this will be made by:

1. Eradicating surplus mouths (Jews, and the population of the large Ukrainian cities) which, like Kyiv, will receive no quota of supplies. (Burleigh 221)

Certainly, there were differences in German approaches to food policy depending on specific local conditions, yet several basic assumptions hold true. German plans regarding food provisioning were realized to no small extent in the occupied Soviet territories (Berkhoff 164-86; see also Burleigh). However, there were exceptions, primarily in the former Baltic states (Kroener et al. 382) and the northern Caucasus (Feferman, "The Food Factor" 87-90), which were singled out for political, strategic, or ideological reasons.

How did the realization of the German plans affect the unfolding of the "Final Solution" in the occupied Soviet areas? Often in areas where German plans were implemented, food scarcity for the entire civil population under German control soon reached a critical point, necessitating drastic decisions, as inaction could prompt enormous opposition to German rule. One solution was to procure food for the entire civil population, but this ran counter to the stance of Nazi ideologues and pragmatists alike (Gerlach 265-88). The elimination of "surplus mouths" was the solution Nazi decision-makers initially came up with, a solution that involved provisioning the local population with food below the subsistence level. This was the case on the Crimean Peninsula in November-December 1941 (Feferman, "The Food Factor" 78-84) where it received the full support of General Erich von Manstein, the highest German military authority in the region: "The food situation in our Fatherland requires that the troops be supplied with food from local resources and, furthermore, that as much stocks as possible be put at the Fatherland's disposal . . . . A considerable part of the population of the enemy's towns will have to starve" (Feferman, *The Holocaust* 238).

It was assumed that local people would be able to live off their own resources, as they were able to significantly augment these resources by looting abandoned Soviet storage facilities and food stores during the interim period (after the Red Army left but before the Wehrmacht entered). Such incidents did take place, but their significance should not be overrated because the retreating Soviet forces, acting on the orders of the high command, either destroyed food storage locations or took considerable food stocks with them. These facts were known to local people and widely employed by Nazi propaganda, which reiterated that only Bolsheviks bore responsibility for the miserable food conditions in the occupied territories. According to a German military expert in Reichskommissariat Ukraine in November 1941, German food policy in the Reichskommissariat was tantamount to the "extermination of Jews" (Berkhoff 167).

Later, when the situation at the fronts worsened, the Germans departed from their rigid, ideologically driven policies and increased the food supply by deporting a portion of the urban population to the countryside (Kroener et al. 383). Yet, this moderate phase was of little relevance to the local Jews, who were mostly murdered by that time. In areas of the Soviet Union where mass murders were carried out early on, German food policies did not have time to impact the Jewish population. However, in places where the Germans allowed a more protracted Jewish existence in the ghettos (such as in Kaunas, Vilnius, and Minsk), local Jews went through sufferings similar to Jews in Poland (Aleksiun). The introduction of maximum rations in towns on 4 November 1941, illustrates the inadequate, in fact starvation-level, food provisioning policy. The nutritional value of these rations was about 1,200 calories per day for those doing "useful work," roughly 850 calories for those not employed in German projects, and 420 calories for children under the age of 14 and for Jews (Müller, "The Failure" 1163). Moreover, even these meagre rations were issued only if the German authorities decided that the local population had exhausted its stocks, and provided that deliveries to the Reich were not affected. These were starvation rations for most non-Jews, but the Jews were usually the first to perish, as their allocation was the lowest.

Conclusion

German theories and policies regarding Jews and food constituted one of the most important foundations of the Nazis' *Judenpolitik*. The mass starvation of Jews in German-dominated Europe was the result of a carefully calculated policy. The Germans aspired to murder the Jews, but their deaths were not to be easy; through attrition and starvation the Jews had to pay for a long list of misfortunes they had allegedly inflicted on the Germans. This policy evolved from a highly restrictive and discriminatory approach toward German Jews in the Reich to a full-fledged starvation policy applied to the Jews in eastern Europe, which unfolded against the backdrop of very harsh food policies applied to the local non-Jewish population.

Works Cited

Aleksiun, Natalia. "Food, Money and Barter in the Lvov Ghetto, Eastern Galicia." *Coping with Hunger and Shortage under German Occupation in World War II,* edited by Tatjana Tönsmeyer et al., Palgrave Macmillan, 2018, pp. 223-47.

Allen, Keith. "Sharing Scarcity: Bread Rationing and the First World War in Berlin, 1914-1923." *Journal of Social History*, vol. 32, no. 2, 1998, pp. 371-93. DOI: 10.1353/jsh/32.2.371

Berkhoff, Karel C. *Harvest of Despair: Life and Death in Ukraine under Nazi Rule*. Belknap Press, 2004.

Braun, Hans-Joachim. *The German Economy in the Twentieth Century*. Routledge, 1990.

Browning, Christopher R. *The Origins of the Final Solution: The Evolution of Nazi Jewish Policy, September 1939–March 1942*. Nebraska UP and Yad Vashem, 2004.

Burleigh, Michael. *Germany Turns Eastwards. A Study of Ostforschung in the Third Reich*. Cambridge UP, 1988.

Cesarani, David. *Final Solution: The Fate of the Jews 1933-1949*. Macmillan, 2015.

Cory, Brant Wamick. *The Food Crisis in Germany and Its Consequences, 1918-1924*. 1999. Virginia Commonwealth University, MA thesis.

Davis, Belinda Joy. *Home Fires Burning: Food, Politics, and Everyday Life in World War I Berlin*. North Carolina UP, 2000.

De Waal, Alex. *Mass Starvation: The History and Future of Famine*. Polity Press, 2018.

Feferman, Kiril. "The Food Factor as a Possible Catalyst for Holocaust-Related Decisions: The Crimea and the North Caucasus." *War in History*, vol. 15, no. 1, 2008, pp. 72-91. DOI: 10.1177/0968344507083994

---. *The Holocaust in the Crimea and the North Caucasus*. Yad Vashem, 2016.

Gerlach, Christian. *Kalkulierte Morde: Die deutsche Wirtschafts- und Vernichtungspolitik in Weißrußland 1941 bis 1944*. Hamburger Edition, 1999.

Goldenberg, Myrna. "Food Talk: Gendered Responses to Hunger in the Concentration Camps." *Experience and Expression: Women, the Nazis, and the Holocaust*, edited by Elizabeth R. Baer and Myrna Goldenberg, Wayne State UP, 2003, pp. 161-79.

Götz, Aly. *Hitler's Beneficiaries: Plunder, Racial War, and the Nazi Welfare State*. Metropolitan Books, 2007.

Gruner, Wolf. *Jewish Forced Labor under the Nazis: Economic Needs and Racial Aims, 1938-1944*. Cambridge UP, 2006.

Janczewska, Marta. "Research on Starvation in the Warsaw Ghetto—Ethical Dilemmas." *Holocaust Studies and Materials*, vol. 2, 2010, pp. 439-50.

Kaplan, Marion A. *Between Dignity and Despair: Jewish Life in Nazi Germany*. Oxford UP, 1998.

Kay, Alex J. "Germany's Staatssekretäre, Mass Starvation and the Meeting of 2 May 1941." *Journal of Contemporary History*, vol. 41, no. 4, 2006, pp. 685-700. DOI: 10.1177/0022009406067750

Kochanowski, Jerzy. "Black Market in the General Government 1939-1945: Survival Strategy or (Un)Official Economy?" *Coping with Hunger and Shortage under German Occupation in World War II*, edited by Tatjana Tönsmeyer et al., Palgrave Macmillan, 2018, pp. 27-47.

Kroener, Bernhard R., et al., editors. *Germany and the Second World War.* Vol. 5: *Organization and Mobilization of the German Sphere of Power,* part 1: *Wartime Administration, Economy, and Manpower Resources, 1939-1941.* Clarendon Press, 2000.

Lower, Wendy. *Nazi Empire-Building and the Holocaust in Ukraine.* North Carolina UP, 2005.

Michlic, Joanna. "Stories of Rescue Activities in the Letters of Jewish Survivors about Christian Polish Rescuers, 1944-1949." *Warsaw: The Jewish Metropolis. Essays in Honor of the 75th Birthday of Professor Antony Polonsky.* Edited by Glenn Dynner and François Guesnet, Brill, 2015, pp. 515-38. IJS Studies in Judaica 15.

Müller, Rolf-Dieter. "From Economic Alliance to a War of Colonial Exploitation." *The Attack on the Soviet Union*, edited by H. Boog et al., Oxford UP, 1998, pp. 118-224.

---. "The Failure of the 'Economic Blitzkrieg' Strategy." *The Attack on the Soviet Union*, edited by H. Boog et al., Oxford UP, 1998, pp. 1081-1244.

Obenaus, Herbert. "Hunger und Überleben in den nationalsozialistischen Konzentrationslagern (1938-1945)." *Der Kampf um das tägliche Brot; Nahrungsmangel, Versorgungspolitik und Protest, 1770-1990*, edited by Manfred Gailus and Heinrich Volkmann, Westdeutscher Verlag, 1994, pp. 361-76.

Oberschall, Antony, and Michael Seidman. "Food Coercion in Revolution and Civil War: How They Do It." *Comparative Study of Society and History*, vol. 47, no. 2, 2005, pp. 372-402. DOI: 10.1017/S0010417505000174

Roland, Charles G. *Courage under Siege: Starvation, Disease, and Death in the Warsaw Ghetto*. Oxford UP, 1992.

Weinreb, Alice. *Modern Hungers: Food and Power in Twentieth-Century Germany*. Oxford UP, 2017.

Food Supply, Starvation, and Food As a Weapon in the Camps and Ghettos of Romanian-Occupied Bessarabia and Transnistria, 1941-44

Paul A. Shapiro
United States Holocaust Memorial Museum

Abstract: The Romanian regime of wartime leader Ion Antonescu concentrated the Jews of Bessarabia and Bukovyna in transit camps and ghettos, and then deported them to the Romanian-administered territory between the Dnister and Buh rivers, in southwestern Ukraine. Of approximately 160,000 Romanian Jews deported to "Transnistria," only 50,000 survived the ordeal. The Romanians, with local Volksdeutsch and Ukrainian collaborators, also massacred and were otherwise responsible for the death of approximately 150,000 local Ukrainian Jews, including the large Jewish community of Odesa. While not comparable to the Jews in number, deported Romanian Roma and local Roma were also subjected to physical brutality, forced labour, and incarceration.

Famine and starvation did not cause all Jewish and Roma deaths in Bessarabia and Transnistria. Mass executions exacted a huge toll. So did exposure to the elements, exhaustion, and typhus. Still, while there was no famine in the region, starvation was a permanent presence. Romanian authorities controlled the food supply and denied it to their targeted victims. This article describes the steps taken by Romanian occupation authorities to isolate Jews and Roma; to limit the flow of food supplies to them; to prevent them from accessing food in local markets; and to prevent help that might have been offered by those local civilians who took pity on the starving victims. Official documentation and testimonies of both officials and survivors provide a vivid picture of the consequences. Specific cases reveal factors that made the situation in one locality better or worse than that in another, or that caused a situation to improve or deteriorate. Variations notwithstanding, however, all sources lead to the conclusion that Romania's goal was to eliminate the Jews and reduce the Roma population. This made starvation, the use of "food as a weapon," an acceptable element of state policy.

Keywords: Bessarabia, Transnistria, Romania, Holocaust, Roma, starvation.

Famine and starvation: does this phrase describe the situation that prevailed in Bessarabia after Romania regained control of the province in mid-1941, following a year of Soviet occupation? Does it adequately describe the realities of the situation in Transnistria, the territory stretching from the Dnister to the Buh rivers that Romania occupied during World War II? Do famine and starvation explain the deaths of between 280,000 and 380,000 Jews and nearly half of the 25,000 Roma from Romania who were deported eastward by the Antonescu regime, or who, as local inhabitants of Transnistria, found themselves in the hands of Romanian authorities between 1941 and 1944?

The answers to these questions clearly must be "no," or at least "it is not that simple." There was no famine in either Bessarabia or Transnistria. Indeed, as the Romanians were shipping immense quantities of foodstuff out of Romania to their Axis ally, Germany, they were simultaneously requisitioning agricultural products from Transnistrian farms and transporting food from Transnistria into Romania proper.[1] Romanian occupation authorities maintained the collective farm system that had been installed by the Soviets, and they levied food delivery requirements, just as the Soviets had, to supply themselves and contribute to the food supply available at home.

Romanian policy toward the Jews of Bessarabia and Transnistria was intentionally demeaning, brutal, and lethal. Control of the food supply and systematic starvation, however, were hardly the only murderous techniques that the Romanians deployed to achieve their policy goals regarding Jews, which had been enunciated clearly by wartime dictator and military leader "*Conducător*" Ion Antonescu and his Vice President of the Council of Ministers Mihai Antonescu. The policy they laid down was carried out without hesitation by their principal accomplices in the territories addressed here—the governor of Bessarabia Constantin Voiculescu, Transnistria governor Gheorghe Alexianu, and General Constantin Z. ("Piki") Vasiliu, Director General of the Gendarmerie in the Romanian Ministry of Interior. Ion Antonescu, in establishing "cleansing the terrain" of Jews ("*curățirea terenului*") as national policy, declared on 4 July 1941, as Romanian forces entered Bessarabia, "The Jews have drained, impoverished, speculated against and prevented the development of the Romanian nation for centuries. There can be no debate regarding the need to escape from this plague against Romanianism . . . ."[2] Four days later, Mihai Antonescu, at a meeting of the Council of Ministers, which he chaired

---

[1] For an early study of the roots and magnitude of Romanian economic obligations to Germany, including food shipments, see Niri. Romania's systematic pillage and removal of Transnistrian economic resources, ranging from industrial facilities and transportation infrastructure to cultural assets and food, is explored in detail, on the basis of documentation that became accessible following the collapse of Communist regimes in eastern Europe and the Soviet Union, in Solonari. The exploitation of food requisitioned from Transnistrian collective farms is addressed in Verenca and in various reports issued by the Antonescu government during the war. Germany's disappointment that these surpluses were not fully available for German use is noted in Axworthy 137. The most authoritative monographic source on Romanian-German relations during the war is Trașcă, *Relațiile Politice*.

[2] Order of 4 July 1941, Ion Antonescu to military and gendarmerie units, in *Evreii din România între Anii 1940-1944: Perioada* 1: 256-57. All translations are my own.

during the Conducător's frequent absences at the front, summarized Ion Antonescu's intentions in an even more menacing tone:

> At the risk of not being understood by any traditionalists who may remain among you, I am for the forced migration of the entire Jewish element from Bessarabia and Bukovyna . . . . I am indifferent if in history we are deemed to be barbarians . . . . There has been no more favourable, more unfettered, more propitious or more unconstrained moment in our history for a total ethnic resolution . . . and for the purification of our nation . . . . If necessary, use machine guns.[3]

Tens of thousands of Jews in Bessarabia and in Transnistria were simply shot on the spot during the advance across Bessarabia and southwestern Ukraine of Romanian military forces and the Einsatzgruppen-like "operational [killing] units" ("*eşaloane operative*") that had been created by Romanian authorities. Jews were murdered on the streets of Chişinău during a week of wild killing before the creation of the ghetto there, and then in massacres of able-bodied Jews from that ghetto, which were designed to reduce the potential for resistance on the eve of approaching deportations. The killing continued during the forced marches of columns of Jews from Bessarabia to Transnistria, and from location to location in Transnistria, where the standing order was to execute any Jew—man, woman, or child—who fell behind the column. On the streets of Odesa and at Dalnic on the outskirts of the city, Jews seeking to escape the warehouses that the Romanians had set ablaze, with some 16,000 Jews inside, were met with machine-gun fire. In the Berezivka (Berezovca) district, Volksdeutsch colonists eagerly participated in executing Jews being evacuated north from Odesa. In Holta (Golta) district, over several weeks in December 1941-January 1942, between 48,000 and 52,000 Jews were shot to death at Bohdanivka (Bogdanovca), Domanivka (Domanovca), and Akmechetski Stavky (Acmecetca).

At Bohdanivka, as at Dalnic, Jews were burned alive. One of the pigsties where they were being held was set on fire by the Romanians, as a means of "encouraging" other Jews interned on that collective farm to proceed more willingly to the shooting site. Jews were hanged from lampposts on the streets of Odesa in retribution for the dynamiting of the military headquarters building, which in reality had been mined by withdrawing Soviet forces, not by Odesan Jews.[4] And many Jews quite simply were left

---

[3] The minutes of the meeting can be found in *Evreii din România între Anii 1940-1944—Problema* 264-68; also excerpted in Carp 3: 92.

[4] For well-documented accounts in English of Romania's involvement in the Holocaust, including these events, see Ioanid, *Holocaust*; Ancel, *History*; Ancel, *Transnistria*; and Shapiro,

exposed to the weather with neither shelter nor heat and froze to death in ghettos and camps across Transnistria, especially during the brutally cold winter of 1941-42. Roma deportees who arrived later were also deprived of adequate shelter and succumbed in significant numbers to cold, disease, and exhaustion.[5]

Yet even within this litany of murder techniques, the impact of the food factor manifested itself at all stages of the persecution and destruction process. Hunger and starvation became a daily reality because of the rules established by the regime, according to which Jews and Roma in most cases were supposed to provide for their own food needs through work. The disproportionately large number of elderly, women, and children relative to able-bodied workers among the victims and the severe restrictions placed on their freedom to go in search of either work or food made this a virtual impossibility. The refusal of potential employers, as well as many actual users of forced labour, to pay or feed Jewish and Romani labourers further aggravated the tragic situation confronting the persecutees. The authorities controlled food supplies, and the needs of everyone else, both locally and in Romania proper, took priority over the needs of Jews and Roma. Both Jews and Roma found themselves in a constant state of panic regarding food. Malnutrition was pervasive, and starvation was common. Moreover, in some specific instances control of diet was used in premeditated fashion as a lethal weapon, designed to kill.

There has been no comprehensive study of this issue, but a wealth of documentary and testimonial resources that address the food issue exists, enough to support a serious monographic study. In the pages that follow, it is possible to present only samples of those sources as they relate to the transit camps and ghettos in Bessarabia, to Jewish deportees and local Jews in Transnistria, and to Roma deportees to Transnistria. The perspectives of Romanian authorities and of their victims emerge clearly from this material.

Kishinev Ghetto. Because the majority of citations in this essay are to sources originally in the Romanian language, when they first appear I have provided in parenthesis the Romanian spellings of Ukrainian localities that were in Romanian-administered Transnistria during World War II.

[5] The recently completed third volume of the *United States Holocaust Memorial Museum Encyclopedia of Camps and Ghettos 1933-1945*, dedicated to the camps and ghettos under European regimes that were aligned with Nazi Germany, includes detailed information, with extensive citations of primary source material, regarding the camps and ghettos established by Romanian authorities in Bessarabia, Bukovyna, and Transnistria, including the majority of those to which reference is made in this article. See Megargee et al. 569-830.

The Bessarabian Transit Camps

According to the 1930 Romanian census, 206,958 Jews lived in Bessarabia. The number had grown to an estimated 225,000 or more a decade later. On the eve of Operation Barbarossa, General Vasiliu informed the leadership of gendarmerie units that were to proceed into Bessarabia with the first wave of the military attack that "cleansing the terrain" meant "the extermination on the spot of all Jews in rural areas, [and] enclosing in ghettos the Jews in urban areas . . . ."[6] Despite the massive killing that followed, not all the Jews in rural towns and villages were murdered in this first wave. A sequence of orders followed, first, to "identify and arrest all Jews, of every age and gender, still found in rural districts,"[7] then, to ensure "the removal of Jews from the villages,"[8] and finally, on the order of Governor Voiculescu, to create camps in which all Jews in rural areas were to be concentrated and subjected to physically exhausting forced labour on roads, bridge repair, earthworks, and similar projects. Jews in cities were to register within three days and were also to be used for forced labour. In Chişinău, Voiculescu ordered "acceleration of the operation of establishing a ghetto."[9]

The concentration and isolation of Jews in restricted rural locations immediately triggered a crisis of food supply, quickly recognized by authorities on the ground and felt by Jewish internees. Transit camps were established in response to Voiculescu's order and encircled with barbed wire. They were intended by the Romanians as temporary holding sites, where Jews would be kept until it was possible to deport them, first across the Dnister into Transnistria and then to German-occupied Ukrainian territory beyond the Buh.[10] The principal transit camps were large.

[6] United States Holocaust Memorial Museum Archive (USHMM) RG-25.004/Romanian Information Service Archives, Roll 16, File 22539, vol. 32, ff. 5-6, Document of [Postwar War Crimes Trial] Indictment—Case 547/1950; the indictment, including the quoted passage, is also excerpted in facsimile in Ancel, *Documents* 5: 2-6 and 6: 441-55.

[7] Circular Order No. 1 of 8 July 1941, from [Teodor] Meculescu, Chişinău Inspectorate of Gendarmerie, excerpted in Carp 3: 92.

[8] USHMM RG-25.003/Archives of the Romanian Ministry of National Defense, Roll 125 (old 655), Fond Guvernămîntul Basarabiei, Cabinet Militar, Folder 25, ff. 520-22, Copy of telegraphic order No. 143 from Vice President of the Council of Ministers to Voiculescu, 12 July 1941.

[9] This order was widely distributed. See, for example, USHMM RG-54.001/State Archival Services of Moldova, Roll 17, Fond 680, Opis 1, Folder 4230-1, f.1, Voiculescu Order No. 61 of 24 July 1941 to Inspectorate of Police Chişinău, registered as received by the Inspectorate on 28 July. The same order went to all county prefectures, mayoral offices, the Military Commander of Chişinău, police offices, and gendarmerie offices. The order has been published in Benjamin 214.

[10] The Romanian government's desire to deport the Jews of Bessarabia and Bukovyna eastward immediately, first across the Dnister and then across the Buh, was frustrated from the start by German unwillingness to have masses of Jews pushed into territories under German control where military operations were continuing. By formal agreement concluded

Statistics have survived in Romanian government records. On 1 September 1941, just a few weeks after the re-entry of Romanian forces into Bessarabia, for example, there were 23,549 Jews in the transit camp at Vertiujeni; 11,762 at Edineţ; 10,737 at Mărculeşti; and 10,356 at Sokyriany (Secureni).

Figure 1. Map of camps in Old Romania, Bessarabia, and Bukovyna. Courtesy of the United States Holocaust Memorial Museum.[11]

On 17 July, General Ion Topor, Grand Praetor of the Romanian Army (chief of the military gendarmerie) reported to General Staff Headquarters that several thousand Jews were already in detention at Bălţi and that additional Jews were being sent in the direction of Bălţi by various advancing army units. He reported that he lacked the manpower to guard them and lacked sufficient food for the 8,500 Jews that he anticipated would

---

on 30 August 1941, the Romanians assumed administrative authority in Transnistria, but were constrained to postpone deportations across the Buh until the conclusion of military operations. The concentration of Jews in camps and ghettos in Bessarabia, and then in Transnistria, was one result of this contretemps between Romanian and German authorities. See Ioanid, *Holocaust*, 115-22.

[11] This and the other two maps reproduced in this article first appeared in United States Holocaust Memorial Museum, *Encyclopedia of Camps and Ghettos 1933-1945*, vol. 3, Indiana UP, 2018.

soon be concentrated there. Describing the situation as untenable, Topor suggested to his military leadership and to the Ministry of Interior that the Jews be sent to the interior of Romania.[12] General Nicolae Tătăranu at General Staff Headquarters responded that the internees were to stay put and indicated that they should be fed by the local Jewish community. This proposed solution to the food problem was totally unrealistic. The Bălţi Jewish community had already lost its leadership and many of its members to shooting squads, and the surviving Jews were being forced into a ghetto.[13] The Ministry of Interior communicated to every gendarmerie inspectorate Ion Antonescu's confidential orders that all Jews in detention were to be put to hard labour and that Jews who did not work were not only to be denied a food ration, but also were to be prevented from receiving food from any other source.[14]

The preponderance of the elderly, women, and children among the internees—able-bodied men having been drafted or evacuated by the Soviets or shot on sight by the advancing Germans and Romanians—as well as the isolation imposed on the Jews gave the lie from the very start to the notion that internee populations would be able to feed themselves through work. Nor was the compensation for labour that the government suggested sufficient for this approach to be viable. Moreover, it rapidly became clear that employers, actual or potential, were not anxious to pay or even feed Jewish labourers when they understood that they were not going to be forced to do so.[15]

The result was predictable. In a postwar testimony, Vertiujeni resident Lida Molceanov described the situation in the transit camp outside Vertiujeni. Surrounded by barbed wire and guarded by soldiers, the Jews were forced to pave the streets of the village. But when Molceanov's mother gave Lida small bags of potatoes, polenta, or other bits of food to throw over the wire, the guards chased her and other children away, sometimes beating them. All the while inside the wire "were little children with their

---

[12] USHMM RG-25.004, Roll 25, Fond 20725, vol. 9, f. 305, Report No. 223 of 17 July 1941 from Grand Praetor Topor to General Headquarters; USHMM RG-54.001, Roll 22, Fond 1607, Opis 1, Folder 3-1, f. 460, Telegram No. 229 of 18 July 1941 Topor to Ministry of the Interior.

[13] See Tătăranu's note in the margin of Topor's report (USHMM RG-25.004, Roll 25, Fond 20725, vol. 9, f. 305, Report No. 223 of 17 July 1941 from Grand Praetor Topor to General Headquarters).

[14] Ancel, *Documents* 5: 19, General I. Popescu, Undersecretary of State, Ministry of the Interior, very urgent/confidential Order No. 5011 to the General Inspectorate of the Gendarmerie, 18 July 1941. The content of Antonescu's order also can be found in an official communiqué of the Ministry of Interior dated 18 July 1942, reproduced in *Evreii din România între Anii 1940-1944: Perioada* 1: 396.

[15] On pay scales set by the government and the reluctance of "employers" to follow them, see Shapiro, *Kishinev* 49-51.

hands stretched out to those passing by pleading, 'Give me a piece of bread! Give me a piece of bread! Please give me a piece of bread to eat!'" Another Vertiujeni resident, Valeriu Bogdan, noted that the Jews had no choice other than to sell their valuables or trade them for food. While some internees were able to work for more wealthy villagers (mostly providing tailoring services) in exchange for food, which they took to their families in the camp, Bogdan remembers that the road he walked to school passed by the camp and that he would share his lunch "with the Jews who were begging by the camp fence . . . ." Even as a child he was shocked by the number of people who died in the camp and were buried in the Jewish cemetery outside the village. About twenty to thirty bodies per day, he recalled, all buried "in a big pit."[16]

Romanian authorities were aware of the rapidly deteriorating situation in the transit camps. On 10 September 1941, Bureau II (Counterintelligence) of the Romanian army reported on the situation in the camps in three Bessarabian districts—Bălţi, Soroca, and Khotyn (Hotin). There were three camps in the Bălţi district—Limbenii Noi, Răşcani, Răuţel—with a total of 9,141 internees; the camp of Vertiujeni in Soroca district, with "approximately 23,000 internees"; and two camps in Khotyn district—Sokyriany and Edineţ—with a total of 22,118 inmates. The mayor's office in the city of Bălţi was feeding the internees, "providing two-thirds of a loaf of bread daily per person and once a day a portion of corn meal cooked in oil." "Both the bread and serving of corn meal," the report noted, were "of very poor quality and totally insufficient." Medical care and sanitary facilities were lacking in the camp, and the death rate in was rising. In the camp at Răuţel, where the survivors of the Bălţi Jewish community had been moved from the ghetto in town, a scarlet fever epidemic had broken out, with ten to fifteen people dying each day and "the cadavers lying in the midst of the internees," for lack of a place to put them. The situation was even worse in Soroca district, where neither the mayor's office nor the district prefecture assumed any responsibility for feeding the internees. "The prefecture gave orders that the Jews obtain their own food," the report stated, and continued, "the majority of internees, however, have no money and are forced to simply endure hunger." In Khotyn, the situation was similar. The report concludes:

---

[16] Testimony of Lida Molceanov, Moldova Documentation Project, USHMM, RG-50.572*0013, Box 1, CD 1; and testimony of Valeriu Bogdan, Moldova Documentation Project, USHMM, RG-50.572*0014, Box 1, Tape 1. I want to express special appreciation to my friend and long-time colleague Radu Ioanid, who graciously shared with me information regarding the unique testimonial sources cited in notes 16, 18, 19, 27, and 39.

> [T]aking into consideration the lack of food, the lack of shelter (in some camps in the current bad weather they must stay outside in the rain), and especially the lack of sanitation, these camps will soon become nests of infection and the spread of all types of contagious diseases which will endanger the population and the troops, even if we establish a cordon sanitaire, since we know that hunger will succeed in breaking through any barrier.[17]

Reports such as this definitely reinforced the Romanians' determination to remove the Jews and hastened their preparations to deport all surviving Bessarabian Jews eastward into Transnistria.

Bessarabian Ghettos

In terms of food policy and access to food, the situation in the short-lived ghettos in Bessarabian cities and towns deteriorated less rapidly than in the transit camps, but in the final analysis was little different. The policy of assuming that Jews would feed themselves through work was flawed for reasons similar to those that applied in the transit camps—there were too few able-bodied Jews relative to the entire ghetto population, and "employers" were unwilling to pay or feed Jewish workers enough to enable them to provide for the ghetto's needs. To these factors was added the sad reality, regularly reported by government officials, that the Christian population in Bessarabian towns was antagonistic and complained when Jews were taken out of the ghetto to work sites. They were fearful that the Jews might attempt to return to their homes, which were already occupied by others, or try to remove items from their former homes to trade for food, when those items had already been appropriated by new inhabitants or former neighbours. This attitude of the local population, the growing fear of epidemics, and orders received by late summer in preparation for deportations to restrict entirely the movement of Jews beyond the confines of the ghettos also limited the number of Jews actually used for labour or able to obtain food (Shapiro, *Kishinev* 23-24).

Many powerful descriptions of the situation in smaller ghettos exist, provided by Jewish survivors, Christian eyewitnesses, and official Romanian government and military reporting. For example, a Christian resident of the city of Orhei, Gheorghe Stratan, born in 1920, recalled in his testimony the establishment of the ghetto, when entire families were arrested throughout the town and taken to the ghetto, allowed to take with them

---

[17] Arhivele Militare Române (Romanian Military Archive-AMR), fond 1693-Comandamentul Etapelor de Est, dosar nr. 16, f.23+verso, "Report of 10 September 1941 on the Situation of the Jews in this Command," published in Trașcă, *"Chestiunea evreiască,"* document 101, 262-63.

"nothing other than food, mostly bread." He remembered acquaintances of Jews sometimes bringing food to those arrested and sneaking it through cracks between the wooden planks that surrounded the ghetto. In the same breath, however, he also described the brutality of the police guarding the ghetto, who did all that they could to prevent the locals from feeding or otherwise helping the Jews. Noting that the Jews were not permitted to exit the improvised camp, he spoke vividly of those who died, emphasizing the authorities' lack of respect for the Jews, even after death, reflected in the way the bodies were simply thrown into a truck and hauled away.[18]

Survivor Lida Burihovici was interned together with ninety-six other Jews in the ghetto of Izmail (Ismail) at the southwestern edge of Bessarabia. She described in frightening detail the abuses to which internees were subjected: shoved, beaten, kicked; sick and elderly taken away and never seen again; young girls raped in front of their families. As for food, she declared:

> [W]e had only what we had brought with us. When we left our home my uncle and I wanted to bring clothes, but mama said to bring food. She put together two small bags with dishes and a sack full of food, but they were very heavy and we abandoned them on the way. So our food was finished quickly. We were lucky that local Ukrainians would throw us something over the fence to shove into our mouths . . . .[19]

The situation in the large ghetto in Chişinău, the provincial capital, was also perilous. At its high point there were 11,525 Jews crammed into a few streets in the very centre of the city, but separated from the world outside by a closely guarded wooden fence. In the first weeks of the ghetto's existence, Romanian authorities made an effort, albeit insufficient, to make food available in the ghetto. The authorities appointed a Jewish Ghetto Committee, and on 1 August, Chişinău garrison commander Colonel Dumitru Tudose agreed to the operation of a bakery, which was to be provided with flour from the Chişinău garrison. The ghetto committee was to use the money from bread sales to Jews who could afford to pay to assist the destitute. Tudose also authorized the establishment of a ghetto marketplace, and peasants were permitted to enter the ghetto to sell produce and other food products. Conditions, however, deteriorated rapidly. After a few weeks even official reports by the Regional Police

---

[18] Testimony of Gheorghe Stratan, Moldova Documentation Project, USHMM RG-50.572*0026, Box 1, Tape 1.

[19] Testimony (part 2) of Lida Burihovici-Havas, interviewed by Andrea Ghita on 3 October 2010, accessible at http://www.acum.tv/articol/18373 under title "Mărturii cutremurătoare despre calvarul din Transnistria." Accessed 15 Aug. 2017.

Inspectorate stated that the availability of food in the ghetto was very limited and the prices very high. The supply of flour to the bakery was inadequate, providing for the distribution of only one hundred grams of bread per internee per day. The Jewish Committee, trying to cope with the deteriorating situation, operated a soup kitchen where two hundred families were fed soup and corn meal mush ("*mămăligă*") once daily. But Romanian authorities reported ten to fifteen deaths daily due to the lack of food, limited medical care, and inadequate sanitary conditions in the ghetto.[20]

A list of Jews who succumbed to the rapidly worsening conditions in the ghetto was prepared daily. Nearly all of the lists have survived. Small children and the elderly were most susceptible, and the death lists reflect their vulnerability: two adults aged sixty-five and ninety, and seven-and-a-half-month-old Victoria Katz died on 18 August; four adults aged sixty-seven to eighty, on 19 August; four women aged fifty-nine to eighty and a four-day-old baby on 31 August. By early October, the death rate among the Jewish internees was averaging thirteen to fifteen per day: twelve people on 1 October, nine over age sixty, and a five-year-old child; nine the next day, including an eighty-nine-year-old man and a one-year-old child; fifteen on 4-5 October, including eleven adults aged sixty-six to eighty-two and a three-week-old baby. The pace slowed only when deportations reduced the ghetto population. The running total of recorded deaths from "natural causes" reached 441 by the time deportations began. A commission of inquiry appointed by Ion Antonescu to report on irregularities in administration of the ghetto considered this number "not very high," although it represented, on an annual basis, a "natural" death rate of fifteen to twenty percent.[21]

---

[20] USHMM RG-54.001, Roll 17, Fond 680, Opis 1, Folder 4230-1, f. 13, Memorandum No. 804a of 3 August 1941 from Chişinău Police Station to the Regional Inspectorate of Police. USHMM RG-54.001, Roll 1, Fond 706, Opis 1, Folder 22, f. 21, "Nota informativă," undated; USHMM RG-25.004, Roll 25, Fond 20725, vol. 7, ff. 297-317, Chişinău Regional Police Inspectorate Counterintelligence Bulletin for 10-20 September 1941.

[21] USHMM RG-25.003, Roll 131 (old 657), Folder 35, ff. 368-72, Report No. 1537 of 23 August 1941, Chişinău Military Commander, Col. D. Tudose, to the Administration of Bessarabia (Voiculescu); USHMM RG-25.004, Roll 25, Fond 20725, vol. 7, "Ministry of Interior, Arhiva Operativă," ff. 288-91, Report No. 2147 of 2 September 1941 from Chişinău Military Commander Eugen Dumitrescu to Leadership and Administration of Bessarabia (Voiculescu). A number of death lists for October are at USHMM RG-25.004, Roll 25, Fond 20725, vol. 7, ff. 277-90. Additional reports regarding mortality numbers and the names of the deceased, covering the period from 16 August to 5 October, are in USHMM RG-25.003, Roll 131 (old 657), Folder 35; see ff. 372, 398, 404, 407, 413, 424-25, 431, 435, 438, 443, 447, 454, 458, 462, 466, 470, 474, 493, 494, 496, 499, 504, 505, 518, 527, 529, 544, 549, 554. For the commission's report and conclusions, see USHMM RG-54.001, Roll 1, Fond 706, Opis 1, Folder 69 (Folder

At the end of August Governor Voiculescu reported to Antonescu that only a few Jews in the ghetto had the money or other possessions necessary to sustain themselves, and that only approximately four hundred men and four hundred women remained physically able to work. The rest had no means to support themselves.[22] Even those who might have worked faced serious obstacles. Bessarabia Police Inspector Alfred Pacsimade reported to Voiculescu that Jews had been "used as forced labourers for public purposes, mainly by the army, official installations, and by city authorities." He continued,

> They were supposed to be paid twenty-five lei per day, which they did not receive, because the authorities for which they worked had no funds. Today the authorities, knowing that Jewish labour is supposed to be paid for, no longer request them, thus depriving the Jews of the single possibility they had to secure their own survival . . . .[23]

The chief of the police unit assigned to work inside the ghetto reported that deprived of any income, the Jews were "selling their last possessions to survive." He signalled the danger the ghetto represented to the surrounding Chişinău community and to the peasants who entered the ghetto to sell food or barter with the Jews: "Everything is crawling with parasites . . . a hotbed of infection . . . [and] the selling of clothing, linens, carpets, pillows, comforters to the peasants . . . makes the ghetto a centre for the transfer of every kind of microbe by the principal carrier of disease, fleas."[24] Inside the ghetto, the internees' concern over the lack of food was reaching desperation. The police chief reported, "they have neither food nor clothes nor money. They are wondering what they will do in the winter."[25]

As the noose around the ghetto tightened with the approach of planned deportations and in response to the growing fear of disease, peasants who had once supplied the ghetto market were denied entry. Even military and police officers were searched on entering and exiting the ghetto to prevent the exchange of possessions, favours, and food. In mid-September,

---

title: *Ancheta neregulilor în administrarea Ghettoului Chişinău, 1941*) (henceforth *Inquiry Report*).

[22] USHMM RG-25.004, Roll 25, Fond 20725, vol. 7, ff. 260-61, Voiculescu Communiqué No. 772/C to the Presidency of the Council of Ministers, 31 August 1941; and same folder, ff. 263-75, Chişinău Regional Police Inspectorate Counterintelligence Bulletin for 20-31 August 1941.

[23] USHMM RG-54.001, Roll 17, Fond 680, Opis 1, Folder 4230-1, ff. 89-90. Report No. 281-C of 27 August 1941 from Pacsimade, Bessarabia Inspector of Police to Voiculescu.

[24] USHMM RG-54.001, Roll 7, Fond 679, Opis 1, Folder 6586, f. 414, Report No. 529 of 6 October 1941 from Chief of the Ghetto Police Station to Chief of Chişinău Municipal Police.

[25] USHMM RG-54.001, Roll 6, Fond 679, Opis 1, Folder 6586, f. 333, Report No. 5915-S[ecret] of 29 September 1941 from Chişinău Police Station to Chişinău Regional Police Inspectorate.

Voiculescu refused the Chişinău garrison commander's request to continue to allow Jews designated by the ghetto committee to leave the ghetto, under escort, to procure food supplies.[26] As deportations began and word spread that the internees would have to provide for their own food for the journey, the Jews' desperation to obtain food to take with them peaked. A local Christian Orthodox high school student who witnessed the scene later described the exploitation of the situation by the local population:

> I watched helplessly the pillaging of a column of Jews on the way to Transnistria in mid-winter . . . . Not all Bessarabians are heartless, but unfortunately there were plenty who for a loaf of bread demanded and got an astrakhan fur collar or fur hat. The price of a roast chicken was at least a fur-lined jacket. . . . I will never forget these images.[27]

Deportations from Bessarabia to Transnistria

Having decided that the Jews would be deported east on foot, and given the rapid deterioration of the condition of internees in the transit camps and ghettos, Bucharest ordered the deportations to begin. On 7 September, Grand Praetor Topor issued a written instruction to Bessarabia Gendarmerie Inspector Meculescu to begin the deportation of Jews on 12 September, starting with the transit camp at Vertiujeni. The abbreviated guidelines in Topor's "Note" of 7 September became the standard for deportations from other locations in Bessarabia as well, including the ghettos. The guidelines are worthy of attention:

1. The evacuation of Jews begins on 12 September with the camp at Vertiujeni . . . .
2. Groups of 1,600 at most, including children; but they will cross the Dnister at a rate of no more than 800 per day.
3. Forty or fifty carts for each group.
4. Groups will leave Vertiujeni every other day.
5. A gendarmerie officer will cross [the Dnister] with every group.
6. Crossing without [completion of] any formalities.
7. [Evacuation] Routes will be established by Lt. Colonel Palade . . . .
8. Two platoons [of gendarmes] will provide supplemental assistance.

---

[26] USHMM RG-54.001, Roll 1, Fond 706, Opis 1, Folder 22, f. 26, Intelligence Note of 19 September 1941; and f. 271, Secret Communiqué No. 244-C of 24 September 1941, from Voiculescu to Dumitrescu.

[27] Blog testimony entitled "Gropile erau deja săpate și au fost împinși în ele și acoperiți cu pământ," 1 November 2009, at https://maghiaromania.wordpress.com/2009/11/01/gropile-erau-deja-sapate. Accessed 15 Aug. 2017. The full blog statement posted on 25 October 2009 by [Dumitru] Stoian can be found as part of the blog of Petru Clej at http://acum.tv/articol/10523. Accessed 15 Aug. 2017.

9. Gendarmes at territorial posts [along the way] to aid in cleansing the terrain and burying the dead, using local inhabitants [for this purpose].
10. Way to deal with those who do not comply? "Alexianu."
11. No customs procedures. Anyone who steals [Jewish goods] will be shot.[28]

On 10 October, as deportations from the transit camps were being completed, Meculescu issued similar, but more elaborately spelled out, instructions for the deportation of Jews from the Chişinău ghetto and from the other ghettos in Southern Bessarabia as well—Bolhrad (Bolgrad), Cahul, Kiliia (Chilia), Izmail, and Vâlcov. Instructions regarding the Tarutyne (Tarutino) ghetto were issued separately a few days later. The routes of forced march and the Dnister crossing points were designated for each camp or ghetto, with hand-drawn maps attached to the instructions illustrating the routes to be taken by each column and the pace at which the columns were to move.[29]

Recognizing that many internees would be unable to endure the deportation on foot and that few internees would be able to carry even the "strictly necessary" personal items they would be allowed to take with them, the instructions called for the gendarmerie and other "administrative authorities" to provide 100 to 120 carts for each convoy leaving Chişinău. Other provisions in the instructions, however, made it clear that cleansing the terrain of Jews in Bessarabia took precedence over any concern regarding the deportees' physical survival. Because neither Voiculescu nor Topor were willing to allocate supplies for the deportees, Meculescu stipulated that the Jews in the convoys would have to feed themselves—a virtual impossibility for many internees, certain to be made even more difficult by the speed and conditions of the deportations. The deportation instructions required that maximum effort be made to avoid having the columns of deportees pass through towns and villages or come into contact

[28] USHMM RG-25.004, Roll 25, Fond 20725, vol. 9, ff. 287-89, Communiqué No. 1550 of 11 September 1941 from Meculescu to Government of Bessarabia (Voiculescu), covering Topor "Note" of 7 September 1941; and f. 278, Minutes of Deposition of Teodor Meculescu, 28 April 1945. A copy of the Topor "Note" is also at RG-54.001, Roll 1, Fond 706, Opis 1, Folder 22, f. 43. The instructions were summarized in *Inquiry Report*, Part 1.

[29] USHMM RG-54.001, Roll 1, Fond 706, Opis 1, Folder 22, ff. 51-66, Secret Communiqué No. 2830 of 10 October 1941 from Meculescu to Gendarmerie Legions at Cahul, Chilia, Ismail, Orhei, and the 23rd Police Company, covering "Instructions relating to the evacuation of the Jews of the Chişinău ghetto and of Southern Bessarabia," with attached maps and schedules of forced marches. A copy of the instructions, with a slightly revised version of the covering Secret Communiqué No. 2830, to include transmittal also to the Eighty-Second Police Company, is at USHMM RG-25.003, Roll 126 (old 656), Folder 29, ff. 608-16 [handwritten]. The special instructions regarding Tarutino, sent by Meculescu to the Gendarmerie legions at Cetatea Albă and Chilia Nouă on 23 October 1941, continue on ff. 617-20 [handwritten].

with the local population, making the procurement of food virtually impossible.[30]

The increasingly dismissive attitude of Romanian authorities toward the survival of the Jews could be seen in differences that appeared between procedures established for the first deportations and those that came later. While the deportation orders for the Vertiujeni camp, for instance, called for arrangements to be made for the Jews to sleep in sheds and stables along the way, no shelter was foreseen for the Jews from Chişinău, who despite exhaustion and low physical resistance, were forced to overnight in late October weather in open fields along the route of march. Recognizing the likely consequences of the orders—that the planned forced marches would become "death marches"—the drafters of the instructions chose to use veiled language when they directed the officials who would manage the deportations to "take appropriate measures during the marches to ensure the cleansing of the terrain, collecting those who fall behind and burying immediately any that may eventually cease living." A final admonition from Governor Voiculescu warned that the units in charge would be "held responsible if a single Jew remains in either an urban or a rural area after the completion of this operation."[31]

A description of the horrendous conditions that prevailed during these deportations was provided by a Romanian officer who participated in the deportations from Edineţ and Sokyriany transit camps. He also revealed the meaning of the code word "Alexianu," which was not only a direct reference to the person who had been appointed governor of Transnistria, but also, indirectly, a reference to the broadly understood anticipated fate of the Jews being sent there. Questioned in December 1941 by the commission of inquiry looking into irregularities in administration of the Chişinău ghetto, Lieutenant Augustin Roşca declared:

> The term we used for the Jews was "crates." We had enough carts because people knew we would pay 250 lei a day, but the drivers took more money [from the Jews], one hundred lei per person, and when they came to the foot of a hill, they would demand another hundred [threatening to put the Jews out, at the risk of their lives]. Cart drivers even came out of the villages without being summoned because for them this was a good way to make some money .... General Headquarters [instructed] ... that those who could not keep up with the convoy, either because they were weak or because they

[30] Minutes of Deposition of Teodor Meculescu, 28 April 1945, USHMM RG-25.004, Roll 25, Fond 20725, vol. 9, f. 278.

[31] USHMM RG-54.001, Roll 17, Fond 680, Opis 1, Folder 4230-2, f. 308, Secret Communiqué No. 368/C of 10 October 1941 from Voiculescu to all Prefectures, the Bessarabian Gendarmerie Inspectorate, Chişinău Police Inspectorate, and the Chişinău Military Command.

> were sick, should be executed . . . . I was ordered to send out, two or three days before the departure of the convoys, a [sergeant] . . . to arrange for pits to be dug big enough to hold about one hundred people, at appropriate locations, that is, far from villages, so that the cries and shots [would] not be heard . . . . The pits had to be at ten-kilometre intervals, where those who could not keep up with the column would be assembled. For those who could not even make it to the pits, it would be "Alexianu," which was code for execution on the spot . . . . Pre-military youths [recruited locally] dug the pits, put the bodies in, and covered them . . . . Peasants stood along the way, like crows waiting to scavenge something . . . . At the first ditch, which was just five kilometres along the way, I left fifty to sixty people behind, guarded by about six gendarmes, who stayed there until evening and then executed them. The columns moved with great difficulty and disorder because of the children, women, and elderly. About 120 Jews from the first convoy were buried in other ditches along the way.[32]

The elderly, the sick, women, and children vied for space in the carts, and those who still had possessions loaded them in as well. Both the escort guards and onlookers along the deportation route were tempted by the "wealth of the Jews" passing within their reach. Robbery of the convoys was a constant problem. Peasants lined up along the road waiting for the column to stop for the night so that they could steal or, more ominously, waited for stragglers who had fallen behind the column to be executed so that they could strip the bodies of possessions, clothes, and shoes. The possibility that those same individuals would feed the Jews was far-fetched indeed. The confusion, the assembled goods, the vulnerability of the deportees, and the pressure created by rigid deadlines all combined to increase the suffering and the number of Jews killed during the deportations. On these forced marches, exposure, illness, exhaustion from the effort to keep up with the convoy, and weakness from a starvation diet before the deportations began took a deadly toll. For the troops and gendarmes escorting the columns, the pressure to meet a deadline set by Ion Antonescu to have all Jews out of Bessarabia by 31 October made shooting Jews preferable to trying to ensure that as many as possible reached the Dnister.

The bodies of thousands of Bessarabian Jews still lie today in those ditches every ten kilometres along the routes the convoys were forced to tread. The Jews who reached the Dnister crossing points arrived in terrible condition. A Jewish woman deported by train from Bukovyna testified of her encounter with a column of Bessarabian Jews at Otachi (Atachi):

---

[32] USHMM RG-25.004, Roll 25, Fond 20725, Folder "Ancheta Georgescu Mihnea şi alţii," vol. 9, f. 286, Declaration of Lt. Augustin Roşca, 23 December 1941.

> *They* came on foot, *we* by train—it made a big difference. They were walking skeletons, dressed in rags, just shreds, and when they saw us . . . they tried to leave the column and come toward us to ask for help. The gendarmes would not permit it and told us that these people were covered in fleas and carrying typhus, which was true. Thus, they extended their hands toward us, and we shied away . . . . Some among us, violating every rule and overcoming fear, approached the column and gave them something to eat . . . . Meeting this group was horrible because we realized that we could become just like them.[33]

Forced Marches in Transnistria

The majority of the Bessarabian Jews who were deported to Transnistria did not survive. Most failed to survive even the first winter. Arriving in weakened physical condition, they were forced to march from place to place through difficult terrain, always with the dreaded "Alexianu" order hanging over the head of any man, woman, child, grandfather, or grandmother who fell behind. Those who survived the forced marches were put to forced labour or concentrated in ghettos and on collective farms in the Holta region along the Buh River, where the conditions for sustaining life were minimal and where food, water, medicine, and outside contact were denied them. The winter of 1941-42 was particularly harsh. Deportees succumbed in massive numbers to freezing temperatures, starvation, and typhus, and tens of thousands of local Jews and deportees from Bessarabia were executed in the districts of eastern Transnistria along the Buh.

Still, Transnistria and Bessarabia were not the same. A recent study, which compared the behaviour of non-Jewish civilians in Bessarabia and in Transnistria, has demonstrated convincingly that the local Ukrainian population of Transnistria adopted a much more humane attitude toward both Jewish deportees from Bessarabia and local Transnistrian Jews than non-Jews had shown toward persecuted Jews in Bessarabia (see Dumitru). One area where the contrast of behaviour was most striking was in the readiness of locals to attempt to provide food and water to the exhausted, parched, and starving Jews in the forced march columns. Recognizing the risk, some people threw food to the Jews from a distance. Peasant women sometimes put food bundles on the roadways in rural areas before the unfortunate columns were driven through. But in many instances, Transnistrian peasants assisted the deportees openly, in full view of the soldiers accompanying the columns. Basing her research on an extensive

---

33 Interview with Sarina Ionescu in *Holocaustul evreilor români* 179.

study of testimonies and on her own interviews with survivors, Diana Dumitru summarized:

> In the majority of testimonies, survivors mention that during the deportations (for example) some Transnistrian locals would come out to the streets and offer the Jews food and water as they passed through. In doing so, local civilians confronted greater danger than Bessarabians [who were mainly ethnic Romanians] of being attacked by the Romanian guards. (191)

Jews in the columns faced the real danger of starvation. As deportees were arriving from Bessarabia, Transnistria governor Alexianu himself described the situation as "quite serious." The Jews were arriving "in bad weather, with the roads impassable," he reported, which made "getting them to their destinations . . . extremely difficult." He described the region to which the Jews were being directed as poor, the sanitary situation there as "very bad," and declared flatly, "I do not have the ability to give them even a piece of bread."[34] While there was no famine per se in Transnistria, Alexianu's comment reflected the reality that multiple significant demands left food in short supply. The Romanians shipped massive amounts of agricultural goods from Transnistria to Romania to support domestic consumption and help fulfill Romanian commitments to Germany. Romanian occupation authorities and military forces had to be provided for locally. The non-Jewish population, although subjected to severe food rationing, also had to be fed from local supplies. In addition, government policy established in Bucharest forbade shipping any food from Romania into Transnistria. Meanwhile, ethnic German ("*Volksdeutsch*") farmers in the territory, whose communities enjoyed semi-autonomy under the protection of the SS and Volksdeutsche Mittelstelle (VoMi), were not subjected to the same forced deliveries of crops and animals that the Romanians imposed on other local farmers, who were often stripped of most of what they produced. And in spite of agreements between the Romanian and German governments to the contrary, German military commanders seized food supplies, as well as other resources, in Transnistria, more or less at will, to provision German forces further east (Solonari 39-50).

---

[34] USHMM RG-25.003, Roll 126 (old 656), Folder 29, f. 331 [handwritten/counter illegible], Order No. 13842/CBBT [Comissariat for Bessarabia, Bukovyna, and Transnistria] of 5 November 1941, Vlădescu at Council of Ministers to Governor of Bessarabia, with excerpts from Alexianu's report on conditions in Transnistria. Alexianu's Report No. 2369 (perhaps 2363/partially illegible) of 1 November 1941, sent from Tiraspol, can be seen at USHMM RG-31.004/Odesa Oblast Archives, Roll 1, Fond 2242, Opis 1, Folder 677, ff. 99-110 [handwritten].

The Jews who were pushed across the Dnister from Bessarabia arrived in Transnistria in terrible shape. Feeding them (and the Roma who came later) was the lowest priority of all in a situation of extreme food scarcity. A confidential report dated 27 September from the commander of border fortifications at the crossing point Rezeni-Râbniţa described their situation in the following terms:

> they have reached such an advanced state of physical weakness following their march that the route which they travelled is dotted with graves. Insects crawl all through the filthy rags they are wearing, and the faces of these people, drawn by hunger, project the presence of disease . . . . The guards accompanying these transports have told me that only about half of the Jews have anything with which to buy food . . . . The others go hungry or survive on help from the others. The guards have also shared with me their impression that only twenty percent of the Jews will survive to their destination.[35]

Even as death consumed large numbers of deportees, it is clear that the food provided by locals to some Jews in the columns was a critical factor for those who survived the ordeal.

Ghettos, Camps, and Killing Sites in Transnistria

The circumstances of Jews from Bessarabia and Bukovyna who survived deportation and forced marches into and through Transnistria and of local Jews from Transnistria itself varied considerably. Deportees from Bessarabia were sometimes put to forced labour and compelled to live out in the open, without shelter, in the dead of winter. Some deportees from Bukovyna were transported to Transnistria by train, arriving in better physical condition and, in the best of cases, able to find a degree of refuge, for longer or shorter periods, in larger towns. Deportees, as well as Transnistrian Jews from rural areas and Jews evacuated from Odesa, were concentrated in stables and pigsties or in the open on collective farms in the Holta district along the Buh River, where Romanian occupation forces denied them food, water, medicine, and outside contact. At the same time, Transnistrian Jews living in larger towns might be confined in ghettos but not expelled from surroundings that were familiar to them and not always completely isolated from neighbours who might offer some aid. Two special cases—the ghetto at Mohyliv-Podilskyi (Moghilev-Podolski) and the camp

---

[35] AMR, fond 1693-Comandamentul Etapelor de Est, dosar nr. 16, ff. 30-31, "Confidential Report No. 166 of 27 September 1941 on Jews Moved from Bessarabia to Transnistria," published in Traşcă, *"Chestiunea evreiască,"* document 106, 268-69.

at Vapniarka (Vapniarca)—also merit attention because of their unique characteristics. It is important to recognize that in all of these locations, Jews suffered and succumbed to exposure, typhus, and other diseases, physical and emotional exhaustion, starvation, and murderous killing rampages. However, the circumstances differed significantly from place to place, including in regard to food policy and access to nourishment.

Figure 2: Map of Romanian camps and ghettos in Northern Transnistria. Courtesy of the United States Holocaust Memorial Museum.

In Râbnița, where the condition of deportees passing through was described above in such dire terms, a report from several months later, dated 19 April 1942, presented the situation of the 1,471 Jews in the town's ghetto in much more positive terms. Of the 293 men, 609 women, and 569 children, 635 were deemed unable to work, but the ghetto had a public kitchen that fed a single meal each day to 230 people, as well as a medical dispensary and a "very well-supplied" pharmacy. There were seventeen workshops in the ghetto employing 130 Jews, who were doing work mainly for the population of the city. While some employers of this forced labour had not paid labourers all of the money due to them, still, the report concluded, "the ghetto is in satisfactory condition, the houses whitewashed, sanitary conditions almost sufficient."

The report provided an even more positive picture of the small ghetto—fifty-six men, forty-two women, nine children—at Tiraspol (an additional seventeen Jews working for outside institutions were living outside the ghetto). The ghetto kitchen was able to serve two meals per day to the entire ghetto population. There were nine workshops inside the ghetto, employing thirty-eight Jews, and fifty-three Jews worked for various institutions of the military garrison and were paid two RKKS ("*Reichskreditkassenscheine*"—the occupation currency issued by Nazi Germany) per day for their labour. Even here, however, the report noted that many of the Jews had been brought to Tiraspol from elsewhere, but that their families, "often including minor children," had been abandoned in other localities. And despite all the positive statements in the early paragraphs of the report, the author also indicated that the ghetto was not able to continue to feed adequately the internees with the "income" it had. The author's final recommendation was that on days when bread was distributed in the city, a ration of one hundred grams of bread per person also be distributed in the ghetto.

The same inspection report provided a description of conditions that were far worse in the ghetto at Balta, second in size among Transnistrian ghettos only to Mohyliv. There were 514 men, 1,234 women, and 898 children in the ghetto. Of the adults, 698 were unable to work, and of the children, 700 were orphans (300 having lost both parents). According to the report, conditions were "bad," "filthy," and the Jews who had performed forced labour for different authorities had not been paid "for months," despite the government guideline that required payment of "two Marks [RKKS] per day for a skilled labourer and one Mark per day for unskilled." Some users of forced labour had "paid" labourers just 600 grams of cornmeal for a day of work, "which is unfair since a kilo of corn meal costs just 24 lei (40 pfennigs)." The central kitchen where 300 people eat, the report continued, "is dirty, poorly equipped, and poorly supplied. It serves a single meal per day, has difficulty obtaining food, and pays a high price for the food it is able to get . . . ."[36]

A year later the situation in Balta had not changed significantly. A report dated April 1943 described the houses in the ghetto as "miserable, with eight to ten people living in each room, infected air, and indescribable filth." The two orphanages were described similarly, with the added note that food was

---

[36] Arhivele Ministerului Afacerilor Externe (Archive of the Ministry of Foreign Affairs [of Romania]—AMAE), fond Problema 33, vol. 21, ff. 455-63, "Note of 19 April 1942 on the Jewish Ghettos in Transnistria," published in Trașcă, *"Chestiunea evreiască,"* document 237, 497-502.

"insufficient, even bread being missing." In Râbniţa, meanwhile, the situation had deteriorated. The houses on the two streets of the ghetto were "filthy," and the Jews had "no clothing." The report noted, however, with what in hindsight can be perceived only as extreme cynicism, that the sanitary situation had improved "following the death last year of ninety percent (of the ghetto inhabitants) of exanthematic typhus."[37] The combination of malnutrition, unsanitary conditions, exposure, disease, and the passage of time proved deadly for Jews in ghettos all across Transnistria.

As problematic as maintaining an acceptable survival diet may have been in Transnistrian ghettos, the situation in camps established in more isolated locations was far more difficult. Neighbours and acquaintances who might have taken pity on the internees or with whom "arrangements" could have been made did not exist, and the food supply in marketplaces, sometimes accessible to ghetto inhabitants if they could sneak out long enough to reach a market, was also generally beyond the reach of the Jews penned up on collective farms or in makeshift work camps. In May 1942 the Romanian army's Bureau 7, responsible for Jewish affairs, provided a report on these camps to the Presidency of the Council of Ministers. The camps for Jews were set up under the direct authority of the Government of Transnistria and located in villages, on isolated terrain, and on collective farms. Guarded by gendarmes and local policemen ("armed Ukrainian guards"), the Jews "were not permitted to leave their localities [or] camps." "Those who violate this," the report continued, "are considered spies in time of war and sanctioned accordingly [underlined in the original] .... Every Jew has to take care of his own food and maintenance. Both hygiene and what it takes to stay alive are lacking ...."[38]

---

[37] Arhivele Naţionale Istorice Centrale (National Central Historical Archive [of Romania]-ANIC), fond Cabinetul Ministrului de Interne, dosar nr. 48/1943, f.7+verso, "Report on the Situation of the Ghettos in Transnistria in April 1943," published in Traşcă, *"Chestiunea evreiască,"* document 380, 768.

[38] AMR, fond 5416-Marele Stat Major, Secţia I-a Organizare-Mobilizare, dosar nr. 3002, ff. 21-22, "Note 42071 of 31 May 1942 from Bureau Seven-Jews," published in Traşcă, *"Chestiunea evreiască,"* document 263, 546-47.

Figure 3. Map of Romanian camps and ghettos in Southern Transnistria. Courtesy of the United States Holocaust Memorial Museum.

In such circumstances, survival could depend on taking the real risk of sneaking out of camp and into a nearby village to beg, barter, or work for something to eat, even in full knowledge of likely execution if caught. Many survivor testimonies focus on the potentially fatal risk required to avoid starvation. One survivor of the camp at Obodivka (Obodovca) told his story this way:

> I arrived in the camp at Obodovca. It was enclosed with barbed wire, with guard observation posts. It was crowded, between 3,000 and 4,000 Jews . . . they put us in a cowshed . . . . At night adults went into the village, the guards fearing partisans [and thus absent], and they were able to bring back something to eat from the Ukrainians . . . . We were not given any food in the camp. They took us out to work . . . on the Subina state farm ("*sovkhoz*"), [and] it was our good fortune that the Ukrainian men had been taken into the Soviet army, and others were partisans in the woods, and there remained only women and children . . . . They [the Romanians] did not have people to do the work. I was twelve years old at that time, and together with my two brothers we worked there and managed to get something to eat. It was food not even a dog would eat, but we ate it then. We were also saved by Ukrainian women working near us who would bring food and hide it in the woods and show us where to look. They were

afraid to hand us the food because there were gendarmes there also . . . . [One boy] was killed because he went into the woods and picked some wild apples. The gendarme saw him . . . . He beat him to death, and we buried him there in the forest.[39]

In her chapter on "Jews and Their Neighbors in Occupied Transnistria," Dumitru provides equally compelling examples of the ways in which Jews in the extreme circumstances of Transnistrian camps survived by begging, trading, working for, or even stealing food. Multiple entries in a collection of survivor testimonies published by the Romanian Institute of Recent History (*Institutul Român de Istorie Recentă*) contain similar examples. "The Pullover," a short autobiographical story by Romanian author and Transnistria survivor Norman Manea, provides a powerfully moving image, as seen through the eyes of a child, of Manea's mother bringing food (and a sweater) back to her family after a week of labour in a Transnistrian village (see Dumitru 196-209; *Holocaustul evreilor români*; Manea 3-15).

If state policy, antisemitic propaganda, the military chain of command, and widespread lack of humanity accounted for the terrible treatment of Jews by Romanian civil and military authorities early on, an added and accelerating factor that led to many of the camps in Transnistria being transformed into mass killing sites was fear, specifically fear of disease, and most particularly, fear of typhus. Significantly, while there is little evidence that German officials, who exercised certain administrative prerogatives that, in fact, infringed on Romanian authority in Transnistria, ever interfered in the formulation of Romanian food policy toward the Jews, they clearly shared the Romanian fear of typhus. They intervened directly to urge extreme action—liquidation of the Jews—in order to remove the danger of the disease spreading to the local population, and, even more importantly, to German military units transiting the territory and operating east of the Buh.[40]

Typhus appeared in the ghettos and camps where Jews from Bessarabia, rural Transnistria, and Odesa were crowded in the late fall and early winter of 1941. Records relating to the Chişinău ghetto show that cases of the disease had appeared there even before deportations began. However, when the number of cases began to rise among the non-Jewish population of Transnistria, fear of an epidemic sweeping across the entire territory became extreme. While sanitary and economic conditions in the

[39] See interview of survivor Şabs Roif by Petru Clej, entitled "Am fost în groapa cu morţi timp de o noapte," 1 November 2009, at http://acum.tv/articol/10505. Accessed 15 Aug. 2017.

[40] On German advisors in Romania and the prerogatives of German authorities in Transnistria, see Solonari 31-62. On massacres carried out by Reich Germans and local Volksdeutsch, and German pressure for the mass execution of Jews in Holta district, see Ioanid, *Holocaust* 182-93.

territory were in general very poor, there is no question that some instances of the disease were the result of civilian contact with the exhausted, emaciated, starving, and disease-prone Jewish persec utees interned in Transnistrian camps and ghettos. A ledger for December 1941-January 1942 listing hundreds of cases of typhus among the non-Jewish population of Berezivka district provides a record, case by case, of where the sick person was being treated or isolated, when the disease was contracted, and how. The notes regarding the "how" question vary somewhat in form, but "contact with Jews," "contact with Jews from the camp," "Jews slept in her house," "from Jews from whom she bought clothes," "from contact with clothes bought from Jews in the camp" are typical of the comments in over ninety percent of the cases.[41] With blame placed squarely on the Jews, and the Jews isolated, sick, and starving in cowsheds, pigsties, and on open ground, it is hardly surprising that mass shootings of Jews of a magnitude rarely seen elsewhere during the Holocaust—tens of thousands of Jews—took place in late 1941 and early 1942 in Berezivka district, on the Domanivka, Akmechetski Stavky, and Bohdanivka collective farms in Holta district, and at other sites in Transnistria (see Ioanid, *Holocaust* 176-94).

Special Case: Mohyliv-Podilskyi

The largest ghetto in Transnistria, at Mohyliv-Podilskyi, was unique in many ways, not least because of the extraordinary efforts made by the chairman of the ghetto committee, Siegfried Jagendorf, to establish a foundry and other enterprises that proved useful to the Romanian occupiers. This allowed Jagendorf, through skilful and constant negotiation, to employ a significant number of Jewish deportees and keep them in the town, in many cases with their whole families, right up to the end of the Romanian occupation of Transnistria. The number of deportees who managed to remain at Mohyliv reached as high as fifteen thousand. At the same time, and in spite of Jagendorf's efforts, Romanian authorities constantly threatened and sometimes actually did expel Jews to other localities, where they were less likely to survive.

Conditions in Mohyliv were poor, and many Jews succumbed to typhus and other diseases, as they did elsewhere. In an official report on "The Situation of Jews in Transnistrian Ghettos," prepared in 1942, the author noted:

---

[41] See "Table of Evidence of Contagious Disease" in USHMM RG31.004, Roll 19, Fond 2361, Opis 1, folder 59/1941.

> In most ghettos there are no toilets, and in Mohyliv there are feces everywhere . . . . The Jews pay rent to the Ukrainians for housing with their clothes, jewelry, and shoes. If they live in houses belonging to the local authorities, they pay rent as well . . . . There are about three thousand children in Mohyliv. The dispensary where sick children are interned made an odious impression on me . . . . It was something horrible to see . . . . I saw on the streets of the ghetto of Mohyliv women and children who had fainted from hunger because the food from the common kitchen is totally insufficient . . . . The authorities provide no help at all because they have to supply the urgent needs of the army.[42]

In a postwar testimony, Roza Schachter, a survivor at Mohyliv who came originally from Chernivtsi, also described the appalling deprivation and plight of the children in the Mohyliv orphanage:

> The children picked through the garbage cans . . . . I think you've seen it on film, often they show how children were, at Auschwitz, too, with legs like sticks, bloated bellies, faces drawn; these children were like walking mummies. Unclothed and naked, in winter too, and they were digging for potato peels and whatever else they could find in the garbage cans, even while assistance was coming from inside Romania, from different organizations, for these children.[43]

Still, conditions in general were better in Mohyliv than in most other localities in Transnistria. The odds for survival at Mohyliv were improved by the fact that while many deportees from both Bessarabia and Bukovyna had passed through the city during the deportations, most of the deportees who managed to remain there were from Bukovyna, especially Chernivtsi and Dorohoi, and had arrived in Transnistria in much better condition than the Bessarabian Jews. In addition, Mohyliv was just across the Dnister from Bukovyna, and the internees managed to maintain communication with relatives and other contacts who remained in the large ghetto in Chernivtsi. Proximity to Romania also made it possible for Jagendorf to plead his case and garner substantial aid from the Jewish community leadership in Bucharest after the Antonescu regime decided to allow money and parcels of food and medicine to be transferred to deportees in Transnistrian ghettos and camps. The number of deportees who survived at Mohyliv exceeded ten thousand, an extraordinary number in light of the fact that only about fifty thousand of all deportees from Bessarabia and Bukovyna combined survived deportation (see Hirt-Manheimer).

---

[42] AMAE, fond Problema 33, vol. 21, ff. 594-98, "Report [undated] on the Situation of the Jews in Ghettos in Transnistria," published in Trașcă, *"Chestiunea evreiască,"* document 361, 728-31.
[43] Interview of Roza Schachter in *Holocaustul evreilor români* 57-70.

Special Case: Food As a Weapon at Vapniarka

Located in northwestern Transnistria, Vapniarka became one of the many locations to which Romanian authorities sent the Jews they were expelling from their homes. In early 1942, nearly 1,200 Jews were sent there from the prison in Odesa. Several hundred Jewish deportees from Bessarabia and Bukovyna also were sent to Vapniarka. Many of these first contingents of Jews died during the typhus epidemic of the winter-spring of 1941-42. Jews who survived the epidemic were removed from Vapniarka in June 1942 and taken to other sites. Then, in August, the character of this specific site changed dramatically. Vapniarka was designated a special camp for "political" prisoners, to which Romanian authorities sent Jews who were incarcerated in Romania for alleged communist activity, Romanian Jews suspected of communist leanings, and Jews who had opted to move from Romania to Soviet-occupied Bessarabia and northern Bukovyna during the year-long Soviet occupation of those territories (June 1940-June 1941).[44]

During September, nearly 1,200 Jews identified as falling within these categories were deported from Romania to Vapniarka. Among them were 407 (406, according to some sources) communist, social democratic, and other "political" prisoners from the Târgu-Jiu prison and seventy-two (eighty-seven, according to some sources) from the Caransebeş prison. Non-Jewish communist prisoners jailed in Romania, often in these same prisons, were not deported. When the new prisoners arrived, conditions at Vapniarka were horrifying. The camp buildings were in disrepair, and there was no running water in the camp. Nor had any food supplies been arranged for the arriving prisoners.[45] Drawing on stocks of animal feed abandoned by retreating Soviet forces, the Romanians fed the prisoners a diet that consisted primarily of a fodder pea ("*Lathyrus sativus*") that was toxic to humans. The fodder pea diet very quickly wreaked havoc on the health of the prisoners, causing lesions, violent stomach cramps, diarrhea, impaired kidney function, spasmodic twitching of the extremities, and paralysis.

In response to this desperate situation and convinced that they were being intentionally poisoned, the prisoners went on hunger strike. Led by a

[44] Documents relating to this last category of internees were found by Romanian authorities in the Soviet embassy in Bucharest following the Axis attack on the USSR on 22 June 1941. For Antonescu's orders regarding the deportation of communist prisoners and the resulting implementation, see Traşcă, *"Chestiunea evreiască,"* document 314, 653-54; document 328, 682-83; and document 338, 696-97.

[45] Transnistria Governor Gheorghe Alexianu reported these conditions to Antonescu; see AMAE, fond Problema 33, vol. 20, ff. 67-68, "Communiqué No. 820 of 9 November 1942 from Alexianu to Ion Antonescu," published in Traşcă, *"Chestiunea evreiască,"* document 347, 709-10.

camp committee dominated by communist activists and with guidance from Jewish doctors who had been arrested and sent to Vapniarka (some of them simply because Romanian authorities perceived all Jews as potential communist sympathizers), the internees refused to eat the fodder pea diet. The doctors in the camp, led by Arthur Kessler from Chernivtsi, addressed a series of written appeals to the camp commandant and directly to Transnistria Governor Alexianu. As a result, the government's medical examiner for Transnistria visited the camp. Persuaded by the diagnostic analysis provided by the incarcerated Jewish doctors, he proposed corrective action. In response, the internees' diet was modified, slightly at first, more significantly later, and prisoners were granted permission to receive packages of food, medicine, and clothing from Romania. Still, according to a report from late February 1943, 611 prisoners continued to show various symptoms of the disease, and 110 were severely afflicted.

In early 1943, the Antonescu regime determined that more than four hundred of the internees had been sent to Vapniarka without justification. They were Jews but neither communists nor communist sympathizers. Instead of repatriation, however, as Jews, these prisoners were moved from Vapniarka to Transnistrian ghettos at Savran (Savrani), Olhopil (Olgopol), and Trykhaty (Trihati) (Ioanid, *Holocaust* 250-51). Then, in late 1943, with the Red Army approaching the region, Romanian authorities decided to close the camp. Some of the prisoners were sent to Transnistrian ghettos. A small group of fifty-four communists was sent to the prison at Rîbnița, where on 19-20 March 1944, in the confusion that reigned as responsibility for the administration of Transnistria passed from Romanian to German control, all were executed by German Schutzstaffel (SS) men. The majority of the communists from the camp, 565 prisoners, were sent first to the Grosolovo ghetto, then taken back to Romania and interned again in the camp for political prisoners at Târgu Jiu, where many of them had been held before their deportation to Transnistria, eighteen months earlier.

There is an extraordinary variety and volume of documentation relating to this special Transnistrian camp, and a substantial share of it relates to the food supply and the consequences of the Romanians' attempt to use food as a lethal weapon. In addition to numerous unpublished memoirs collected by Romanian Jewish community organizations shortly after the war, sources range from camp administrative records of every kind to unique exchanges of memoranda between Jewish doctors in the camp and the government's medical examiner, to postwar trials of the officers who ran the camp. A postwar register of Jews interned in the camp on 1 September 1943, prepared by the World Jewish Congress office in Bucharest and based on a hand-written wartime list, records the names of the 706 internees who remained in Vapniarka after the removal of the prisoners deemed to have been improperly sent there. The diagnostic notes kept by Dr. Kessler as he tracked the paralysis and other afflictions the prisoners suffered have also survived.[46]

Details of the prisoners' diet are provided in files of "Supporting documents for expenses paid to feed the internees in Vapniarka camp" from the Odesa branch of the Ukrainian state archives. The December 1942 file, for example, reveals that only thirty lei (half of one RKKS) per day were allocated to feed each prisoner, and provides a daily accounting of the number of prisoners who had to be fed and the supplies purchased to feed them. On most days, purchases per prisoner consisted of four hundred grams of fodder peas, two hundred grams of bread, fifteen grams of salt, and five hundred grams of wood to feed the stoves. Every few days, between two and ten grams of oil were allotted per prisoner. On rare days, such as Christmas, meat was added to the supplies purchased. The meat was horse meat, and special documentation, still in the files, was required to record the purchase and slaughter of the horses. The documentation also reveals that on Christmas day in 1942, small amounts of carrots, onion, and potato were added to the diet. Subsequent files for the first three months of 1943 reflect a slight improvement in the diet, mainly through the more regular addition of potatoes and sour cabbage. A unique document records the slaughter of a thirty-eight-kilogram ram on 2 March to add some meat to the diet of the most severely afflicted internees in the prisoner infirmary.[47]

There are 450 files of former Vapniarka internees among tens of thousands of compensation claim files that were assembled by Romania's communist government in the early 1970s for the purpose of seeking a lump sum hard currency settlement from the Federal Republic of Germany. Many of these files include detailed medical records showing the decades-long paralysis, as well as other ailments, that were the legacy of Vapniarka's toxic diet.[48] Recognizing that the Romanian government was unlikely to pass any payments on to the actual victims, the German government refused the claims.

---

[46] The "Register of Jews interned in the Camp at Wapniarka-Transnistria on the 1st of September 1943" and Dr. Kessler's diagnostic notes are in the collections of the International Tracing Service at Bad Arolsen, Germany, and can be consulted in the ITS Digital Collection, List Material of various camps, 1.1.47.1, Folder 19, DOI 5160365-76 (VCC 176/c Ordner 19 in the paper records) and Folder 19a, DOI 5160449-5160553 (VCC 176/c Ordner 19a in the paper records), respectively.

[47] USHMM RG-31.004, Reel 8, Fond 2255, Opis 1c, Folder 1617.

[48] The collection of claim files is in the archives of the International Tracing Service. For a detailed survey of Vapniarka-related sources, see Shapiro, "Vapniarka."

Roma Deportees to Transnistria

The deportation of Roma to Transnistria by the Antonescu regime began later than the deportation of Jews. Starting in May and ending roughly at the end of October 1942, the Romanians deported approximately 25,000 Roma, some nomadic, others non-nomadic. According to the extraordinarily well-documented research of Romanian scholar Viorel Achim, eleven thousand deported Roma perished in Transnistria, while approximately fourteen thousand survived and were permitted to return to Romania in the spring of 1944, as Romania lost Transnistria to the advancing Red Army.[49] It is frequently asserted that among all of the groups that were persecuted as groups and deported to ghettos or camps by Nazi Germany and her Axis allies, the treatment meted out to Roma most resembled the treatment of Jews. The similarities could not be more striking than when the issues of food supply, malnourishment, and starvation among deportees to Transnistria are considered. Excerpts from the reports written by Romanian authorities illustrate this point.

In December 1942, an agent of the Romanian security police who spent two weeks on assignment in the Ochakiv (Oceakov) district of southeastern Transnistria, where many Roma deportees had been taken, reported:

> While they were in the barracks at Oleksandrodar (Alexandrudar), the gypsies were living in indescribable conditions. They were insufficiently fed. Those able to work got 400 grams of bread per day, children and old people got 200. They also got a bit of potato or salted fish, but in extremely small quantities. Due to malnutrition, some of the gypsies—the majority—have lost so much weight that [they] have become mere skeletons. Every day, especially recently, ten to fifteen die. They were full of parasites. They received no medical visits . . . . They are naked . . . . In general the gypsies' situation is terrible and almost unimaginable. From this misery many of them have become mere shadows and almost wild. This is due to poor living conditions and poor food, and the cold as well. Because of the hunger to which they are subjected, they have frightened the Ukrainians by stealing . . . . (Achim, *Documente* 2: 24-29)[50]

[49] Achim has published extensively on the subject. He contributed the chapter on "The Deportation of the Roma and Their Treatment in Transnistria" to the *Final Report* of the International Commission on the Holocaust in Romania. His two-volume study and document collection, *Documente privind Deportarea Ţiganilor în Transnistria,* was awarded the Romanian Academy's prestigious Euxodiu Hurmuzaki Prize for a work of history. His *Munca forţată în Transnistria: "Organizarea Muncii" evreilor şi romilor decembrie 1942-martie 1944,* which deals with forced labour in Transnistria, is one of the rare works in which the experiences of Jews and of Roma during the Antonescu regime are treated in a fully integrated manner.

[50] Document 249, Report of 5 December 1942, "On service executed in Oceakov district from 19 November to 4 December 1942."

Another report, filed a few days later by a special commission sent to Transnistria to investigate the situation of the non-nomadic Roma among the deportees, was even more grim. The colonel who authored the report noted that many of the Roma had been deported to Transnistria without the opportunity to bring any household items, extra clothes, or other possessions with them. While making short reference to orders regarding treatment of the Roma which, if implemented, might have offered the possibility of survival, the colonel then continued:

> What is the reality? The gypsies are receiving 400 grams of oat or corn flour, and 200 grams for children. They have received nothing else—if they die they will die from hunger and cold . . . . [S]ince they arrived they have not been given a single gram of salt, even though the prefecture has salt . . . . In general, the gypsies do not even have a pot in which to prepare food. With their funds exhausted, they have sold the clothes off their bodies, and now half of them are completely naked . . . . If the food supply for the gypsies does not improve, soon almost all of them will die. (Achim, *Documente* 2: 51-54)[51]

In the spring of 1943 conditions seemed only to have worsened. A gendarme in the Berezivka district reported the result of sending Roma from the camp at Kovalivka (Covaliovca or Covalevca) to surrounding villages to work:

> Nothing was arranged in the communes to which they were sent, so the gypsies mostly just stood around outside, and because the temperature was very low, hundreds of gypsies died . . . . [A]ll the fields were strewn with corpses . . . . In the communes where they went, they are given no food . . . . The locals hate them, and when they find them alone, they beat them up; in general, they are left to die of hunger. The local [raion] authorities pay no attention to their fate. (Achim, *Documente* 2: 147-48)[52]

There is a remarkable consistency to all of the reports regarding the food situation. A report notes that in the camp at Holta neither the Jews nor the Roma had been given food for months, but "they are required to work while they are fainting from hunger" (Achim, *Documente* 2: 186-87).[53] At Variushyne (Varuşino), where some food distributions were taking place,

---

[51] Document 267, Report of 17 December 1942 of Commission No. 1 for investigation of the situation of non-nomadic gypsies evacuated to Transnistria.

[52] Document 342, Report No. 91 of 17 March 1943 from Gendarmerie post Covalevca to Gendarmerie legion Berezovca.

[53] Document 375, Report of 10 May 1943 from Gendarmerie Legion Golta to the Inspector General of the Gendarmerie.

"the corn meal that is given to the gypsies is impossible to eat; the grain is just broken into quarters, many grains are whole, and there is an immense amount of sand in [it]" (Achim, *Documente* 2: 200).[54] At Kovalivka, the chief of the gendarmerie post reported:

> Today is the eighteenth day since the gypsies at Kovalivka have been given food. The gypsies have sold everything they had to buy food, now they have nothing left to sell and are eating the buds off fruit trees . . . . Because of hunger many gypsies are fleeing . . . even at the risk of their lives, of being shot, because they are condemned to die of hunger anyway. (Achim, *Documente* 2: 196-98)[55]

Consulting the memoirs and testimonies of Roma survivors of Transnistria adds the perspective and authentic voice of those who suffered, as well as details that even the gendarmes, soldiers, police, and civilian officials who observed and perpetrated the crimes against the Roma hesitated to put into their reports. Every one of the thirteen Romani survivor testimonies in a volume published in Romania in 2009 deepens the reader's understanding of the horrendous injustice and unspeakable suffering inflicted on these people during the war and the pain with which they saw, and later related, the agonizing and brutal deaths of their family members. In this regard, as in others, the fate of the Roma mirrored that of many Jews in Transnistria under Romanian rule (see Ioanid et al.).

Anghel Nedelea was a non-nomadic Roma deported from Pitești, west of Bucharest, and survived internment in Mykolaiv (Nicolaev), Volodymyrivka (Vladimirovca), and Bohdanivka in Transnistria. In her testimony she returned repeatedly to the reality of hunger and the search for food:

> Old people and children were dying of hunger, and we also . . . . In the winter there was no work, we just headed out to the villages . . . . You went to every house, and someone would give you a bit of corn, some "*mămăligă*" [polenta], that was all there was to eat. No other kind of food . . . . I got sick with typhus and was going to die, from minute to minute I was going to die. Because most people died from the typhus. And they found a horse, frozen by the Buh, left by the Russians. And the gypsies went and got it, cut it up and divided it up, and father managed to get 200-300 grams. And he gave it to me to make me well. And I ate that meat in that

[54] Document 386, Report of 20 May 1943 from the Gendarmerie post Covalevca (stamp of Zlatonstove Gendarmerie post used) to the Military Gendarmerie of Landau district.
[55] Document 383, Report No. 216 of 18 May 1943 from Gendarmerie post Covalevca to Gendarmerie Legion Berezovca.

> cold in that swarm [of people], and I got well. After that, what can I tell you, the fleas ate us alive . . . . (Ioanid et al. 214)

Another survivor, Gheorghe Irimia, who was eight years old when his family was deported from Medgidia in Dobrogea to Korenykha (Caranica) in Transnistria, spoke of the importance of each kernel of grain:

> We were kept in captivity like prisoners; if you left the camp, they shot you; you did not have permission to leave the camp, but staying there you had nothing to eat. They gave you 600 grams of food a week . . . . You could see people picking up kernels of grain in the courtyard, on the street, wherever they were. And what they found they stuffed right into their mouths, because they were beside themselves with hunger and were dying of hunger. (Ioanid et al. 231-32)

Even these testimonies were not the most extreme. Pavel Zgonea, who was seventeen when he was deported to Fedorivka (Feodorovca), stated simply, "We found horse droppings, combed through the manure, scrubbed the kernels, and ate, biting our tongue; we ate grass like animals" (Ioanid et al. 260). In another case, Enuţa Spiridon described cannibalism as a consequence of the extreme starvation that afflicted Roma deportees during a typhus outbreak in 1943:

> Whoever survived, survived; whoever did not, did not. We could hardly wait for someone to die to cut up and eat him, if you had nothing to eat . . . . [My father] died . . . . And when he died, I stayed and kept watch because they would come and cut him up and eat him; and I stayed and watched until they came and buried him . . . . From hunger, from hunger they were eating one another. And until they came and buried him I was worried. (Ioanid et al. 155-56)

Under normal circumstances one might be inclined to doubt such testimony. However, during a review of thousands of claim files submitted by Romanian Roma to the International Organization for Migration during the processing period of both Swiss and German forced labour settlements in the late-1990s and early-2000s, I personally encountered similar stories in a number of files, some relating to the same incident, and all convincing in their detail. Additional testimony and references to cannibalism in Transnistria appear in a recently published issue of the journal *Etudes Tsiganes* (*Gypsy Studies,* Paris), which is focused on "Territories of Extermination in Eastern Europe, 1941-1944" (nos. 56-57, 2017). Thus cannibalism, too, was a result of Romanian food policy and the starvation it produced among Jews and Roma deportees in Transnistria.

***

Famine and starvation were not the entire story in Romanian-occupied Bessarabia and Transnistria during World War II, but they were a permanent presence. Both Jewish and Roma deportees from Romania as well as Transnistrian Jews struggled to find enough food to survive.

Romanian state authorities, having established national policies of discrimination and deportation of both Jews and Roma largely independently of German influence, controlled the food supply available to these victims of persecution, on the basis of ethnicity. Prejudice against both targeted groups had deep roots in Romanian society.[56] With the rise of Nazi Germany to dominance in Europe, the antisemitism and anti-Roma prejudices long present among Romanian elites and widespread in the general population became government policy in Bucharest. This background, more than any control exercised by Germany, shaped the murderous policies of the Antonescu regime and the attitudes of Romanian civilians who witnessed the concentration and deportation of the Jews of Bessarabia.

Bessarabian Jews suffered hunger, malnutrition, and disease in transit camps and ghettos before their deportation. In Transnistria, the Romanians shipped food out of the territory to Romania and also prioritized the food requirements of their occupation authorities and the Romanian military. Providing food to Jews and Roma was a lower priority than meeting the needs of the local non-Jewish population that lived between the Dnister and the Buh. Indeed, feeding Jews and Roma was the lowest priority. The extreme steps taken by both civilian and military occupation authorities to isolate the Jews and Roma, to prevent them from accessing food in local markets and punish those who tried, and to limit the help that might have been offered by those local civilian individuals who took pity on the victims all lead to the same conclusion. Romania's goal was to eliminate the Jews and reduce the perceived problem represented by the Roma. This made starvation of these ethnic groups an acceptable element of state policy.

Most of the Jewish and Roma victims of the Antonescu regime perished in Bessarabia and Transnistria. Many died of starvation or from the diseases that afflicted people subjected to extreme malnourishment. Others were the victims of mass shootings that the Romanians justified as necessary to prevent epidemics spreading to their own forces and the local

[56] On the history of antisemitism in modern Romania, see the chapter I authored on "Background and Precursors to the Holocaust. Roots of Romanian Anti-Semitism. The League of National Christian Defense and Iron Guard Anti-Semitism. The Anti-Semitic Policies of the Goga Government and of the Royal Dictatorship" in *Final Report* 17-55.

population from the camps and ghettos where the perpetrators had concentrated their victims. At Vapniarka, the diet imposed by Romanian authorities was a particularly clear manifestation of the regime's use of "food as a weapon." Elsewhere in the territories that the Antonescu regime transformed into killing zones, the use of food policy as a weapon may have been less explicit, but it was no less deadly.

The Commission of Inquiry appointed by Ion Antonescu to investigate irregularities in the administration of the Chişinău ghetto asserted that in Bessarabia the lives of the Jews "ceased to represent a notion worth defending."[57] Long after the events discussed in this paper took place, some members of the Roma community continued to use the expression *"Du-te la Bug!"* ("Go to the Buh!"), when they wanted to tell someone to go to hell.[58] Bessarabia and Transnistria were territories not of life, but of death during the Antonescu regime. What transpired there truly was a hell for the hundreds of thousands of Jews and tens of thousands of Roma who had the misfortune to find themselves in those territories under Romanian rule.

Works Cited

Achim, Viorel. *Documente privind Deportarea Ţiganilor în Transnistria.* Enciclopedică, 2004. 2 vols.

---. *Munca forţată în Transnistria: "Organizarea Muncii" evreilor şi romilor decembrie 1942-martie 1944.* Cetatea de Scaun, 2015.

Ancel, Jean. *The History of the Holocaust in Romania.* U of Nebraska P and Yad Vashem, 2011.

---. *Transnistria.* Editura Atlas, Yad Vashem, 1998. 3 vols.

57 *Inquiry Report,* Part 1.

58 Use of this expression was first brought to my attention at a conference in 1981 by Nicolae Gheorghe, who was already establishing himself as a future leader in the Romani civil rights movement. A sociologist by training, Gheorghe was treated as a dissident during the communist era in Romania. Later he emerged as an important spokesperson for Romani rights internationally, including at the Organization for Security and Cooperation in Europe. Gheorghe impressed with his sensitivity and humanity, and he saw use of this expression as particularly painful to survivors of deportation to Transnistria. Gheorghe delivered an amazing paper at the conference, which sensitized me to the importance of including study of the fate of the Roma in study of the Holocaust era. Gheorghe feared the consequences he would suffer if his paper was published, however. The volume that emerged from the conference in 1981, unfortunately without Gheorghe's presentation, is Karnoouh, *Paysans et Nations d'Europe centrale et balkanique.* Born in 1946, Gheorghe passed away in 2013. His death was marked by a statement in the United States Senate on 11 September 2013 by Senator Ben Cardin, Chairman of the United States Commission on Security and Cooperation in Europe.

Ancel, Jean, editor. *Documents Concerning the Fate of Romanian Jewry during the Holocaust*. Beate Klarsfeld Foundation, 1987. 12 vols.

Axworthy, Mark. *Third Axis-Fourth Ally: Romanian Armed Forces in the European War, 1941-1944*. Hailer, 1995.

Benjamin, Lya, editor. *Comisiunea Internaţională pentru Studierea Holocaustului în România: Documente*. Polirom, 2005.

Carp, Matatias. *Cartea Neagră: Fapte şi Documente—Suferinţele Evreilor din România, 1940-1944*. Socec, 1946-47. 3 vols.

Dumitru, Diana. *The State, Antisemitism, and Collaboration in the Holocaust: The Borderlands of Romania and the Soviet Union*. Cambridge UP in association with the United States Holocaust Memorial Museum, 2016.

Evreii din România între Anii 1940-1944: Perioada unei Mari Restrişti, 1940-1942. Federaţia Comunităţilor Evreieşti din România, Centrul pentru Studiul Istoriei Evreilor din România, Hasefer, 1997. 2 vols.

Evreii din România între Anii 1940-1944—Problema Evreiască în Stenogramele Consiliului de Miniştri. Federaţia Comunităţilor Evreieşti din România, Centrul pentru Studiul Istoriei Evreilor din România, Hasefer, 1996.

Final Report. International Commission on the Holocaust in Romania, Polirom, 2005.

Hirt-Manheimer, Aron, editor. *Jagendorf's Foundry: Memoir of the Romanian Holocaust 1941-1944*. By Siegfried Jagendorf, HarperCollins, 1991.

Holocaustul evreilor români: Din mărturiile supravieţuitorilor. Institutul Român de Istorie Recentă, Polirom, 2004.

Ioanid, Radu. *The Holocaust in Romania: The Destruction of Jews and Gypsies under the Antonescu Regime, 1940-1944*. Ivan R. Dee in association with the United States Holocaust Memorial Museum, 2000.

Ioanid, Radu, et al., editors. *Tragedia Romilor Deportaţi în Transnistria, 1942-1945*. Polirom, 2009.

Karnoouh, Claude, et al., editors. *Paysans et Nations d'Europe centrale et balkanique*. Maisonneuve et Larose, 1985.

Manea, Norman. "The Pullover." *October, Eight O'Clock*, Grove Weidenfeld, 1992.

Megargee, Geoffrey P., et al., editors. *The United States Holocaust Memorial Museum Encyclopedia of Camps and Ghettos, 1933-1945*. Vol. 3: *Camps and Ghettos Under European Regimes Aligned with Nazi Germany*, Indiana UP in association with the United States Holocaust Memorial Museum, 2018.

Niri, A. *Istoricul unui tratat înrobitor*. Ştiinţifică, 1965.

Shapiro, Paul A. *The Kishinev Ghetto, 1941-42: A Documentary History of the Holocaust in Romania's Contested Borderlands*. Alabama UP in association with the United States Holocaust Memorial Museum, 2015.

---. "Vapniarka: The Archive of the International Tracing Service and the Holocaust in the East." *Holocaust and Genocide Studies*, vol. 27, no. 1, 2013, pp. 114-37. DOI: 10.1093/hgs/dct003

Solonari, Vladimir. *A Satellite Empire: Romanian Rule in Southwestern Ukraine, 1941-1944*. Cornell UP, 2019.

Trașcă, Ottmar. *"Chestiunea evreiască" în documente militare române, 1941-1944*. Institutul European and Institutul Elie Wiesel, 2010.

---. *Relațiile Politice și Militare Româno-Germane, Septembrie 1940-August 1944*. Argonaut, 2013.

Verenca, Olivian. *Administrația civilă română în Transnistria*. Universitas, 1993.

Hunger Habitus: State, Society, and Starvation in Twentieth-Century Bengal

Janam Mukherjee
Ryerson University

Abstract: This article offers a brief summary of the complex factors leading to the famine in Bengal in the 1940s and discusses its longer-term impacts—the afterlife, so to speak—of famine. This episode of starvation claimed as many as five million lives in Bengal, and had long lasting social, political, and economic consequences. Several different paradigms emerged that impacted the socio-political landscape of Bengal in the midst of the famine. Famine studies often focus on causality and on peaks of starvation deaths. However, periods of mass starvation such as the famine in Bengal do not simply end when mass starvation ends. Rather, famine inscribes itself into a famine society in elaborate fashion, impacting post-famine societies in abiding ways for generations to come.

Keywords: India, colonialism, gender, political economy, famine, culture.

The insistence on causality as a primary (and at times even exclusive) focus in famine studies often distorts the complexity of famine as a multivalent human event. The death of millions of people in a most inhuman manner—through the absolute deprivation and the relentless torture that famine represents—cannot be settled by isolating individual culprits or by analyzing structural factors. Famine represents a limit situation that if studied closely and minutely as an unfolding event, reveals the anatomy of power from top to bottom in kaleidoscopic dimensions. For this reason, I detail the course of the famine in Bengal by examining the political, economic, governmental, and social factors that contributed to mass starvation in this region during the mid-twentieth century (see Mukherjee).

In what follows, I will first summarize the complex factors leading to famine in Bengal, a populous province on the eastern front of British rule in India, the earliest region of South Asia colonized by the British. I will then extend the analysis to a discussion of the longer-term impacts of famine—the afterlife, so to speak, of this episode of starvation that claimed as many as five million lives in Bengal. In this latter exercise, I hope to demonstrate that famine studies would do well to move beyond a narrow focus on famine as a circumscribed historical event, and historians would do well to move beyond analyses of famine that focus exclusively on causality. Periods of mass starvation such as the one Bengal went through in the 1940s do not simply end when mass starvation ends. Rather, famine inscribes itself into a famine society in elaborate fashion, impacting post-famine societies in abiding ways.

The Famine

On 3 September 1939, when England declared war on Germany, it also declared war on behalf of its far-flung empire. Subsequently, the idea of Total War began to underwrite all domestic and colonial policy. Though an attack by Germany on India was highly improbable, large-scale mobilization in India began immediately. An air raid precaution (A.R.P.) service was established in all cities of Bengal, which, together with the Civic and Home Guards, amounted to an ad hoc militia of more than 200,000 by 1943. Mock bombings, complete with phosphorous bombs, ambulance services, and corpse disposal crews, were staged throughout Calcutta, the capital city of Bengal, and the colonial economy was quickly retooled for wartime production. Meanwhile, the Indian National Congress (INC), the country's primary nationalist organ, withdrew from participation in colonial governance, protesting that it had been forced into Britain's war. Without the participation of the INC in Britain's experimentation with democracy in India, much of the country reverted to "emergency rule," which allowed colonial authorities to wield power with especially authoritarian zeal during the entire course of the war. India, in this sense, amounted to an occupied nation for the duration of World War II.

When Japan entered the war in December 1941, and Singapore and Burma fell just a few short months later, Bengal became the front of the Axis/Allied conflict in Asia, and Calcutta became the main source of supplies in a war against a formidable enemy. Calcutta also became a prime target for further Japanese advance, which bred considerable administrative unease in the former colonial capital. The British were shocked by the sound defeats they were dealt across southeast Asia and dug their heels into Bengal with particular resolve. Calcutta was now of paramount geopolitical importance to the British Empire, and its potential loss to Japan could not be countenanced. The call went out for all hands on deck, and the Calcutta population was goaded into reluctant mobilization. Indian residents of Calcutta responded in less than patriotic ways, however: those who had roots outside the city, the middle class, mostly caste Hindu gentry, began to flee in large numbers, while those who had no village to retreat to—the poor, and the working classes—treated A.R.P. drills with disregard, and at times open disdain (WBSA W-72/41).

As the native quarters were becoming ghost towns, the city was filling up with British and American troops, and the factories that supplied the war machine kicked into overdrive. Subsequently, the need for labour pressed hard on industrialists, who were now turning record profits in war-related industries. Labourers were recruited from the far reaches of Bengal's impossibly vast hinterland to keep the supply train running. By this time, the province of Bengal had been labelled a "dangerous area," and colonial officials themselves were making plans to move their families out of harm's way. Whereas the rhetoric of defence escalated, military protection of the all-important city of Calcutta remained minimal at best, with only ad hoc measures taken to thwart a Japanese attack. The plan that the colonial government came up with—in lieu of actual military preparation—amounted to a scorched earth campaign in Bengal. This scheme of "Denial," as it was called,[1] would have disastrous consequences for the people of the entire region.

The first measure of the "Denial Scheme" was to confiscate all "surplus" rice in coastal districts so that the Japanese could not appropriate it in the event of an attack and a land-march on Calcutta. To this end, the British government agents, backed by law enforcement and the military, went into the countryside and snatched up all the rice that could be found, paying whatever price they deemed appropriate, and wreaking chaos on existing market structures in the process. No real effort was made to establish which rice was "surplus" and which rice was essential, and as such, the scheme appeared to the people of Bengal to be open looting. The rice was to be used to feed labour forces in Calcutta, but much of the confiscated rice seems to have been hoarded in corporate and government warehouses, even while starvation in Bengal began to mount. Already, by April 1942, the price of rice had risen dangerously, and there was distress—and even starvation—in both the city and the countryside. The Denial Policy upped the ante, putting further pressure on prices, disorganizing the traditional market system, and alerting an already uneasy population to the State's mounting anxiety.

After "rice denial" the British colonial government moved on to a scheme of "boat denial." The idea here was to deny potential Japanese landing forces the opportunity of appropriating local conveyance in the event of an advance on Calcutta. The delta of Bengal is one of the most

[1] This official policy, conceived by the War Cabinet in London, was intended to deprive possible Japenese invading troops of what they might acquire in the event of a naval landing in coastal Bengal and a subsequent march to the industrial city of Calcutta. The Denial Policy was implemented through government and military channels.

complex waterways in the world, and the "country-boats" of Bengal represented the essential form of transport across much of the region. During the Denial schemes, in the period of a few short months, a total of more than 46,000 boats were requisitioned (for military purposes), sunk, destroyed, or otherwise removed from service, crippling the riverine economic infrastructure of deltaic Bengal (Famine Inquiry Commission 26). As life in the districts began to deteriorate without local transport, those who had fled Calcutta months earlier in fear of Japanese attack began to straggle back into the city in search of increasingly scarce resources. Accordingly, the needs of the city, already serving as a war base for tens of thousands of Allied soldiers, escalated still further. It was at this time that war came home to Calcutta.

On 20 December 1942, Calcutta was bombed for the first time by the Japanese. According to official reports, the damage was "slight,"[2] but panic gripped the city. Most alarmingly, rice merchants and large holders of stocks of rice fled the city for safer harbours—even while the colonial government worked to keep the war machine functioning. Concerned about access to supplies to feed industrial labourers and the military in and around Calcutta, government agents broke into shuttered private warehouses and requisitioned all the rice they could find (Testimony of L. G. Pinnell, Nanavati Papers 553). Two thirds of the available stocks in Calcutta were summarily seized; in the process, the influential and well-connected Indian merchant class of Calcutta was deeply estranged from the colonial authority. The trade system from root to branch was thrown into complete disarray, and as prices skyrocketed, more and more supplies found their way into the thriving black market. In Calcutta, as rice markets became increasingly volatile, government and industrial interests descended again and again on the countryside to raid it of rice and paddy[3] to offset the uncertainty of rice supplies in the city. The military presence in Calcutta needed to be maintained at all costs.

As conditions in the countryside grew ever more ominous, middle-class Bengalis who had fled the bombings in Calcutta now returned to the city to

---

[2] Official instructions promulgated to minimize panic after air raids stated: "where necessary to publish any mention of damage the general terms 'slight,' 'moderate,' and 'heavy' or synonyms of these will be used" (WBSA, Home Political File W-296). Newspapers accordingly reported air raid damage to be "slight" ("Calcutta's First Raid").

[3] Paddy is rice in the husk, before being milled. Although the paddy can be stored much longer than milled rice, it is expensive to transport and so was often left at the place of purchase, and thus removed from the open market. Records exist indicating the amount of rice that was moved to Calcutta but not the amount of paddy that was purchased and withheld from the market in the countryside.

parlay their influence and status into stockpiles of rice—their entitlement thus putting increased pressure on rice markets in the city. Close on the heels of the returning gentry was a tidal wave of starving villagers who began to crash onto the shores of Calcutta by May 1943. They came naked or draped in rags and filled the lanes and by-lanes of the city with their broken bodies, human skeletons uttering plaintive moans. Despite extraordinary measures by the colonial state to stem the influx of famine refugees and to censor the inconvenient truth of their wretched arrival in the city, the hunger—and indeed starvation—that had been haunting the rural districts of the region for some years could no longer be denied. In August 1943, Calcutta's premier English newspaper, *The Statesman,* defied a censorship order to publish a photo essay of starvation on the streets of the city, and the "Bengal Famine of 1943" came into usage.

Causality

In this brief summary, the centrality of colonial policies related to the war in Asia is paramount to understanding the course of famine. War created the conditions for an authoritarianism in Bengal that justified extremely predatory economic practices that threw rice markets into chaos and created the conditions for runaway inflation. In addition, according to the calculations of war, priorities were set that greatly disadvantaged those not seen as directly involved in the war effort—namely, the rural poor, who, it might be said, became a kind of "collateral damage" during the famine. War in a colonial setting, moreover, could be conducted with a particularly strong hand and with a pronounced disregard for the native population. While in Britain there had been provisions for rationing and public health since the very commencement of the war, in colonial India, few, if any, precautions were taken to shield the population from the entailments of a wartime economy. In colonial India, the entire governmental apparatus could be fashioned according to the prerogative of Total War without concern for how this fashioning would impact the colonized population. We thus see a dovetailing of colonial and martial ideologies in Bengal at the crux of the massive starvation that erupted in 1943.

One can identify central actors and specific decisions with direct relevance to an analysis of famine in Bengal. A relatively recent focus of such an investigation is Winston Churchill (see Mukerjee). Churchill, a staunch defender of colonialism, hated the Indian National Congress and all discussion of independence for India. He also repeatedly scuttled calls for the import of food into India at the crucial juncture when prices were skyrocketing in Bengal. Beneath Churchill were a host of colonial officials, who through active malice or idle disinterest failed to stem the escalating material distress of the people of Bengal just prior to 1943. From the Viceroy on down to the most local officer, concern for the wretched masses of India was tepid and often laced with a Malthusian fatalism, energized by social Darwinism. As the starvation of the poor in Bengal did not prove a threat to the colonial regime or to the British war effort, it was almost completely ignored at every level of colonial governance.

But apart from the crimes of commission, the historical record is replete with evidence not only of venality and culpability in relation to the famine in Bengal but also of the sheer incompetence of the colonial state. Far from establishing a hegemonic presence in India, the colonial state, as late as 1943, had little knowledge of the local population and limited capacities of governance or management. This leant a persistent aspect of confusion, as well as overreach, to the problem of executing wartime policies. The defeats of World War II in Asia had served to demoralize spirits further. Miscommunications, petty squabbling, and trained indifference defined a colonial administration in total collapse. In sum, it might be said, the colonial government had neither the will nor the capacity to contend with the far-reaching breakdown of order that the famine in Bengal represented.

What we see in Bengal in 1943, however, cannot be explained by merely examining the enactments of colonialism and war. There were clear indications of chronic hunger, and even starvation, in Bengal that went almost completely unheeded. We must also look to the self-interest of colonial and colonized actors. While the extent of the impoverishment of Bengal's rural masses can be traced to the colonial economy, the invisibility of the poor within the colonial society also must be closely considered. Evidence of acute hardship and even starvation had been reported in rural districts of Bengal as early as 1934 (see Mitter). By the end of that same decade, many small tenants had lost their lands to unscrupulous money lenders and were already insolvent. Meanwhile, in Calcutta, middle-class, white-collar workers were increasingly insulated from the miseries of the rural poor. Politics, elite society, and even nationalism most often failed to address the poverty that was hollowing out the countryside, and rigid caste and class distinctions defined a partition of concern that rendered the hunger of millions invisible to those enjoying relative prosperity. When, in 1942, Gandhi fasted in the name of the "privations of the poor millions," a "Leaders Conference" was called in Delhi. Many of the scions of Indian industry and politics attended to express their support for Gandhi, but none made any mention whatsoever of Gandhi's concern about the material welfare of the now starving population.

In fact, when we look beyond colonialism and its relation to famine in Bengal, we find a class of Indian capitalists who themselves were deeply invested in Calcutta's wartime economic boom, making fantastic profits in textiles, armaments, and other manufactured goods. They deeply imbricated themselves into the colonial state apparatus and peddled influence far and wide in order to maximize their fortunes. During the war, these interests repeatedly partnered with government and military authorities to ravage the Bengal countryside in the quest for rice. A conflict between the government and Indian owners of rice mills also had a great impact on rice supplies (Testimony of Representative of the Bengal Rice Mills Association, Nanavati Papers 1211). As industrial interests were amassing their stockpiles, white-collar workers in Calcutta began to hoard. In short, the extent to which the social structure of Bengali society contributed to famine is an interesting subject, one that has important implications even today, with large sectors of Bengali society still on the margins of survival, while remaining all but invisible to priviledged sectors of society.

If one looks at how famine unfolded, many different causal factors can be identified. What is more, the architecture of not only the colonial state but also of the Bengali society and economy is revealed in stark relief. If we take the four factors outlined here into account—colonialism, war, capitalist profiteering, and existing structures of inequality—we begin to approach a better understanding of the causes of the Bengal famine. We also discover more about the anatomy of colonial rule, the ideological mania of total war, unfettered capitalism, and the structural mechanisms of Bengali society that mask the suffering of the poor. The interplay of these factors is extremely complex and tortured, and they are far from exclusive. Armatya Sen's work on the Bengal Famine of 1943 highlighted the economic factors from a theoretical standpoint. There were also environmental factors (see Iqbal) and international factors outside of colonialism (such as the blocking by the USA of UNRRA funds to Bengal in 1944) that might help to assess the causes of the Bengal famine (see Venkataramani). In fact, famine represents a unique lens for examining social, political, and economic structures at large, revealing the mechanics of a given social order in deathly relief.

In the Wake of Famine

It is here that many studies of famine tend to conclude. Famine is understood as a delimited disaster: its causes are assessed, remedies are discussed, and it is often left at that. Catastrophic famine, however, cannot be understood as a historically circumscribed episode with a beginning, an apex, and a neat conclusion. Rather, famine is a historical event that has very long legs. An intense period of starvation and death from disease, like that which Bengal endured in the 1940s, continues to affect the lived reality of famine-stricken societies for many years to come, with impacts on a people's political and social realities that can extend for generations.

Given that famine does not end when starvation abates, I move beyond questions of causality to questions of longevity. Famine, while stemming often from military occupation, colonialism, and foreign rule, might be said to represent a kind of "occupation" with which famine societies continue to struggle after starvation is brought under control. The sheer magnitude of famine becomes mapped onto the collective psyche of a surviving population, and famine transforms societal structures in abiding ways. Hunger remains a persistent spectre, a societal haunting that is inflected in the ongoing collective experience of post-famine societies. This is especially true in Bengal, a region of the world that has grappled with famine throughout its modern history, and where acute hunger, malnutrition, and even starvation continue to plague those on the economic margins. In Bengal, famine is written deeply into the societal script and continues to reverberate distinctly a full seven decades later. In public discussions on famine in Bengal, I have often posed the question of whether or not the Bengal famine ever *did* come to an end. The question is relevant, as hunger and material deprivation continue to plague the poor in Bengal, and the profound collective experience lives on in memory, art, and intergenerational discourse. For the British, on the other hand, marking an end to the famine in Bengal took on great political importance.

In 1943, when famine in Bengal finally came to wider public notice, it created something of a scandal and embarrassment to the brokers of power—locally, nationally, and internationally. How could it be that Britain's great "civilizing mission" in Asia had gone so wrong? The United States, jockeying throughout the war for geopolitical advantage over Britain in Asia, touted colonialism as the moral scourge of European hegemony. Famine at the heart of empire served this rhetorical purpose well. The British, who had been desperate to keep the conditions in Bengal from the front pages of newspapers, shifted into full damage control mode when the news could no longer be suppressed. Bodies of the starving were rounded up from the streets of Calcutta by force and warehoused in bleak death camps on its outskirts, where they could be hidden from public view. High profile relief campaigns were undertaken by the British military and splashed across international newspapers. By the end of 1943, even though mortality rates were on the rise, Britain strove to call a quick end to famine to stem its own diplomatic bleeding on the international stage (Sen 200-02). Famine in Bengal was simply not consistent with the moral claims of an empire at war. Meanwhile, in Bengal, many of the elite Indian class, for varying reasons of self-interest, were happy to follow suit. The ruling party, at that time the Muslim League, was eager to declare victory over famine in order to legitimize its efforts at remediation, while opposition parties were happy to call an end to famine because they well knew that a "second famine" (which could have been declared at any moment at least until 1946) would destroy the ruling party's claims of having ended famine. In a more general sense, Bengal had grown weary of death, and those with the means to move forward wanted to leave famine behind.

Famine, however, did not simply slink into a cave like some sad dragon, but continued to take a massive toll, hammering a devitalized population deeper into uncharted despair. Death and dislocation by hunger had altered the very demographics of the region, with whole villages wiped out or abandoned and many millions on the move. Malaria, smallpox, and other epidemic diseases were making fast work of the depleted population, and several million would die even after the dreadful year 1943 had been put to rest. By 1944, however, other dramas took centre stage, and the moans and meanderings of the devastated underclasses fell on deaf ears. With the war seemingly winding down and independence for India expected on the near horizon, famine (as catastrophe now survived) was bandied about for political gain, ladening an already rancorous debate with the weight of several million destroyed bodies. In this sense, for many of the Bengal elite, once widespread starvation had been contained, famine became merely a tool of power—a rather cynical means of mobilizing constituencies and winning popular support. During the entire period of starvation, the political establishment of the region had been deadlocked in bitter rivalry. With ongoing material deprivation and death from starvation and disease, famine was an extremely cheap and easy way to tar one's political opponents. In particular, blame for famine was enthusiastically slung back and forth between the Hindu Mahasabha and the Muslim League, weighing down already bitter debates with the immensity of famine deaths. Famine thus intensified Hindu/Muslim tension in Bengal at an extremely critical juncture.

For the almost exclusively Hindu middle class of Bengal, sandwiched precariously between those who were damned and those who sat in privileged denial, life was harrowing, anxious, and uncertain. This Hindu middle class was positioned between a mass of wretched misery and the competing cabals of self-serving patricians who clung to what they held in terms of resources, influence, and "priority" with a sometimes ruthless resolve, while crippling scarcity continued to make life bitter well into 1946 and beyond. The plight of Bengal's middle class during the famine fostered a congealing of Hindu identity that had lasting, and ultimately, pernicious results. The sufferings of the middle class became easily equated with the claim of disproportionate suffering of Hindus in general, particularly in the context of a Muslim League-dominated Ministry. Government relief for the poor was considered inappropriate for middle-class Hindus because of dietary taboos (upper-caste Hindus will only eat food prepared according to certain caste restrictions, which relief kitchens did not enforce), and as such, it was resented as biased. Moreover, as most of the impoverished agriculture workers, particularly jute planters in eastern Bengal, were Muslims, the famine exacerbated the politically expedient equation of class and religious community. Government relief for the rural poor could be touted as "Muslim relief" by opposition parties, while relief for the middle classes could be coded as "Hindu." The claim of social difference, long embedded in the socio-political structure of the region, was increasingly lodged in a biopolitical struggle for survival. At length, the Hindu Mahasabha, while distributing relief almost exclusively to the "middle classes," was able to gain a populist foothold throughout Bengal that all previous efforts to consolidate a popular Hindu political front had failed to do—even while the Bengal government, with substantial help from the Government of India and the military, could claim its dedication to assisting the Muslim lower class majority.

It should come as no surprise that further violence, anarchic and annihilating, finally exploded in August of 1946 at the congested and contentious urban core of Bengal in the city of Calcutta. The Calcutta riots, which saw Hindu-Muslim violence on a scale never before witnessed on the subcontinent, cost the lives of perhaps 10,000 people in the former colonial capital, with as many as 200,000 dislocated.[4] These riots provided the initial spark for the further more apocalyptic Hindu-Muslim violence that accompanied the partition of British India. From where did all that sudden, life-annihilating hatred come? Although these same riots have most often been interpreted through the narrow lens of communalist manipulations, I argue that the Calcutta riots, although distinct from the annihilating structural violence of famine and war out of which they emerged, have to be read from within the context of a cumulative violence that began with chronic, multi-generational poverty compounded by war, and brought to a catastrophic head in devastating famine (Mukherjee 209-34). The riots in Calcutta refracted the complex ruin of Bengal in violent colours and with

[4] The number of those killed is extremely difficult to ascertain. The total number of dead bodies reported to have been processed through official channels was 3,468 (WBSA, Home Political File 351/46 [Part B, IX]). Many of the dead, however, were disposed of in a non-offical manner (stuffed into manholes or burned in buildings, for example). In my work (*Hungry Bengal*) I have estimated the dead at 10,000 at least. Several hundred thousands were displaced (see Home Confidential, File W-351/46 [Part B, VII], "Activities of the Civil Supplies Department").

novel forms of cruelty, self-interest, and heartlessness. They did not emerge out of the thin blue sky of manufactured "communalism."

The impact of the injustice and structural violence of famine that characterized Bengal in the 1940s hardly ends there. In late 1946, while the nationalist clouds were rumbling above and scalpels were being sharpened for the vivisection of the subcontinent, an armed agrarian uprising, the Tebhaga Movement, was unfolding across still undivided Bengal. At the bottom, the primary concern was neither partition nor independence, but economic justice. By early 1947, sharecroppers, a group decimated by famine throughout the preceding years, were burning down their landlords' threshing houses, seizing crops, and demanding a fairer share of the fruits of their own labour. The intensity and persistence of this uprising has to be understood as a legacy of famine. There could not have been one amongst the peasantry who had not been touched by hunger, and all had watched thousands around them perish of starvation and disease. As such, the experience of famine proved extremely fertile ground for the Communist Party of India (CPI), which had long been struggling to gain a political foothold in Bengal. The Tebhaga movement is often understood to represent the party's first effective stand in Bengal, gaining its first momentum in the context of famine. Although the Tebhaga movement was ultimately crushed, it simmered below the surface for decades to come, energizing the communists' rise and their long rule in West Bengal three decades later.

It was famine that finally brought the Communist Party out of the shadows in Bengal. Prior to the 1943 famine, the party's strategy of a "People's War" to defeat global fascism had gained only tepid support from a beleaguered population in wartime Bengal. In the early 1940s the Communist Party—at the bidding of the Communist International—had vigorously promoted the allied war effort, had acted to rally labour "morale" in and around Calcutta, had argued against labour action during the war, and had even enthusiastically advocated for policies directly linked to the creation of famine, including denial. This policy of complicity with the colonial state garnered little approbation from a skeptical and increasingly despairing public, and the ideological vagaries of the CPI's internationalism won little popular support. By 1944, however, with the end of the war in sight, and the continuation of dire scarcity still breeding widespread anguish, the Communist Party in Bengal began a cultural turn that directly focused on the intractable plight of the rural poor. It was this turn away from an abstract internationalist ideology and toward recognition of material conditions in agrarian Bengal that established the CPI's first popular foothold in the region. In doing so, it also gave the party a largely autonomous scope in organizing across the state; the idioms of the communist movement being heavily entrenched in cultural work specifically related to the famine.

With widespread relief operations set up mostly from Calcutta, Dhaka, and other cities of Bengal, famine also created the conditions for the urban elites of the early People's War movement to "de-class" in the countryside, which gave leftist intellectuals a new perspective of the inequality that had laid waste to the region. A cultural effervescence emerged among young people associated with the Communist Party, who had often been at the front in famine relief operations. This translated into considerable cultural capital that would serve the party well for years to come. The depictions of famine by artists like Chittaprosad, Somnath Hore, and Zainul Abedin (to name a few) became icons of the post-colonial era, and many artists who had directly associated themselves with the CPI became stalwarts of the party. In addition, by 1944, the Indian People's Theatre Association, established directly by the CPI, was touring villages and towns, staging trenchant dramas that portrayed the despair and injustice that had wracked Bengal. This novel experiment in folk theatre brought the Communist Party in close contact with the rural poor and created a template for artistic expression informed by social reality. It also won the Communist Party considerable support among the rural poor.

At the other end of the spectrum, the consolidation of capital and the boom in industry that accompanied war—so fundamental to the policies that engendered famine—resulted in lasting political and economic formations that would impact the history of South Asia for decades to come. The exact extent of profits made and the relation of these profits to the immiseration of Bengal is a topic for further research. It is safe to say, however, that fortunes were made among the industrial elite of India and that these fortunes were funnelled into (and became the backbone of) the nationalist movement. With this confluence of political and economic purposes came certain ideological configurations of influence that remain central to the Indian power structure even today. In some definite sense, the rise to power of this class of industrialists and their influence in Delhi were concocted in the crucible of famine. The claim of "priority" in the face of war made by the industrialists of Calcutta was directly linked to the hunger, dispossession, and despair of the countryside. It was during the war (and the famine) that Indian industrialists consolidated the economic and political powers they still wield today. Famine, in this respect, continues to have important entailments in the structural and political makeup of India.

Gender relations in Bengal also went through a radical transformation during this period of war and famine. In Bengal, as elsewhere, the typical picture of famine has most often been a feminized one: an anonymous woman's emaciated face stares dully into a waiting camera lens, her rail thin arm supports a wasted infant who seeks vainly for sustenance from a sunken, withered breast. It is a barren picture of utter hopelessness: both mother and child will surely perish. However, such artists' depictions do not concur with the data. The historical record reveals that women were less likely than men to die of starvation. While I leave the question of why and how women seem to have had a better chance of surviving famine for another time, I analyze below the consequences of the persistent idea that women were the primary victims of famine.

Gender and Famine

The most complete picture of differences in mortality based on gender was given in a report published by the University of Calcutta's Department of Anthropology in 1949 (Das). This study has long been regarded as one of the most thorough demographic works compiled during the Bengal famine. The survey was meticulously conducted by eleven well-trained field workers and sponsored by the University of Calcutta. It has remained an important primary source for almost all studies of the Bengal famine, including Amartya Sen's, which relies heavily on this work in reconstructing a demographic picture of the class basis of destitution during the 1943 famine.[5] According to the data gathered, out of every 1,000 dead, 651 were men and 349 were women (Das 93). The 1951 census figures support the gist of these findings, pegging annual female deaths for the decade as a whole at 918 to every 1,000 male deaths (Srimanjari 210). Death, however, was not the only (or perhaps even the worst) victimization that women, as a whole, were perceived to have suffered in the context of famine.

With American and British military troops stationed throughout the Bengal region during World War II, war and famine created the conditions for a booming sex industry in Calcutta that has long been depicted as the ruin of millions of women across Bengal. Hindu nationalist Shyama Prasad Mookerjee and others made great hay of the scourge of prostitution during the war and the famine. Subsequently, literary and filmic representations of the 1943 famine followed suit, making iconic the image of the poor village woman who sells her "honour" for material survival. By 1946, the

[5] In his chapter on the Bengal famine in *Poverty and Famines*, under the subheading "The Class Basis of Destitution," Amartya Sen draws data from three works, the data for two of which were collected post-1943. In introducing the sources of his data, Sen states, "while these two [other] studies were conducted after the famine was over, a study of the destitutes in Calcutta during the famine was carried out in September 1943 by T. Das (1949) . . . covering 820 destitute family units" (70). Sen goes on to draw statistics from Das that are fundamental to his arguments.

"protection of women" from the depredations they were said to have suffered during famine became a recurrent rhetorical framework of the Hindu Mahasabha in Bengal. Accounts of women entering into sex work were greatly exaggerated, and the spectre of a "ruined" Hindu womanhood was used as a wedge against the Muslim League Ministry, which had operated government relief. Moreover, by the end of the decade, the idea of women's economic agency had become stigmatized with what might be called the famine-taint of dishonour. In this light, women's new-found engagement in the labour force—a phenomenon that was seen across the world during and after World War II—in Bengal became entangled with a moral suspicion and a patriarchal disdain that lingers today. Famine, it can be said, created the conditions for a heavier patriarchal hand in shaping these perceptions.

The 1960 Bengali film, *Meghe Dhakka Tara* (*Cloud Covered Star*), by Ritwik Ghatak, has become emblematic of the post-famine, post-partition period. In the opening vignette, the heroine of the story, Neeta, is seen shuffling off to her work wearing broken sandals, demonstrating her family's acute poverty. In subsequent scenes we learn the backstory to Neeta's employment. Her father is past his prime, and her younger brother, an aspiring singer, cannot earn a living for himself, much less for the family. Facing abject destitution, Neeta takes the bold decision to get an office job. Throughout the course of her short career, she suffers repeated humiliations and ultimately is forced to forgo marriage and personal care in the name of group survival. The pressures of her economic stewardship break her in the end, and in the last scene she is seen begging in a sanatorium somewhere in north Bengal. Her entry into the work force is thus portrayed as her undoing—both morally and materially. That the heroine in *Meghe Dhakka Tara* has long served as a popular representation of suffering womanhood in post-colonial Bengal is a testament to the ways that famine has impacted gendered understanding of economy in Bengal.

Conclusion

Apart from structural and political considerations, the extent to which famine has affected Bengali collective self-understandings and popular culture is a subject for study that may well be inexhaustible. The decades following the famine and riots, and then partition, were a period of intensive change and struggle, and memories of famine and its myriad entailments remain deeply lodged in Bengali hearts and minds. Famine and hunger were central motifs around which creative thought constellated for generations. "Hungry Bengal"—the title of Chittoprasad's compilation of sketches and essays of famine-ravaged Midnapore—became the label chosen by the following generation of writers, painters, and poets who in the 1950s, 60s, and 70s struggled to come to grips with the enormity of the tragedy that had unfolded in the 1940s. The names of many of these artists are as ubiquitous in Bengali households as the individual stories, passed down by grandmothers and grandfathers, and now great grandmothers and great grandfathers. Thus, famine has written a rich text into the culture of Bengal and continues to do so.

In the years that followed acute starvation, famine became a sort of self-conscious banner of the whole of Bengal for generations—a sign under which the province has long laboured. Even today, seventy years later, it is remarkable the alacrity with which youth in Bengal take to conversations about the famine. Few of them have not heard of it, and many of them have a fair understanding of the event and speak about it with a passion and indignation that keeps the famine fresh and relevant in modern Bengal. It is obvious that youth have been learning about famine, probably from as early as they can remember—at the foot of some auntie, or grandfather, or parent, or neighbourhood teller, but also from movies, popular reference, music, and art. The means and modes of famine transmission, and the ways that famine continues to impact social, political, cultural, and economic facets of individuals and communities, lay grounds for further research and analysis.

In assessing and analyzing the collective impacts of famine on Bengali society and culture, the work of Pierre Bourdieu comes to mind, in particular, his concept of "habitus," which figures in the title of this paper. In 1990, Bourdieu defined habitus as "a system of acquired dispositions functioning on the practical level as categories of perception and assessment or as classificatory principles [that inform] the organizing principles of action" (12-13). Habitus, in less technical language, might be described as those dispositions of being and communication that are ingrained in any society by their collective experience, collective memory, and collective representation. It is the lens through which a culture views and expresses itself. Habitus informs the way people speak, the way they think, their gestures, and other unconscious representations of self. The collective memory of famine, as I have seen it in Bengal, has created a strong collective memory that has now spanned several generations, becoming a particularly powerful kind of habitus, the hunger habitus. Again, the event of famine in this sense does not end when starvation ends. Rather, famine writes itself deeply into a culture, with a productivity of energies that also promise possible redemption in the face of almost unimaginable loss.

Overall, I argue for a better historical appreciation of the complexity of famine, in terms of both causality and consequences. Perhaps because it had long been thought that famine resulted only from environmental factors, its imbrication in social, economic, and political structures has received relatively scant attention. On the other hand, if we understand famine as a human (all-too-human) event, we are more inclined to examine its considerable complexities. In this mode, famine becomes an extremely important lens through which we can view structures of inequality, political mobilizations that hinge on resource allocation, and many other aspects of structural violence. In sum, the political economy of famine is a key to the understanding of power structures at large. The concurrence of factors, policies, and enactments that deny large sectors of a population the bare means of existence are essential clues in understanding constellations of power that both precede and follow famine. Moreover, in addressing the complexity of famine more rigorously, it is possible to imagine we are redressing—in a small way—the dismissal of the value of human life at the margins. If the study of the death of many millions in Bengal can shed light on critical aspects of the structural violence of famine more broadly, it might be seen as some small redemption of lives lost so senselessly and brutally.

Works Cited

Bourdieu, Pierre. *In Other Words: Essays towards a Reflexive Sociology.* Stanford UP, 1990.

"Calcutta's First Raid." *The Statesman,* 22 Dec. 1942.

Das, Tarakchandra. *Bengal Famine (1943): As Revealed in a Survey of the Destitutes in Calcutta.* University of Calcutta, 1949.

Famine Inquiry Commission of India. *Report on Bengal.* Government of India, 1945.

Ghatak, Ritwik, writer and director. *Meghe Dhakka Tara.* Chitrakalpa, 1960.

Iqbal, I. *The Bengal Delta: Ecology, State and Social Change, 1840-1943.* Palgrave Macmillan, 2010.

Mitter, S. C. *A Recovery Plan for Bengal.* The Book Company, 1934.

Mukerjee, Madhusree. *Churchill's Secret War: The British Empire and the Ravaging of India during World War II.* Basic Books, 2010.

Mukherjee, Janam. *Hungry Bengal: War Famine and the End of Empire.* Oxford UP, 2015.

National Archives of India (New Delhi), Nanavati Papers.

Sen, Amartya. *Poverty and Famines: An Essay on Entitlement and Deprivation.* Oxford UP, 1981.

Srimanjari. *Through War and Famine: Bengal, 1939-45.* Orient Black Swan, 2009.

Venkataramani, M. S. *Bengal Famine of 1943: The American Response.* Vikas Publishing House, 1972.
West Bengal State Archives (WBSA), Home Political Files.

Stalin's Faminogenic Policies in Ukraine: The Imperial Discourse

Liudmyla Hrynevych
Institute of the History of Ukraine, National Academy of Sciences of Ukraine

Translated from Ukrainian by Andrew Sorokowski

Abstract: Because Stalin's policy of famine creation in the early 1930s has been viewed through the prism of communist theory and practices, scholars have paid less attention to the imperial/colonial discourse of the period. This essay attempts to show the suitability of applying theoretical models of dependence and imperialism to analyze the dynamics and consequences of the collectivization of agriculture and the Holodomor (the mass deaths through starvation in Ukraine). The pressure applied to all regions of the USSR, resulting from the "communist experiment," was in Soviet Ukraine supplemented and intensified, and, at some points, determined by a system of centre-periphery relations, characterized by political domination, control, the subordination of regional political elites to the centre, and the exploitation of economic resources. The appropriation of sovereignty over the Ukrainian republic by the central government in Moscow included establishing full control over Ukraine's food resources, such as determining grain harvesting and distribution. The ongoing exploitation of Ukrainian economic resources and the anti-Ukrainian terror caused the Ukrainian famine of 1928-29. These also became significant factors in the onset of the 1932-33 Holodomor.

Keywords: faminogenic policy,[1] Holodomor, genocide, Ukraine, famine, imperialism, colonialism.

In the last thirty years, our knowledge and understanding of the causes and nature of Stalin's famine-inducing policies in Ukraine have grown significantly (Applebaum; Kulchytsky; Kul'chyts'kyi; Mace; Makuch and Sysyn). Nevertheless, while the 1932-33 famine in Ukraine, known as the Holodomor, has been examined through the prism of theories and practices of communism and totalitarianism, it has for the most part remained outside of academic discussion of imperial and colonial discourses.

Given that for decades Stalinist faminogenic policies were not the subject of scholarly attention, the study of the Holodomor is only beginning to benefit from theoretical models that could contribute to understanding

[1] The term "faminogenic" was coined by David Marcus to describe state policies and activities that create famine conditions or support their creation (245n 9).

its complexities. In addition, the academic community is far from unanimous in how concepts of empire and colonialism apply to the USSR. Finally, political and psychological factors must be taken into account. Since the time of the Cold War, the "politicization" of the topic of the Ukrainian famine of the early 1930s has received attention, with the terms "Soviet empire," "Soviet imperialism," and "Soviet colonial practice" sometimes employed for political purposes. The combination of these factors, I would argue, has shaped a reluctance in academia to discuss the Ukrainian famine in terms of imperialism and colonialism.

Paradoxically, for decades the USSR built its ideology upon anti-imperial and anti-colonial rhetoric. As noted by Ronald Suny, the denial of its own imperial nature made the Soviet Union a truly unique empire in the twentieth century (191). With the dissolution of the USSR and the rise of nation-states upon its ruins, interest in "empire studies" in general and in the imperial nature of the Soviet Union in particular increased significantly. There are three basic approaches to addressing the question of the imperial nature of the USSR. The majority of scholars in North America and Europe consider the Soviet Union as a state of the imperial type (Applebaum; Etkind; Hirsch; Hosking; Kappeler, *The Russian Empire*; Lieven; Martin; Vishnevskii). Some scholars propose that the USSR be regarded as a hybrid entity: both an empire and a nation state (Kaspe). Finally, there are researchers who preserve a view of Soviet history that is nation-state oriented, ignoring the imperial essence of the USSR (Tishkov).

Contemporary scholars have proposed various typological designations of the Soviet empire: polyethnic (Kappeler), neo-Russian (Hosking), colonial (Thompson), post-colonial (Etkind), post-theocratic (Iakovenko), uninterrupted and totalitarian (Motyl), an affirmative action empire (Martin), an empire of nations (Hirsch), and an authoritarian and disciplinary empire (Batalov 12), among others. As well, scholars have expressed different and, at times, diametrically opposed views regarding the status and role of the Ukrainian SSR in the Soviet Union, especially as to the question of its colonial nature. Here the spectrum of opinions is particularly wide, from declaring Ukraine part of an "East Slavic metropolia" within "Great, Little, and White Rus'" (Vishnevskii 278-79) to confidently designating it as a typical peripheral colony (Motyl').

These discussions are further complicated by the absence of scholarly consensus on classification criteria and typological markers, or even on the definition of the concept of "empire" itself. Dominic Lieven describes the methodological difficulties in arriving at clear formulas that capture the phenomenon of empire in all its complexity. "Empire," he writes, "is a fine subject, peopled by leopards and other creatures of the wild. To reduce all this to definitions and formulas is to turn the leopard into a pussycat, and even then into an incomplete but misshapen pussycat with three legs and no tail" (Lieven 417). Of key significance is the nature of relations between the centre (metropolia) and the periphery (colony), which Michael Doyle describes as "a relationship, formal or informal, in which one state controls the effective political sovereignty of another political society. It can be achieved by force, by political collaboration, by economic, social, or cultural dependence" (45).

This essay aims to stimulate academic discussion on the topic of whether one can view Stalin's faminogenic policies in Ukraine in the late 1920s and early 1930s through the prism of imperial discourse. It compares the Holodomor with other instances of "imperial" famines in modern world history. My key thesis is that theoretical models of dependence and imperialism can be employed fruitfully to elucidate important aspects of the Stalinist policies that created famine in the national republics and, in particular, the Holodomor of 1932-33 in Ukraine. It is my belief that in the epoch of Stalin's "revolution from above" and the Holodomor, the pressure resulting from the "communist experiment," indisputably shared by all regions of the USSR, was amplified and at certain moments defined by a system of centre-periphery relations characterized by political domination and control, and exploitation of economic resources (in this case, food resources, grain being chief among them). This circumstance (in interaction with anti-Ukrainian terror, the analysis of which is beyond the scope of this article) became the essential factor leading to mass human mortality during the Holodomor.

In my work, I rely primarily on the theories of dependence and imperialism developed by Doyle and the theoretical approaches and evaluations formulated by Alexander Motyl and Lieven. In his article "The Soviet 1931-1933 Famines and the Ukrainian Holodomor: Is a New Interpretation Possible, and What Would Its Consequences Be?" Andrea Graziosi points to the imperial factor as key to understanding Stalinist faminogenic policies, emphasizing the need to differentiate famine as an all-Union phenomenon in 1931-33 from the Holodomor in Ukraine, the unique consequences and dynamics of which were a direct result of Moscow's decisions. This raises the question: to what degree can the Stalinist policies that led to famine, be seen as a means of consolidating the Soviet empire and ensuring its existence through violence?

In pursuing the research goal outlined above, this article addresses the following tasks (insofar as the limited scope of an article permits). A brief excursus into the history of the Russian Empire is in order to elucidate the role of the Ukrainian gubernias as leading grain-producing and grain-exporting regions and to sketch out in general terms the nature of relations between the central government of Russia and Ukraine during the processes of modernization. I then turn to an examination of the circumstances of the fall of the Russian Empire, the appearance of the Ukrainian People's Republic as a national state-building project, and the formation of the Soviet empire, including particular features of its expansionist policy vis-a-vis Ukraine. Next, citing hitherto unknown archival documents, I examine the manifestations of political and economic inequality in the relations between the all-Union (central) government and the Ukrainian SSR, focusing on the famine of 1928-29 and then touching on the Holodomor of 1932-33 in Soviet Ukraine. Finally, I will consider how these events were perceived by representatives of various social strata at the time, from the peripheral elite to ordinary people. In particular, I address the question of whether Stalin's faminogenic policies were understood by the population as manifestations of Moscow's imperial rule and of Ukraine's colonial dependence.

Ukraine in the Russian Empire As the Breadbasket of Europe: Possibilities and Limits

Before World War I, the Ukrainian gubernias produced 25 percent of the grain in the Russian Empire, close to 30 percent of the wheat, 40 percent of the barley, and nearly 50 percent of the beans and corn (*Kontrol'nye tsifry* 41). Ukraine (chiefly its steppe zone) provided nearly one-eighth of the world's imports in the five principal seed crops (wheat, rye, barley, oats, and corn) and thus was a significant force in producing profits to fund the modernizing of the empire.

The proportion of Ukrainian grain on the world market was particularly notable for certain crops. Barley and rye constituted a third, while wheat and wheat flour made up nearly a ninth. Ukrainian wheat seed was exported to European countries—England, France, Italy, Germany—while flour was shipped to Turkey, Greece, and Egypt. Germany purchased the greatest portion of the rye and barley exported from Ukraine, and France and England imported the greatest portion of Ukrainian oats. Ukrainian corn was shipped to England, Germany, and the Netherlands. France, Germany, and the Netherlands bought beans.[2] It is thus no wonder that before World War I, Ukraine was sometimes referred to as the "breadbasket of Europe," and any news of poor weather or possible crop failure in the steppe gubernias disturbed the world grain market, causing a jump in prices.

---

[2] Al'terman 21-22. On the export policy of the Russian Empire, see Den; Shevchenko; and Thompstone.

And yet, despite their great potential, the Ukrainian lands of the Russian Empire suffered from underdevelopment. As Lieven has observed, entering the age of industrial modernization, the Russian Empire, which combined the traits of European overseas colonies and the characteristics of an autocratic land empire, long remained economically and politically backward. The Russian Empire possessed nearly a third of the earth's arable land. Yet, it provided little more than a fifth of the global grain yield (21.8 percent in 1910-14) (Den 46). Compared with other grain-producing countries, the crop yield was extremely low. According to data from the international agricultural institute in Riga, in 1905-14 Russia had the lowest average yield per hectare (in quintals) for the six chief crops (wheat, rye, barley, oats, corn, and sugar beets). The situation with wheat is illustrative. During these years, the average yield was 30.2 in Denmark, 24.5 in Belgium, 21.8 in Great Britain and Ireland, 20.6 in Germany, and 13.6 in France, while in European Russia it was 6.6. The French harvested twice as much wheat, and the British and Germans, three times as much. The Russian Empire was last not only in comparison with industrially developed countries but also compared to those with extensive agricultural development, even colonies and former colonies: during the four pre-war decades, the wheat harvest in Canada, for example, yielded 12.8 quintals per hectare; in Australia, 7.6; and in British India, 7.7 (Den 48).

An indicator of the backwardness of the Russian Empire was the fact that its population constantly suffered from an insufficiency of grain resources, especially during the frequent crop failures. The years 1891-92, 1897-98, 1901, 1905-06, and 1911 clearly confirm this, at the same time demonstrating the difference between the situation in the Russian Empire and that in the more developed European countries, where crop failures meant lower profits but no longer caused famine among the population. The Russian Empire too, however, gradually evolved in this direction, chiefly in its Ukrainian gubernias: as agronomists observed, they "stood above the greater part of the rest of the Russian gubernias not only in population density, industrial development, and concentration of the population in the cities, but also in the superiority of their agriculture" (TsDAVO 337/1/8085/2).

In fact, after the 1880s the number of major crop failures in the Kyiv, Podillia, Poltava, Kherson, Iekaterynoslav, and Tavriia gubernias, as well as in the Don region, fell by half (1880s: 11, 1890s: 2, 1900-15: 3) (TsDAVO 337/1/8085/8), while from 1883 to 1915, the crop yield in the Ukrainian gubernias rose significantly, in most by a factor of two and even more (TsDAVO 337/1/8085/4).

Before the beginning of World War I, the crop yields of the principal grains in the three Ukrainian gubernias was the highest among the fifty gubernias of European Russia: 84.4 *puds* (1 *pud* = 36.11 pounds) per *desiatyna* (1.1 hectares or 2.7 acres) in the Kyiv gubernia, 81.8 *puds* in the Podillia gubernia, 72.2 *puds* in the Poltava gubernia. In the Volhynia, Iekaterynoslav, and Kharkiv gubernias, over 60 *puds* per *desiatyna* were gathered; the Tavriia gubernia was sixteenth (54.8 *puds* per *desiatyna*); and the Kherson gubernia, nineteenth (54.3 *puds* per *desiatyna*) (TsDAVO 337/1/8085/3).

Nevertheless, by the beginning of the twentieth century, the Ukrainian lands within the empire had reached the peak of their crop yield and export capabilities. The combination of a practical exhaustion of the fund of virgin soil, sharp rise in industry, and increase in the urban population made a reduction of marketable grain from the Ukrainian gubernias inevitable. It became evident that any increase in the size of the harvest would be dependent on the intensification of agricultural production. At the same time, the orientation toward external markets—and as a result, the growing predominance of grain production in Ukraine, with the accent on wheat and barley as the chief cash crops (in 1916, they constituted 29.1 percent and 23.3 percent, respectively, in the sowing area of the Ukrainian gubernias, and in the steppe zone, 36.7 percent and 35 percent)—did not foster a rise in agricultural production (Vol'f and Mebus 69). In fact, the increasing focus on exporting grain undermined the development of cattle breeding, which contributed to the exhaustion of fertile lands.

Hard currency obtained through exports was prioritized for the modernization of the industrial base of the Russian Empire despite the chronic undernourishment of the population. The phrase "we will go hungry, but we will export," attributed to the minister of finance Ivan Vyshnegradskii (1832-95), conveys the essence of imperial government policy on the eve of World War I: in 1909-13, each year an average of 323.8 million *puds* of grain was removed from Ukraine, of which only 55.2 million *puds* ended up on the empire's internal markets, while the rest was exported (Al'terman 21).

As Austrian historian Andreas Kappeler notes, the colonial nature of the polyethnic Russian Empire intensified along with modernization (*Rosiia* 249). Accordingly, Ukraine more clearly took on the traits of a colonial/dependent territory. The centre extracted finances and raw materials from the Ukrainian gubernias more and more energetically, at the same time taking advantage of them as a market for production from Russia that was not competitive on world markets.

In the pre- and especially the post-revolution years, Ukrainian scholars and civic activists were attentive to the marked disproportions in the relations between the centre (Moscow) and Ukraine, to the detriment of the latter. Not infrequently, these relations were termed colonial and served as an argument for Ukrainian autonomy. For example, Oleksandr Mytsiuk, in his brochure *Pro avtonomiiu Ukrainy v federatyvnii Rosii* (*On the Autonomy of Ukraine in a Federal Russia*), which became the notes for two public lectures he delivered in 1917 in Kyiv, pointed out that in 1903, 519 million rubles were transferred from Ukraine to the state treasury, while only 279 million rubles were expended for Ukraine's needs. Accordingly, 240 million rubles, that is, 46 percent of Ukrainian revenues, were spent on the needs of other regions. The author compared the situation with the fate of "luckless Ireland, which in the course of centuries of English oppression has lost even its native old-Celtic language" (Mytsiuk 17).

Other Ukrainian experts expressed similar thoughts. Analyzing statistical data for 1900-13, the economist and social activist Petro Mal'tsiv pointed out that the portion of revenue received from Ukraine constituted, on average, 20.8 percent of the overall Russian amount, while expenses came to only 11.8 percent (Iefimenko 38). L. Bukhanovs'kyi published data showing that in the Russian Empire between 1900 and 1914, an average of 16 rubles 97 kopecks was received annually from each inhabitant of Ukraine, while the state spent 8 rubles 65 kopecks per inhabitant. In comparison, in Russia, the amount received per inhabitant was 13 rubles 90 kopecks and 13 rubles 99 kopecks was expended (Iefimenko 38).

In a study published in Petrograd in 1918, the scholar and publicist Petro Stebnyts'kyi noted another problem: "Ukraine supplies the neighbouring districts with raw materials and semi-manufactured goods, and itself serves as a market for their finished products" (18). The following data supports the assertion: in 1915-16, 96.7 percent of Ukraine's rolled metal, 68 percent of its shaped metal, 99 percent of its I-beams and U-bars, 53 percent of its salt, 81 percent of its tin, 90 percent of its silver, and 75 percent of its general supplies of cast iron went to factories in Russia (V. Hrynevych et al. 85). In his detailed analysis of economic relations, Stebnyts'kyi concluded that in the pre-war years, imperial policy toward Ukraine had assumed the character of colonial exploitation:

> The entire system of Russia's posture toward Ukraine is analogous to the relationship of a metropolia imbued with imperialistic tendencies and a colony, which aspires to emancipate itself from the oppression that it experiences on the part of the metropolia. Of course, official Russia, proceeding in its policy from the idea of state and national unity, did not consciously treat Ukraine as a colony and did not aim at its economic exploitation. But such is the power of the centralizing principle that, in spite of the desires of the circles which direct economic life, economic imperialism grows independently in close connection with political imperialism, and under its pressure, urgent interests are muted and the vital powers of the peripheries atrophy. In the national question, old

> Russia always consciously conducted a policy that was hostile to Ukraine and its culture. (36-37).

Finally, with the onset of modernization in the second half of the nineteenth century, two disparate tendencies, which increased political and social tensions, were growing and also becoming more visible in the polyethnic Russian Empire at the start of the twentieth century (Kappeler, *Rosiia* 247). On the one hand, the centre desired to achieve uniformity based on Russian ethnic dominance. On the other hand, diversity was enhanced by the social and national mobility of the numerous non-Russian ethnic groups, which were gradually turning into contemporary nations with their own elites, literary languages, and highly developed cultures (Kappeler, *Rosiia* 247). In the new epoch of nation states, these contradictions would wind themselves into a tight knot that the imperial government could not untie and that would contribute to the fall of tsarist Russia.

The Fall of the Russian Empire, the Formation of a Ukrainian National State, the Birth of the Red Empire and Its Expansion into Ukraine

World War I was the catalyst of fundamental changes, as the era of nation states began to succeed the era of empires. After the fall of the Russian Empire and the revolution of 1917, the Ukrainian national movement, which rapidly became a mass movement, made itself heard.[3] World War I and the revolution accelerated the process of the formation and consolidation of the Ukrainian nation. Like other European nations, the Ukrainians took up the construction of their own nation state, establishing first the Ukrainian Central Rada as its parliament, which then formed Ukraine's autonomous government—the General Secretariat of the Ukrainian People's Republic (UNR).[4]

The Bolshevik seizure of power in Petrograd in the fall of 1917 hastened the rupture of Ukraine and Russia. In its Fourth Universal

---

[3] On the creation of the Ukrainian People's Republic and the Bolshevik invasion of Ukraine, see Reshetar; Borys; and Kappeler. *Rosiia* 273. See also the collection of essays in Hunczak.

[4] *Ukrains'ka Tsentral'na rada*, vol. 2; *Dyrektoriia*. Contemporary Russian historiography has traditionally minimized the role of the Ukrainian revolution and the UNR as a nation state. While the significance of the UNR as a project of Ukrainian state building is acknowledged in the works of some Western specialists on Russia, these sometimes include claims about its brief existence. For example, in *Rulers and Victims: The Russians in the Soviet Union*, British historian Geoffrey Hosking writes that the UNR lasted three months, when in fact, after a short hiatus (during the period after the declaration of the Ukrainian State of Hetman Pavlo Skoropads'kyi), the UNR was renewed (16). Its government left Ukrainian territory at the beginning of the 1920s under Bolshevik pressure and continued its existence abroad as a government in exile. It formally ceased to exist in 1992 with the creation of an independent Ukrainian state.

(January 1918), the Ukrainian Central Rada declared Ukraine to be an independent state. With the signing of the Brest-Litovsk peace treaty in March 1918, the government of the Russian SFSR acknowledged this. Lenin's government thereby obligated itself to recognize the right of the Ukrainian people to self-determination and the legality of the Ukrainian Central Rada's rule over the territory of Ukraine. In supporting Ukraine, the governments of the Central Powers undoubtedly considered Ukraine's status since pre-revolutionary times as a producer and potential supplier of foodstuffs, chiefly grain. Their desire for access to grain prompted them to support a regime change in Ukraine in the spring of 1918 and the creation of the Hetmanate of Pavlo Skoropads'kyi.[5]

Ukraine's declaration of independence triggered war with Soviet Russia, which sent its armies into Ukraine in January 1918. The determination of Lenin's government to keep Ukraine under Russia's control had not only ideological but purely pragmatic motives—access to essential resources. "For god's sake, use the most energetic and revolutionary means to send bread, bread, bread!!! Otherwise St. Petersburg may perish. Special trains and detachments. Collection and amassing. Accompany the trains. Report every day. For god's sake!" wrote Lenin on 15 (28) January 1918 to the extraordinary commissar of the Russian SFSR Council of People's Commissars in Ukraine, Serho Ordzhonikidze, in Kharkiv, and the commander of the southern Bolshevik forces Vladimir Antonov-Ovsienko (30).

During January-April 1918 over 17.3 million *puds* of grain and 5 million *puds* of other foodstuffs (meat, bacon fat, sugar, and oil) were shipped from Ukraine to Russia. In January 1918 alone, detachments of the People's Commissariat of Food Supply headed by G. N. Kudinskii dispatched 240 train cars of grain and 140,000 *puds* of sugar; at the beginning of February, 200,000 *puds* of flour and 40,000 *puds* of sugar. At the beginning of March 1918, Kudinskii informed Lenin by telegram that his food supply detachments had sent thirteen regular trains with close to 500,000 *puds* of grain to Petrograd (V. Hrynevych et al. 85). According to a statement by Lenin himself, Moscow succeeded in procuring 95 million *puds* of grain from Ukraine in 1918 (*V. I. Lenin pro Ukrainu* 213).

In late 1918, after the capitulation of Germany, Soviet Russia simply annulled the peace treaty of Brest-Litovsk and resumed its offensive in Ukraine. Simulacra of Ukrainian national governments, and a Ukrainian state created under Moscow's aegis (first, a Soviet UNR, then, by analogy with the RSFSR, a Ukrainian SSR), provided a cover of legitimacy. As in 1918, the advance into Ukraine was accompanied by requisitioning of

[5] For a detailed discussion, see Malynovs'kyi; Rafalovs'kyi; Borisov et al.

foodstuffs and their shipment to the north. Although there is no precise information on how much grain Russia managed to ship out of Ukraine into the RSFSR during 1919, the Ukrainian scholar Hennadii Iefimenko, relying on data available in Soviet historiography, estimated at least ten million *puds* (130).

The second attempt of Soviet Russia to establish Soviet rule over Ukraine likewise failed. In a letter of 12 November 1919 to the Central Committee of the Russian Communist Party (Bolsheviks) and personally to Lenin, a group of Ukrainian Bolsheviks, analyzing the reasons, noted "a policy that cannot be characterized otherwise than as colonial." "Ukraine," they wrote, "has been regarded exclusively as an object for the extraction of material resources."[6]

In 1920, the expansion of Soviet Russia into Ukraine was finally successful. Lenin's government had to declare respect for national rights while bringing in substantial contingents of the Russian SFSR's Red Army onto Ukrainian territory. A census of the Red Army and Fleet conducted in August 1920 showed that "the armies of the Ukrainian gubernias were characterized by the presence of a rather small number of local natives and were filled up by natives of the inner regions of the Russian SFSR, as were the forces located in the zone of military operations" (RGVA 40442/3/2/25). Altogether, in the Kharkiv and Kyiv military districts and the Red Army field units stationed in Ukraine at that time, there were 995,882 Great Russians, 130,914 Ukrainians, 28,229 Jews, 41,850 Tatars and others (RGVA 40442/2/3/43). The census data reveal as erroneous the assumption by the British historian Geoffrey Hosking that significant masses of Ukrainians supported Soviet rule (54).

In accord with the report of the Ukrainian Economic Consultation to the RSFSR Council on Labour and Defence, in 1920-21 a plan for grain collections in the amount of 160 million *puds* was established for the Ukrainian SSR, which was later lowered to 105 million *puds*; 76.7 million *puds* were apparently delivered to the state (*Narodnoe khoziaistvo* 509, 512). Aside from grain, the allotment covered potatoes, oil seed, meat, fowl, eggs, and dairy products. The amount of the grain that was shipped out of Ukraine was not reported. From this same source we learn, however, that in 1921, 18,903 rail cars of grain left Ukraine for the RSFSR, 1,653 for the Caucasus, and 1,134 for the Crimea—altogether 21,690 (*Narodnoe khoziaistvo* 598).

---

[6] Letter of representatives of the Ukrainian Communist organization in the Moscow committee of the Russian Communist Party (Bolsheviks) to the Central Committee of the Russian Communist Party (Bolsheviks) and personally to Lenin with an analysis and evaluation of the Communist Party's policy in Ukraine in 1919. 12 Nov. 1919. TsDAHO 57/6/15/1-17. Cited in Iefimenko 192.

The report states that the famine in the Volga region of Russia, which began in 1921, "demanded that Ukraine render significant assistance" (*Narodnoe khoziaistvo* 607), and also that "crop failure in Ukraine was determined relatively late, when its manifestations in the form of famine took on the dimensions of a great national calamity" (*Narodnoe khoziaistvo* 659).

In considering the circumstances that enabled the Bolsheviks to reincarnate the imperial project, Kappeler noted that "[t]he gathering of the lands of the tsarist empire by the Bolsheviks was carried out with the well-tried methods of the carrot and the stick and *divide et impera* (that is, by exploiting social and ethnic antagonisms)" (*Rosiia* 282). Contemporary scholars have also pointed out that in 1920 the Bolsheviks' communist slogans were closely bound up with Russian imperial rhetoric. "The territory the Red Army was fighting to reclaim," writes Hosking in this connection, "was, with a few modifications, the former Russian Empire, so that old-fashioned Russian patriotism was an acceptable motive for service within it" (54). The Bolsheviks' imperial expansionist rhetoric was also aimed at the Russians in the Red Army. A brochure published in 1919 for dissemination among the Red forces entitled *Na iug! Na iug!* (*To the South! To the South!*) explained to soldiers mobilized in the inner gubernias of the Russian SFSR the necessity of reclaiming the "national borderlands" for the control and exploitation of resources—grain, coal, etc.—needed by the north. "It turns out that our chief resources are located at the borders," it states, adding "and in the centre we have almost nothing. The centre cannot survive without the peripheries" (Baratov 8).

The question of how such slogans could have contributed to the development of an imperial mentality among Russian Red Army peasant soldiers, as well as the question of the perception in Ukraine itself of the offensive of the Russian SFSR Red Army as an imperial intervention, remain to be studied. Some documents, different in origin, testify to the manifestation of both imperial and anti-colonial attitudes.

Ukraine in the Soviet Union As the Breadbasket of the USSR: Imposition of Grain Specialization as an Indicator of Dependence and a Prerequisite of Famine

One can confidently assert, ex post facto, as a glaring example of Soviet imperial-colonial rule, the cotton "specialization" imposed by Moscow on the Central Asian republics in the 1920s and the refusal to diversify agricultural production, which led to a large-scale ecological catastrophe and the devastation of the Aral Sea. A consensus seems to have been reached in recent scholarly historiography characterizing Soviet policy in Central Asia as imperial and colonial (Cameron; Edgar; Khalid; Kindler; Sahni; Slezkine). The Ukrainian situation in the 1920s and 1930s was to a certain extent analogous. For Ukraine, it was "grain specialization" imposed by the Union centre, the purpose of which was provision of grain resources to the growing industrial regions of the north and for the procurement of currency for industrial modernization.

During the years of war and revolution, Ukraine lost its position as a leading grain exporter. By 1926-27, as a republic of the USSR, it had reached only 25.6 percent of its pre-war grain exports, 55 percent of its exports of eggs, and 38 percent of its sugar exports.[7] Although exports abroad had fallen, from the beginning of the 1920s a clear tendency was noticeable on the part of Moscow to reorient Ukraine toward grain deliveries to internal USSR markets, chiefly to the industrial regions of the Russian SFSR that were experiencing rapid urban growth. In 1923-24, 83.4 million *puds* of the chief grain crops were shipped from the Ukrainian SSR to internal USSR markets, while 85.1 million *puds* were exported; in 1925-26, the figures were 89.6 million and 42 million *puds*, respectively; in 1926-27, 84.6 and 56.2 million *puds* (Al'terman 40-41). The largest shipments out of Ukraine were of wheat: in 1926-27 they constituted over 50 percent of the grain sent to the union republics, and 40 percent of grain exports (Al'terman 43).

This role of exporter and "breadbasket of the USSR" created stresses for Soviet Ukraine. In fulfilling the centre's shipment orders, the Ukrainian SSR, even in years of good harvests, was left without evident transitional grain reserves, which undermined its grain market (TsDAVO 3/1/5038/8). A survey carried out by the Ukrainian SSR Central Statistical Administration in the spring of 1925 showed that two thirds (68.1 percent) of all peasant households in the forest-steppe region had sown enough grain only for their own needs. Even in the most commercially productive region of the Ukrainian SSR, the steppe, such households constituted just over a quarter (27.3 percent) (Al'terman 27). Thus, a significant portion of Ukrainian peasant households were able to sustain only themselves, with very modest amounts left for the market.

The causes of the weakness of the Ukrainian grain economy can in part be found in the radical social changes resulting from the 1917 Bolshevik revolution: the dissipation and destruction of effectively functioning landed estates and the redistribution of their land among five million peasant households. Ongoing crop failures, caused by a combination of unfavourable natural-climatic conditions and the policies of the communist regime, also shook the Ukrainian grain economy. Large-scale crop failure and famine afflicted Ukraine in 1921-23. The crop failure and famine of 1924-25, the circumstances of which are yet to be researched, dealt a

[7] Chernov. On the specifics of USSR foreign trade, see also Frumkin.

considerable blow to agriculture in the Ukrainian SSR. Agrarian overpopulation, too, remained a problem for Ukraine: according to some prognoses, by the end of the first Five-Year Plan there could have been a "surplus population of nearly 8.5 million" (Popov).

All this undoubtedly actualized the problem of reorganizing and intensifying agricultural production in Ukraine. Ukrainian economists, agronomists, and national-communist politicians viewed this problem in the context of the reconstruction and modernization of the Ukrainian SSR as an integral economic unit where the disproportions in economic development, deemed to be a "colonial legacy," would be addressed. The official position of Moscow was in direct opposition, proceeding from the intention to create a strictly hierarchical economic space with a single centre and zones of agricultural production as well as raw material extraction for industry, to be demarcated by the centre. Thus, despite the status of the USSR as a federation of republics with equal rights, the traditional view of Ukraine from the times of the Russian Empire as simply the south of Russia, the resources of which were to be exploited according to all-Union interests, determined by the centre's Gosplan, prevailed (Hirsch 98).

The perpetuation of the traditional imperial view of Ukraine as the "south of Russia" and a supplier of raw materials caused tensions in relations between Moscow and Kharkiv (which was since 1923 the capital of the Ukrainian SSR), especially in the second half of the 1920s during discussions and confirmation of the first Five-Year Plan. An analogous situation arose in the other former Russian "national borderlands." According to Francine Hirsch, "[t]he tension between the economic and the ethnographic paradigms for regionalization would remain at the heart of Soviet state-building throughout the next decade" (98).

In Ukraine in the 1920s, scientists from various institutions and officials of Derzhplan (the State Planning Committee) of the Ukrainian SSR participated in discussions of Ukraine's economic specialization and ways to improve the effectiveness of the republic's agricultural sector. Proceeding from rational assumptions about a Ukrainian economic organism formed by natural-climatological and historical factors, Ukrainian economists proposed that the Ukrainian SSR should, already during the first Five-Year Plan, (a) reorient itself to the development of technical crops as a raw materials base for the republic's economy, (b) intensify the commodification of livestock management, (c) take measures to improve technical support of agricultural production; and (d) significantly lessen the focus on grain, the vulnerability of which, due to frequent crop failures and low marketability, was evident (Al'terman 101-10; Soloveichyk; Kononenko 184).

Calls for the "decolonization" of Ukraine's agricultural production were closely correlated with proposals for the reconstruction and development of industry. Ukrainian economists and planners thus disagreed with projects outlined in the Five-Year Plan proposed by all-Union authorities, which, in their opinion, would limit and slow Ukraine's industrial development, and perpetuate its role as a supplier of industrial raw materials for the north. These projects were also viewed as irrational and economically problematic and were thought to create disproportions in the development of the Ukrainian economy in favour of the Russian SFSR.

At the beginning of 1928, an article by the economist Mykhailo Volobuiev entitled "Do problemy ukrains'koi ekonomiky" ("On the Problem of the Ukrainian Economy") was published in two issues of the political and theoretical journal *Bil'shovyk Ukrainy* (*Bolshevik of Ukraine*), in which the author presented ideas, facts, proposals, and also complaints of Ukrainian experts. Volobuiev described Ukraine as a former Russian "colony of the European type" and accused the Soviet government of continuing the colonial practice of exploiting Ukrainian economic resources. Volobuiev's basic thesis was that "the essence of the effects of colonial dependence for a colony of the 'European type' is chiefly the denial of the development of its productive powers for the benefit of the metropolitan economy" ("Do problemy" 167). The article presented the "Moscow" and "Kharkiv" projects as in competition. Given the formality of the federative status of the republics and their full subordination to Moscow, Kharkiv had no chance of success.

"Volobuievism" was soon denounced, along with "Khvyl'ovism" and "Shums'kyism."[8] At the end of November 1928, Volobuiev published a letter of recantation in the same periodical *Bil'shovyk Ukrainy* ("Lyst"). A few days later, on 26 November 1928, the Fourth All-Union Consultation of People's Land Commissars was held in the Ukrainian capital, at which the representative of the USSR State Planning Committee Moisei Vol'f defined the position of the Union centre: "In the historical perspective, we think that Ukraine should, for a prolonged time, even in conditions of increased crop yield, remain a country that exports grain to the North, and if the North does not need it, then abroad? I think that for the next five to ten years that is precisely how it will be" (TsDAVO 1/4/635/6 *verso*). This strategy for the next decade was confirmed in the consultative body's resolution, by which

[8] The three "isms" associated with the economist Volobuiev, the national communist and advocate of Ukrainization Oleksandr Shums'kyi, and the writer Mykola Khvyl'ovyi are discussed in three chapters of James Mace's *Communism and the Dilemmas of National Liberation* (86-190). On the "Shums'kyi affair" and on Khvyl'ovyi, see also Terry Martin's *The Affirmative Action Empire* (96-98, 212-28).

the USSR's State Planning Committee Gosplan was designated the right to determine the "grain balance of individual districts" and the list of districts that "should be ensured grain supplies by way of shipments" (TsDAVO 1/4/635/52 *verso*).

On 7-14 March 1929, at the Fifth Congress of State Planning Committee Presidiums in Moscow, Vol'f—now the chief of the agricultural section of the USSR Gosplan—presented a plan for the agricultural subdivision of the USSR into seven groups. In keeping with the strategy of creating a single economic space, the Ukrainian SSR was not regarded as an integral whole; its lands were divided between the third group (the Central Black Earth Region and Ukraine's Forest-Steppe Region) and the fourth (the Ukrainian Steppe, North Caucasus, and Crimea). The principal tasks for the latter group were determined to be the reconstruction of grain agriculture, increased grain exports (75 percent of total grain exports), and grain deliveries to internal USSR markets—to Belarus, the Transcaucasus, and the Central Industrial Region. It was foreseen that the relative weight of these districts in producing commercial grain could be lowered at the end of the First Five-Year Plan from 74 percent to 53 percent because of an anticipated rise in production in the East (*Problemy* 291-92).

Effective imperial leadership depends on the participation of local and regional elites. In the Ukrainian SSR of that time, the administrative elites were in part local cadres, but Moscow sent its emissaries, entirely in keeping with imperial tradition, to the most important posts, which in Ukraine was the position of the first secretary of the Communist Party (Bolsheviks) of Ukraine (CP(b)U). At the beginning of April 1929, at a plenum of the Central Committee of the CP(b)U in Kharkiv, Stanislav Kosior, recently deputized by Moscow as the first secretary in Ukraine, harshly criticized the advocates of diversification of agricultural production—those who sought to reduce the volume of grain production: "I think that the grain question," stressed Ukraine's chief communist, "is absolutely the fundamental and chief question for us *not only in the next five years, but in the next ten*. We are the basic grain district, and for us, the issue of the grain problem is the central issue" (TsDAHO 1/1/324/108-109; emphasis added).

A resolution of the Party Central Committee plenum stated that "For a long time to come, Ukraine will be the most important base for meeting the internal food supply needs of the USSR, as well as a supplier of grain for export" (TsDAHO 1/1/322/87). The same was stated in the resolution of the Eleventh All-Ukrainian Congress of Soviets on the Five-Year Plan for the development of the republic's national economy. The "central and most important task" for Ukraine was to be the development of grain crops, chiefly for food, and among the latter, rye and wheat were the most valuable ("Na zahal'nu dopovid'"; *Zbirnyk*). Thus, the Union centre, through indirect administration of the Ukrainian republic, imposed grain specialization as the Ukrainian SSR's priority, with an emphasis on supplying grain for export and to internal USSR markets for five to ten years, which included the years of mass starvation—the Holodomor.

Those who actively opposed the centre's plans were punished or repressed. Many non-party specialists—economists, historians, agronomists—had already been repressed in 1930 in the affair of the "counter-revolutionary organization" sabotaging agriculture of the Ukrainian SSR" (Marochko; *Sprava*). Arrests continued as the Holodomor gained momentum in 1933, including of those who had argued that Ukraine's narrow grain specialization was a sign of its colonial status.

In the criminal case file of the convicted vice-president of the All-Ukrainian Academy of Agricultural Sciences Andrii Slipans'kyi (1896-1942), we find admissions, beaten out of him by his interrogators in private conversations, that the agronomist had spoken of the need "to destroy the colonial status of Ukraine in the USSR, and to regulate the situation of Ukraine in the USSR in accordance with its economic resources." He admitted that "with harmful intent," he had advocated the development of pig-farming in the steppe "in order to curtail the sowing of grain there and by that means to reduce the significance of Ukraine as a grain-producing region."[9] Finally, in interrogations on 17 and 20 August 1933, Slipans'kyi acknowledged his "guilt," saying that "he had created a harmful plan of specialization of Ukraine's agriculture in which a policy of intensified development of technical crops was undertaken to the detriment of grain" (DAKhO P-6452/3/1555/57, 63).

This same theme was evident in a campaign launched in the press to defame "exposed enemies." One of the articles appearing in the periodical *Bil'shovyk Ukrainy* stated that "[t]he wrecker Slipans'kyi advises us to direct reconstructive reforms in the steppe region of Ukraine towards the decisive elimination of grain farming and the maximum development of technical crops and the feed base for livestock . . . ." The same article states:

> By means of these destructive aims, Slipans'kyi opposed the general national-economic tasks of the Union with his policy favouring the "independence of Ukraine" (one of the most important grain-producing regions in the USSR), and sought to detach the economic development of the Ukrainian SSR from the economy of the entire Union. At the same time, by way of these aims Slipans'kyi seeks to transfer the orientation of

[9] DAKhO P-6452/3/od. b. 1556/44, 64. I am grateful to the Kharkiv historian Ihor Shuis'kyi for his assistance in obtaining materials from the criminal case file of Slipans'kyi.

Ukraine's agriculture toward the Western capitalist countries, and especially Germany. (Borodaev et al. 119)

The danger inherent for Ukraine in its grain specialization became clearer upon the confirmation by the USSR government in April 1929 (*Izvestiia TsIK*) and the Fifth All-Union Congress of Soviets in May 1929[10] of an optimal plan for the first Five-Year Plan. It was based on extraordinarily high planning targets, especially regarding increases in crop yield. According to the plan, the average crop yield was to increase by 35 percent by the end of the Five-Year Plan, while for all types of peasant households in Ukraine it was to increase by 36.6 percent ("Na zahal'nu dopovid'"; *Zbirnyk*). In order to carry out this unrealistic plan, Ukrainian peasants would have had to ensure an annual increase in crop yields of 6.5 percent. For comparison: in the most favourable pre-war years, an annual increase never surpassed two percent. The measures to be taken to achieve such high crop yields, especially the collectivization of 30 percent and the conversion to co-operatives of at least 85 percent of peasant households, were manifestly inadequate and did not take into consideration the possibility of unfavourable natural-climatological conditions.

In the final version of the First Five-Year Plan announced in 1930, the strategy of treating the USSR as a single economic space was fixed. The territory of the USSR was divided into four production zones: industrial, agricultural, agro-industrial/industrial-agrarian, and forest. Ukraine was allocated partly to the first and partly to the second zone type. The plan declared the goal of raising the level of grain farming and turning Ukraine and the North Caucasus into "primarily zones for export" (*Piatiletnii plan* 63). It also confirmed "the supply of grain by Ukraine, the North Caucasus and the Trans-Volga region to the consumer zone of European Russia" "over the next eight-ten years" (*Piatiletnii plan* 23-24). By 1933, the crop yield in Ukraine for the eight chief grain cultures was to increase by 36.3 percent, and in the collective farms, by 53.6 percent (*Piatiletnii plan* 126-27).

The projected increases in expected crop yields found in the Five-Year Plan concealed no small threat to the Ukrainian peasants, as planned high crop yields foretold significant increases in grain procurements. In view of the increasingly clear tendency to "legalize" imperfect statistical methods for determining the size of the harvests, the indiscriminate seizure of grain resources from the Ukrainian peasants, even in conditions of their absence, became a predictable prospect. Together with the imposed grain specialization, with a distinct determination to exploit grain resources,

---

[10] *O piatiletnem plane*. See also *Sobranie*; *S"ezdy Sovetov* 155-61.

these expected crop yields foreshadowed the disorganization of the Ukrainian grain market and elevated the risk of eventual famine.

Intra-Union Grain Deliveries from the Ukrainian SSR in 1927-28 and 1932-33: A Blind Spot in Research on Stalinist Collectivization and Famine

Did Excessive Exploitation of Ukrainian Grain Resources Take Place, and How Could This Have Affected the Onset of Famine?

In his landmark work *Poverty and Famines*, economist Amartya Sen proposed that the onset of famine is connected to the deprivation of economic rights and to unjust distribution. Through the example of the actions of the British colonial administration in Bengal, India in 1943, Sen demonstrated that it is not the lack of food as such but the inability to obtain it that causes famine.

Applying Sen's approach to the situation in the USSR at the end of the 1920s and the beginning of the 1930s, one can see the deliberate actions of the communist government directed toward depriving an entire social stratum, the agriculturalists, of their economic entitlement. The forced liquidation of private farmsteads, the deportation of the so-called kulaks, the creation of collective farms, the setting of extraordinarily low wages for the labour of the collective farmers (in "labour days"[11]), high targets for grain deliveries to the state, in effect its forcible seizure—these caused the phenomenon that Graziosi refers to as the all-Union famine of 1931-33.

Sen's principle of economic entitlement applies to relations between the USSR centre and the national peripheries, especially Ukraine. *De jure* a republic with equal rights within the federative USSR and its own government and declared rights, *de facto* the Ukrainian SSR was prevented from managing its own grain resources, a result not only of the communist but also the imperial nature of the USSR, where Moscow was the metropolia, ruling over Soviet Ukraine as a subordinate periphery. It was the intentional actions of the central government in establishing total control over the republic's grain market that led most directly to the deprivation of economic entitlement in Soviet Ukraine.

In this context, the liquidation in 1928 of Ukrkhlib (Ukrainian Bread), the powerful grain procurement and flour milling trust of the Ukrainian republic, must be mentioned. Created by a resolution of the All-Ukrainian

---

[11] Payments for labour performed by collective farm workers on collective farms (mostly in-kind payments), were calculated according to a formula—given the name "labour days"—which was based on the time spent working and the type of work.

Central Executive Committee of 1 September 1926, Ukrkhlib played a key role in grain procurement and in supplying the Ukrainian population, as it was responsible for intra-Union deliveries and export operations. At the beginning of 1928, the Ukrainian trust had at its disposition ninety-four enterprises, at least fifty mills, and a similar number of grain collection stations (TsDAVO 778/1/280/219), with profits in 1926-27 of 3,278,548 rubles and 33 kopecks (TsDAVO 778/1/280/425). Moscow terminated Ukrkhlib's activity, and its shares were confiscated by Soiuzkhleb (Union Bread), thus depriving the Ukrainian SSR not only of a major portion of its own capital but also of critical levers of influence on its own grain market.

The process of total subordination of the Ukrainian grain market to Moscow was completed by the beginning of the 1930s. On the eve of and during the Holodomor, the incredibly high grain procurement quotas for the Ukrainian SSR, the reduced and extremely insufficient plans and volumes of food supply deliveries to the population, the plans and volume of exports, and also the plans and volume of shipment of Ukrainian grain to intra-Union markets—all was decided not in Kharkiv, but in Moscow. The peripheral elites in the Ukrainian SSR, some sent from Moscow and some of local origin, lacked real influence over the situation and essentially served as instruments of indirect rule or administration.

Given what we know about the grain specialization imposed by the Union centre on the Ukrainian SSR (at a minimum during the first Five-Year Plans) and about the declared aims of intensified shipment of grain resources out of Ukraine, the question logically arises: can one speak in terms of the economic exploitation of Ukraine through control of its grain resources to the benefit of the ruling metropolia, and if so, how did this impact the onset of the Ukrainian famine of 1928-29 and the Holodomor of 1932-33?

To understand how famine arose in the Ukrainian SSR in 1927-28 and 1932-33, the volume of grain removed in the course of state grain procurements is of prime significance. Contemporary research confirms the substantial dimensions and the consistently high proportion of Ukrainian grain in deliveries for central government's stores or funds of grain. In 1927-28 in particular, 260.2 million *puds* of grain were procured from the republic, which constituted 40 percent of the procurement total for the USSR. This reached 46 percent in May ("Na Ukraini"). In 1930-31, after the gathering of the first collective farm harvest, 468.5 million *puds* of grain were procured from Ukraine—39 percent of the all-Union procurement, and in 1931-32, 442.7 million *puds*, or 31.7 percent (*Ezhegodnik* 7). Grain procurement from the Ukrainian SSR continued both in the famine years 1928-29 (124.6 million *puds* of grain, or 18.9 percent of all-Union grain procurement) (TsDAVO 3/1/6433/104, 1/5/472/1), and during the

Holodomor of 1932-33 (258.4-262.2 million *puds*, or 22.9-23.1 percent of all grain deliveries to the state) (*Ezhegodnik* 19). Altogether, over the course of six years, at least 1,833 million *puds* of grain were procured from Ukraine (29.8 percent of the all-Union amount procured).

The central government directed a significant portion of the grain procured in the Ukrainian SSR for export to finance ambitious plans for military-industrial modernization. In 1927-28, the amount of Ukrainian grain exported abroad was still rather modest—only 20 million *puds* (TsDAVO 23/4/164/26-27); in 1930-31 it had risen by a factor of five, reaching 103.7 million *puds* (30.3 percent of the USSR export of 341.8 million *puds*) (Kondrashin 97). "Force the export of grain to the fullest. That is the key now. If we export grain, we will have credits," wrote Stalin in a letter to Molotov on August 6, 1930, during the gathering of the first collective farm harvest (Kosheleva et al. 147).[12]

As is evident from the statistical annual devoted to grain, *Ezhegodnik khlebooborota,* in 1931-32 the Ukrainian portion of the grain exported constituted 151.4 million *puds*, which was 51.8 percent of the total USSR export of 292.2 million *puds* (*Ezhegodnik* 65). In 1932-33, during the Holodomor, 45.6 million *puds* of grain from the Ukrainian SSR went for export (46.6 percent of the USSR shipments abroad of 98.0 million *puds*) (*Ezhegodnik* 67). One can see that the volume of exported Ukrainian grain leading up to and during the period of massive famine and human mortality was enormous.

In the years 1927-28 and 1932-33, Ukrainian grain was shipped not only abroad but also to internal USSR markets. Despite the considerable Western, Ukrainian, and Russian historiography on collectivization and famine in the early 1930s, the subject of internal USSR grain shipments, particularly the deliveries of Ukrainian grain to the industrial districts of the Russian SFSR and other Union republics, has yet to be examined. This may be due in part to an unconscious tendency to avoid issues that cast doubt on the sincerity of the anti-imperial and anti-colonial slogans loudly declared by the USSR. In the USSR itself, the practice of censoring information about the volume and characteristics of internal USSR grain shipments emerged at the end of the 1920s. One indication was the cessation of hitherto regular publications with accompanying diagrams on the pages of the specialized periodical *Statisticheskoe obozrenie* (*Statistical Review*). As supported by descriptions I have studied of holdings of the Central State Archive of Higher Organs of Government and Administration (TsDAVO) of Ukraine, there are reasons to suspect that archival documents

---

[12] See also Kondrashin 96, 280.

that could shed light on this topic were destroyed or transferred to Moscow in the postwar years, in the course of periodic inspections and "purges" of the Ukrainian archives.

These observations, however, pertain to the situation for the years 1932-33. Fortunately, archival documents related to the intra-Union grain shipments on the eve of and during the Ukrainian famine of 1928-29 have been preserved fairly well. Their diligent study opens significant perspectives for a better understanding of the mechanisms that triggered the onset of the Holodomor. A considerable increase, in accordance with directives from Moscow, in the volume of shipments of Ukrainian grain to the north began in the second half of 1926-27, during an intensification of the "grain crisis" and crop failures in the grain-producing regions of the USSR. In the summer of 1927, after a prolonged drought, a crop failure took place in Ukraine, which according to the report of the People's Commissariat of Land of the Ukrainian SSR "On the Crop Failure and Measures for the Struggle with Its Consequences," engulfed close to eighty thousand farms in the Kherson, Mykolaiv, Odesa, Mariupol, Melitopol, and Staline regions (TsDAVO 582/1/2567/232-233).

Nevertheless, during the grain procurement campaign of 1927-28, the USSR centre chose the path of intensifying the exploitation of Ukrainian grain resources. During a meeting in Kharkiv, the representative of the USSR People's Commissariat of Foreign and Domestic Trade Izrail' Veitser, having arrived from Moscow, declared,

> We are not shutting our eyes to all the difficulties that Ukraine faces . . . . We are aware of all these difficulties and we do not want to conceal or minimize their significance. All the same, we face the following task: we have to remove as much grain as possible from Ukraine; this is the goal we have set ourselves. (TsDAVO 337/1/5762/110-111).

At this point Kharkiv was still trying to challenge Moscow and demanded a reduction of shipment orders. On 22 July 1927, the Ukrainian Economic Consultation sent the USSR Council on Labour and Defence a report regarding Ukraine's limited ability to supply grain, directly stating that "the chief cause of the aggravation of the situation in Ukraine's grain market is the increased shipment of grain to the northern markets" (TsDAVO 337/1/5762/139).[13]

---

[13] I have discovered similar petitions, mostly in "special files," dated 21 February; 2, 9, 27, and 30 March; 2, 7, 9, 12, and 27 April; 11 and 18 May; and others (TsDAHO 1/6/142/48-49, 60, 68, 75, 81-82, 96, 101-102, 105-106; 1/20/2769/1-2; 1/20/2771/52; 1/20/2772/47-48; 337/1/6414/47; 539/6/7/26; et al.).

In the spring of 1928, as summer neared, the situation in the Ukrainian grain market became acute, and it was understood that the republic was facing large-scale crop failure. Famine ensued in a number of districts of the Ukrainian SSR. Nevertheless, Moscow continued to demand grain shipments. Realizing the obvious deficit of resources in the republic, the central government invented the tactic of "lending" grain to Ukraine from the State Fund, to which Ukraine had previously contributed to fulfill its shipping orders. The "grain debts" it thus accumulated for deliveries of grain to the state reserve funds were not written off, but only deferred. For example, in mid-March 1928 the Collegium of the USSR People's Commissariat of Foreign and Domestic Trade permitted the Ukrainian SSR to defer 800,000 *puds* of wheat planned for shipment out of the republic to the first ten days of April (TsDAVO 423/4/342/66; 423/5/15/171). On 24 April 1928, during a meeting in Moscow on grain procurement presided over by Viacheslav Molotov, the Ukrainian representatives Vlas Chubar and Mikhail Chernov were informed of the deferment of this debt and were offered a loan from the State Fund of 150,000 to 200,000 *puds* of wheat seed for the fulfillment of the shipment orders in May (TsDAHO 1/20/2769/2). On 4 May 1928, the Collegium of the USSR People's Commissariat of Trade confirmed the May plan for the Ukrainian SSR to ship out of Ukraine 4.2 million *puds* of grain. The plan provided for the deferment of 800,000 *puds* of "owed" grain as well as for new "loans": 400,000 *puds* of wheat seed to be shipped to Central Asia, Tambov, and the Central Black-Earth Region, and another 160,000 *puds* "for shipment to the north per orders of the USSR People's Commissariat of Trade" (TsDAVO 423/4/340/95). The next day, the Collegium of the USSR People's Commissariat of Trade let Ukraine borrow 850,000 *puds* of wheat from the State Fund in order to carry out the shipment plan (TsDAVO 423/4/340/88-89).

It was only on 26 May 1928, that, by a decision of the All-Union Communist Party Central Committee Politburo, the shipment of wheat and rye out of the Ukrainian SSR was officially stopped (up to 1 August 1928). The Commission for the organization of grain supply to the republic, created on 29 May 1928 by the Ukrainian Economic Consultation, issued a resolution instructing the Ukrainian SSR People's Commissariat of Trade to select, in June, fall-sown wheat from the State and Special Funds for distribution within the republic. However, on 30 May 1928, the Collegium of the USSR People's Commissariat of Trade formally transferred jurisdiction over Ukrainian grain to Soiuzkhleb and ordered it to ship all grain reserves out of Ukraine during the month of June, so that they should arrive as reserves at the bases of the USSR People's Commissariat of Trade. In the end, 127.7 million *puds* of grain, including 118.7 million *puds* of rye and wheat, were shipped out of Ukraine in 1927-28 to intra-Union markets, chiefly to industrial districts of the Russian SFSR (TsDAVO 1/1/308/11 *verso*).

This rather detailed description of the relations between Moscow and Kharkiv on issues of grain delivery at a time when Stalin's military-industrial modernization was accelerating, illustrates the inequality of relations and the subordination of the Ukrainian peripheral elite to the central government. The exploitation of grain resources by order of the USSR government, their shipment beyond the borders of Ukraine, the assertion of control over Ukrainian grain resources, and the deprivation of the Ukrainian government of evident liquid resources were the essential factors in the destabilization of the Ukrainian grain market and contributed to the onset of the Ukrainian famine of 1928-29, which took place against the background of a large-scale crop failure.

The question arises whether Ukrainian grain was being supplied to the intra-Union markets as well as for export, and if so, what if any role did it play in the onset of the Holodomor of 1932-33? This topic requires careful research that would greatly benefit from examination of a significant body of documents, in particular, from the archive of the president of the Russian Federation, which are not fully accessible to scholars. However, the amount of Ukrainian grain that might have been shipped to internal USSR markets in 1931-32 and 1932-33 can be arrived at on the basis of an analysis of statistical materials in the *Ezhegodnik khlebooborota* published in 1934. In 1931-32, 442.7 million *puds* of grain were procured in the Ukrainian SSR as a whole; 151.4 million *puds* were removed for export, while 148.6 million *puds* were allocated for internal needs of the republic (food supplies, seed, industrial needs, and forage, not counting allocations for the army, or bran). Accordingly, 142.7 million *puds* hypothetically could have been directed to supplying the army and for satisfying the internal needs of the rest of the USSR. We can make analogous calculations regarding 1932-33: out of 258.4 million *puds* of grain procured, 45.6 million were exported, 162.6 million went for the republic's internal needs, and 50.2 million *puds* of grain could have constituted the remainder for supplying the army, shipment to other republics, etc. (*Ezhegodnik* 7, 19, 65, 67, 81, 131). In sum, for two years, 192.9 million *puds* is a fairly significant amount of grain, even if one subtracts from it annually 5-6 million *puds* of grain for the army.

Documents preserved in the Ukrainian archives suggest that even in the famine conditions of 1932-33, the shipment of grain out of Ukraine to other regions of the USSR may have continued. According to orders of the USSR centre, beginning with 1 October 1932, Zahotzerno and Souizboroshno were to ship 31.7 million *puds* of wheat and rye to Moscow, Leningrad, the Central Black Earth Region, Crimea, Belarus, and the Transcaucasia. This grain was to be sent for export, and internally to the

GULAG, to Torgsin, and to replenish the State and Reserve Funds in Moscow, Leningrad, the Northern and Western regions, Belarus, and so on (*Sovetskaia derevnia* 880-81; *"Sovershenno sekretno"* 196-97, 246-47).

Worth noting here is that grain was not the only "article" in the planned deliveries of the countryside to the state. In 1927-28 and 1932-33, there was massive procurement of "secondary agricultural production" from Ukraine and shipment to other regions of the USSR and for export. This included meat, poultry, butter, eggs, honey, nuts, fruit, vegetables, and so on. The structure, dimensions, and results of the seizure of "secondary products" from the Ukrainian village remain unstudied by scholars. We do know that in the year of the Ukrainian famine of 1928-29, there were 2,020 freight-cars of eggs, 164,000 *puds* of butter, 305,800 *puds* of bacon, 747,400 *puds* of meat products, 2,986,000 *puds* of potatoes, 9,389 *puds* of mushrooms, 4,231 *puds* of honey, 2 million 549.8 thousand rubles' worth of sunflower oil, 94.2 thousand rubles' worth of cow and sheep's milk cheese, 89.5 thousand rubles' worth of conserves, 2 million 518.1 thousand rubles' worth of poultry, 7.6 million *puds* of sugar, 248.1 thousand rubles' worth of fresh fruit, 131.8 thousand rubles' worth of pastry, etc., shipped from Ukraine for export (TsDAVO 3/1/6041/112-114).

Finally, according to information from the Procurement Committee, in 1930-31 the Ukrainian SSR provided two-thirds of all the grain contributed to the state reserves (Vasyl'iev 241). The republic's share in the replenishment of the Reserve and Mobilization grain funds could have been significant in 1931-32 as well. From October 1931, both funds were under the authority of the Reserves Committee of the USSR Council on Labour and Defence. Where these funds were located, whether Ukrainian grain was shipped to them, and in what amounts, whether it was expended and where it was directed during the Holodomor—all of these remain open questions.

All-Union Aid during the Ukrainian Famine of 1928-29 and the Holodomor of 1932-33: An Element in the Strategy of Exploitation of Resources[14]

During the crop failure and famine of 1928-29, the central government did render aid to the Ukrainian SSR. Based on this fact, the American scholar Mark Tauger, in an article on the Ukrainian state commission for rendering aid to the victims of the crop failure, came to the following unambiguousconclusion: "in terms of food supplies, Ukraine in 1928-1929 was not in the extractive-colonial relationship with Russia that Volobuiev

[14] Some of the material in this section is discussed in my study *Holod 1928-1929 rr. u radians'kii Ukraini* (215-24). See also my criticism of Tauger in the same study (7-10).

described at the time. As already noted, Ukraine received more in food supplies during this famine crisis than it exported to other republics" (168). Tauger also sees in this episode "another side of the Soviet regime, one concerned with alleviating suffering rather than creating it," and among other examples in support of his thesis cites a story of Moscow's speedy reaction to the petition of the Ukrainian side for aid to starving children (168). "Sovnarkom SSSR," writes Tauger, "acted on this request rapidly, authorizing Ukraine on 5 February to use an additional 1,316,500 rubles to feed children in the crop-failure districts" (159).

Tauger is mistaken. Attentive study of a broader range of archival sources reveals Soviet aid to Ukraine under famine conditions in 1928-29 to have been a typical imperial practice. The centre's exploitation of the territory under its control continued—merciless and deaf to the sufferings of the population, including children—even during cataclysms and mass hunger. In 1928-29, Union-republic co-operation in the development of plans for state assistance to Ukraine, suffering from crop failure, took place in conditions of clear dominance by the All-Union centre, and was determined by the Stalin group in the Party leadership, whose primary goals were to accelerate military-industrial modernization. It is in this context that the strategy imposed by Moscow on Kharkiv must be understood—of the Ukrainian SSR surviving in conditions of crop failure and famine at the expense of its own resources. The USSR's People's Commissar of Trade Anastas Mikoian openly announced this strategy at the November 1928 Communist Party of Ukraine Central Committee plenum, whose participants, as the documents show, expected information on the rendering of All-Union aid. Mikoian instead declared: "I have said—procure bread and eat it!" (TsDAHO 1/1/306/63). Another remark by Mikoian indicated that Moscow was fully aware of the possibility that famine could arise in Ukraine: "If you cannot feed yourself in November, then what will happen in March, April, June? I can imagine what will happen in Ukraine in those months" (TsDAHO 1/1/306/53).

Despite the modest petitions of the Ukrainian side for assistance to the republic in 1928-29, the USSR Council of People's Commissars, by its resolution of 4 September 1928, reduced delivery of the most important items by half, including those earmarked for the feeding of children (TsDAVO 1/4/72/23). Further, during the budgeting process, it substantially reduced the volume of aid, essentially transferring a part of the financial burden of assistance to the republic itself. Chubar openly stated this at the Party Central Committee plenum on 19 November 1928, pointing out that while the All-Union organs had inserted certain amounts for aid to Ukraine in the budget, they simultaneously reduced expenditures by practically the same amount: "It turns out that the lion's share of these expenditures are also the Ukrainian expenditures that have been eliminated," he concluded (*Kak lomali NEP* 173). Thus, the expenditure portion of the Ukrainian SSR draft budget for 1928-29 in the amount of 415.8 million rubles, which was characterized by the Ukrainian side as a "miserly minimum," was approved by a resolution of the USSR Central Executive Committee, but for an even lesser amount of 388.3 million rubles. The republic's actual budget expenditures though came to 403.9 million rubles (*Kak lomali NEP* 173). The deficit was covered indirectly from funds allocated in the budget as USSR assistance.

During the entire year of 1928-29, a hungry year for Ukraine, the centre continued with bureaucratic delays in financing assistance measures from the All-Union budget, and time and again resorted to resolving the issue "of additional aid" at the expense of Ukrainian resources. The issue of the designated 1,316,500 rubles for starving children mentioned by Tauger is a vivid example of this, which I explore in more detail.

The question of feeding children was not a straightforward matter. At the beginning of the 1928-29 period, the Ukrainian government determined the minimum number of children to be supported as 342,000; after the USSR Council of People's Commissars twice reduced the volume of aid, however, the number of children to whom aid was to be rendered was lowered to 185,000 (TsDAVO 3/1/6414/196; 27/10/71). On 17 January 1929, at the request of the Ukrainian Red Cross, the Ukrainian government sent to Moscow a report "On the Issuance of Additional Funds for Aid to the Child Population in Districts of the Ukrainian SSR Suffering from Crop Failure," requesting an additional 1,573,000 rubles from the USSR's budget to increase the quantity and improve the quality of children's food allocations, and for aid to infants and pregnant women (TsDAVO 27/9/523/32). The document stated, "In view of the shortage of funding, this aid, from the point of view of its quality, represents the bare minimum and could be regarded only as limited support, and not as providing the needed food" (TsDAVO 27/9/523/29).

In fact, at the beginning of February 1929, the USSR Council of People's Commissars adopted a decision to issue for the children of the crop-failure districts of Ukraine 1,316,500 rubles (TsDAVO 27/9/523/29), requiring, however, that the local budgets of Ukraine be the source of these funds, which in conditions of crop failure had been greatly reduced. The essence of this matter can only be understood by way of a deeper study of archival materials that reflect the history of the long-term standoff between the all-Union and republican governments concerning the creation of the State Grain Fund from local budgets.

In 1927-28, the government of the USSR decided to create a State Grain Fund from contributions of the local budgets of the republics. Of the 40 million rubles it planned to obtain in this way, 28.6 million were assigned to the Russian SFSR, 8.9 million to the Ukrainian SSR, 0.9 million to the Belarusian SSR, 0.6 million to the Transcaucasian SFSR, 0.8 million to the Uzbek SSR, and 0.2 million to the Tatar SSR (TsDAVO 3/1/5111/1, 6). The Ukrainian side repeatedly petitioned for a reduction of the republic's contribution to 7.2 million rubles, complaining about the injustice of a situation in which the central government compensated for the reduced contributions from four republics with weak local budgets at the expense of the Ukrainian SSR exclusively. At the same time, the budgets of 17 out of 41 Ukrainian districts also suffered deficits (TsDAVO 3/1/5111/12).

Despite this, by the end of July 1928, Ukraine had transferred 5.9 million rubles from its local budgets to the State Grain Fund (TsDAVO 3/1/5111/33). In connection with the massive crop failure, on 26 July 1928, the Ukrainian government appealed to the USSR Council of People's Commissars to release the republic from the remainder of its payments in the amount of 2.9 million rubles. The Ukrainian side also pointed out that up to that point only 3 million rubles of the 28.6 million due from the local budgets of the Russian SFSR had been paid to the Fund (TsDAVO 3/1/5111/33). On 27 November 1928, the USSR People's Commissariat of Finance presented a report to the All-Union government from which it emerged that the Ukrainian SSR had already transferred 6,283,500 rubles to the State Grain Fund by 1 October, and that it was to pay the remaining 2,616,500 rubles by 1 April 1929 (TsDAVO 3/1/6079/22). The Ukrainian side protested. On 5 January 1929, the permanent representation of the Ukrainian SSR in Moscow submitted to the USSR Council on Labour and Defence a petition for the elimination of the debt based on the extraordinary situation that had arisen as a result of the crop failure, noting, "Any further removal of funds . . . for the creation of a State Grain Fund in a Ukraine struck by catastrophe could create a disastrous situation for the local budget" (TsDAVO 3/1/6079/22).

On 8 January 1929, the USSR Council of People's Commissars issued a resolution reducing Ukraine's debt to the State Grain Fund to 1,316,500 rubles (TsDAVO 3/1/6079/13-14). At the beginning of February 1929, as a supplement to this resolution, the USSR Council of People's Commissars finally resolved "to release the Ukrainian SSR from the transfer of 1,316,500 rubles for the financing of the State Grain Fund, permitting it to use these funds for food supply assistance to children in crop failure districts of the Ukrainian SSR" (TsDAVO 3/1/6079/20). Thus Ukraine, having finally succeeded in securing the cancellation of its remaining debt to the State Grain Fund, turned out to be in debt to itself, or rather, to the starving children, whose feeding now came as an additional burden on local Ukrainian budgets that were already exhausted by the crop failure.

Yet this is still not the entire story of Soviet aid to children. From the summer of 1928, the Ukrainian government had persistently petitioned Moscow for permission to hold an all-Union lottery to collect 2.5 million rubles to support the children. After the approval of the 1,316,500 ruble reduction in financing the State Grain Fund, on 5 February 1929, the People's Commissariat of Finance sent a report to the USSR Council of People's Commissars proposing that it abstain from organizing a lottery, instead giving the Ukrainian SSR permission to withdraw 1,316,500 rubles from regional budgets,[15] to which sum 1,000,000 rubles would be added from the V. Lenin Fund of the USSR Central Executive Committee (GARF 5446/17/144). The decision regarding local budgets had been approved a few days earlier, but judging from the financial reports of the Ukrainian SSR's government, money for aid to hungry children from the fund named after the proletarian leader never arrived (TsDAVO 27/10/49/19).

And yet, the payment of various sums out of the all-Union, republican, or local budgets for carrying out the assistance plan did not solve the problem inasmuch as only real provisions, forage and seed, and not rapidly devalued Soviet money, could assure support for the hungry. And there was not enough of any of these in famine-stricken Ukraine. It would have been possible to improve the situation only by shipping in sufficient grain—essentially, by returning to the Ukrainian peasants at least part of the emergency reserves that had been taken from them in 1927-28.

During the Ukrainian famine of 1928-29, the central government had agreed initially to ship 22.3 million *puds* of wheat and rye to the Ukrainian SSR, but in the spring of 1929 reconsidered on the pretext that the Ukrainian population had already on its own "by means of carts and sacks brought in 5.0 million *puds* from the Crimea, Northern Caucasus and other regions" (TsDAVO 337/1/5941/46). In the end, 12.722 million *puds* of wheat and rye were shipped into the republic—and if one counts other comestible crops, 13.686 million *puds*. At the same time, 10.008 million *puds* of grain and flour (rye and rye flour, wheat and wheat flour, barley and barley flour, corn and corn flour, beans, semolina, buckwheat and barley groats, millet, etc.) were shipped out of Ukraine.[16]

Altogether, according to information reported by the Ukrainian SSR People's Commissariat of Trade, during 1928-29, five million *puds* of grain were expended as food aid for the population of the crop-failure districts

---

[15] The word "regional" used in the text refers to an administrative unit called an "okruha," equivalent in size to a small province. Soviet Ukraine was divided into 41 such units in 1925.

[16] TsDAVO 337/1/6433/10; 1/5/36/6. The information that Tauger adduces from *Ezhegodnik khlebooborota* is somewhat different, but in general the tendencies are analogous to the documents of Ukrainian provenance presented here.

and the poorer peasants of other regions of Ukraine, half of which was provided by a 10 percent deduction from milling fees (TsDAVO 1/5/472/2). As evidenced by report materials of the Government Committee, the planned deliveries of provisions to crop-failure regions, which were significantly lower than actual needs, were not carried out fully: 84 percent of the flour for adults specified by the plan was delivered, 88.2 percent of that for children, and 53.2 percent and 51.3 percent of the potatoes for adults and children, respectively (TsDAVO 27/10/49/4, 8-9). Seed aid for the peasants during the autumn and spring sowing campaigns accounted for something over 30 million *puds* (TsDAVO 1/5/472/2), and 5.5 million *puds* of this was shipped in from other republics, chiefly from Russia, while the rest was ensured by forcible "mobilizations" of local resources; 9.384 million *puds* went for cattle feed, and 2.526 million *puds* for the needs of Ukrainian industry. Centralized bread deliveries to city-dwellers in the Ukrainian SSR in 1928-29 constituted 34.654 million *puds* (TsDAVO 337/1/6433/46). Traditionally, a certain amount of grain was expended on deliveries to units of the Ukrainian Military District. Thus, state expenditures of grains and flour in Ukraine in 1928-29 came to something over 81.5 million *puds*. In this regard, the share of USSR aid in these expenditures, according to my calculations and taking into account the practice of the compensatory removal of grain, constituted 3.7 percent (according to Ukrainian report data) or 11.5 percent (according to central Soviet data).

Indubitably, the grain imported as assistance to Ukraine from other republics, chiefly the Russian SFSR, mitigated the situation, but it did not compensate even minimally for the losses that Ukraine, already experiencing partial crop failure, had suffered in 1927-28 through the shipping out of a substantial portion of its emergency reserves. The central government's "compensatory practice" was denounced in a letter of 7 February 1929, to the USSR Council on Labour and Defence from the Ukrainian Economic Consultation, signed by Ukraine's head of government, Vlas Chubar. In essence, the shipping into Ukrainian territory of "Union aid" was accompanied by the simultaneous shipping out of practically the same amount of seed grain and forage (TsDAVO 423/5/798/151).

The strongest proof of the negative effects of the exploitation of Ukrainian resources in 1927-28 and of the insufficiency and ineffectiveness of the aid rendered by the centre in 1928-29 was the onset of famine and starvation. According to estimates, more than twenty thousand people may have died from hunger in 1928-29. Judging from special reports of the OGPU (Joint State Political Directorate, i.e., secret police), the situation was most acute in April and May of 1929 (*Sovetskaia derevnia* 880-81; *"Sovershenno sekretno"* 196-97, 246-47).

In the case of the Holodomor, scholars have examined the decisions of the central government aimed at rendering aid to the Ukrainian SSR in the winter and spring of 1933, as well as the dimensions of this aid. In their thorough monograph on Soviet agriculture in 1931-33, Robert Davies and Stephen Wheatcroft include a series of tables that provide us with the following information: in February to July 1933, the Ukrainian SSR received loans and assistance in the amounts of 19.8 million *puds* of seed, 10 million *puds* of provisions, 5 million *puds* of fodder—altogether up to 35 million *puds* (479-85).

Without a doubt, the provision of aid saved lives. Nevertheless, knowing the causes of the Ukrainian famine of 1928-29 and Moscow's utilization of assistance as another element of exploitation—a strategy that used the resources of Ukraine for its own rescue—many questions arise. These include the possible cause-and-effect connection between the Holodomor and the massive procurement and shipping of Ukrainian grain for export and to the other union republics; the deliveries of Ukrainian grain to state grain reserves in 1931-32 and 1932-33; the actual sources of USSR assistance given Ukraine; and the possible application by the central government, as during the Ukrainian famine of 1928-29, of "compensatory practices." While these issues have yet to be clarified by scholars, documents about the extent and destination of the food aid rendered by the central government to the Ukrainian SSR at the height of the Holodomor in the spring of 1933 demonstrate that the aid was absolutely insufficient and that its distinct targeting of certain categories of the population (the collective farmers) was intended to further purely pragmatic aims: to support carrying out the sowing and harvesting—that is, the further exploitation of Ukrainian grain resources.

In general, it is not of primary significance whether in the years of the first Five-Year Plan, grain and other food products were shipped out of Ukraine by order of the central government for export or to the union republics. In either or both cases, it was a matter of the ruination of Ukraine's economic base and the disorganization and exploitation of its grain resources to the advantage of the interests of the ruling metropolia, namely Moscow. According to the calculations of demographers, the victims of this policy in the Ukrainian SSR numbered some 3.9 million people. The highest level of mortality in Ukraine was in the first half of 1933, when about 3 million people died due to hunger (Rudnytskyi et al.).

Imperial/Anti-Colonial Identities: Setting a Research Task

In March 1927, the editorial offices of the newspaper *Chervona armiia* (*Red Army*) received a typical letter from a soldier of one of the regiments of the Ukrainian Military District describing the frequent clashes between

Ukrainians and Great Russians over the Ukrainization policy. "The Russians are displeased with Ukrainization, but the Ukrainians defend it," wrote the author and then continued:

> Thus, arguments begin. The Great Russians, even Komsomol members, say, "What good has that Ukrainization done, why is it necessary?" But there are bizarre Ukrainians who declare that if there is to be Ukrainization, then you have to Ukrainianize everything. Newspapers, literature—every last thing has to be Ukrainianized. So that there is nothing left in Russian. One non-Party Red Army soldier even declared, "What is your Lenin compared to Petliura?" (V. Hrynevych et al. 301).

The newspaper never published this unknown soldier's letter, but it did make it into one of the secret bulletins that, together with other similar documents, were compiled to inform the USSR's higher Party and government leadership of the social and political moods of the population in the various regions. In fact, the content of this letter was fairly symptomatic, for it reflected a situation that had been developing since the end of the nineteenth century, which, under the influence of the events of 1914-21, had become a reality. Its essence lay in the definitive affirmation of identity by Great Russians and Ukrainians, and the rapid consolidation, unexpected by many, of the latter as a separate nation, and moreover with a clear antipathy on a noticeable part of it towards the Soviet state project.
What remains often overlooked is that although the Ukrainian SSR had entered the union of Soviet republics, armed anti-Soviet units were active there until the middle of the 1920s.[17] Relations between the government and the peasantry after the announcement of the New Economic Policy were rather wary, characterized by the expression "We've become used to it, we can somehow live and farm." "Ukrainian separatism," common among some of the intelligentsia, "cultivated" by the Ukrainian Autocephalous Orthodox Church, and rapidly disseminated among the student youth and in the countryside, remained a constant problem for the Bolshevik regime. Ukrainian nationalist attitudes, which were invariably characterized as manifestations of "Petliurism" and "Ukrainian chauvinism," simply could not be rooted out. Moreover, despite its specific ideological content, the policy of Ukrainization carried out by the Bolsheviks objectively accelerated the development of national consciousness among Ukrainians. So indeed did the slogans about a union of equal Soviet republics and their right to secede. The Ukrainian political emigration (chiefly the Government-in-exile of the Ukrainian People's Republic, located on the territory of the unfriendly

[17] See Arkhireis'kyi; Bohan; Isakov; Krasnosilets'kyi; Plazova, Stehnii, and others.

neighbour Poland), also remained an irritating factor for the Bolsheviks. Its spokesmen declared the Soviet government in Ukraine illegitimate and worked against it, engaged in an information campaign in the West, and established and maintained illegal contacts on the territory of the Ukrainian SSR, carrying on intelligence and agitational activity.

The persistence of nationalist attitudes invites more questions related to attitudes and identities. Did the phenomena of imperial and anti-colonial identities exist in the USSR in general and in Soviet Ukraine specifically? If so, how widespread were they, how were they manifested, and how did they interact? Were anti-imperial and anti-colonial motifs present in the attitudes of the Ukrainian population with regard to the Stalinist faminogenic policies?

Researchers continue to explore the place and role of the Great Russians in the Soviet Union, particularly in Ukraine, as an "imperial ethnos." In the opinion of the Russian scholar Evgenii Anisimov, the acceptance of an imperial identity by ethnic Russians first in the Russian Empire, and then in the USSR, was obvious, and it was based on the perceptions that the Russian Empire was Russia, and that Russia was an empire; the Soviet Union, accordingly, was a great Russia with its "borderlands," where Great Russians and "others" live. With the victory of the Bolsheviks, notes this scholar, "new but essentially old" imperial stereotypes fit rather easily into the framework of imperial consciousness of the past: "proletarian messianism" with the centre of the worldwide socialist republic in Moscow, "the empire as a fraternal, hierarchical family" headed by the elder brother, the Great Russian, as well as the complexes of "colonial ingratitude," the "innocence" of the Great Russian people, and so on (Anisimov).

Hosking holds a somewhat different view, emphasizing the complex identity of the Great Russians and stressing the considerable damage done to them by the imperial project. Although he does not define the Great Russians as an "imperial ethnos," the lengthy list he provides of factors that gave rise to feelings of national identity among the Russians in the USSR fits fully into the context of its most essential characteristics. In particular, the communist project was painted in noticeably Russian colours; its international messianism can be considered a Russian peculiarity, whose roots reach to the fifteenth-sixteenth century idea of Moscow as the Third Rome; the ideal of socio-economic egalitarianism, which was enshrined in the official ideology of the Soviet state, likewise had noticeably Russian traits; the status of a great state was a Russian concept; the territory of the USSR was nearly coterminous with the Russian Empire; the majority of Soviet leaders, especially after the 1930s, were Russians; the Russian language was the language of the state and the armed forces, and of international communication; finally, in the course of the Five-Year Plans, Russian specialists and workers settled in significant numbers throughout non-Russian regions. Although Russians did not have the status of a "master race," like the British in India, they nonetheless served as a constant reminder that in the Soviet Union, the Russians were the dominant ethnos (Hosking).

All in all, the scholarly problem of imperial/anti-imperial self-identification in the USSR requires thorough research. Here, I focus on the dissemination of anti-imperial and anti-colonial attitudes among a discernible section of the Ukrainian population, chiefly of its largest stratum, the peasantry, with regard to the Stalinist policies of famine creation in 1928-29 and 1932-33. Although with the beginning of Stalin's "revolution from above," negative political activities of an anti-communist and anti-Soviet bent were noticeable in all regions of the USSR, in Ukraine their distinctiveness lay in the interweaving of social and national motifs. A central theme from the beginning was the shipment of grain to Russia—the pillaging of Ukraine as the precondition and direct cause of the famine.

Already in March 1928, the leader of the republic's Party organization Lazar' Kaganovich admitted that in Ukraine, the initiation of extraordinary measures in the agrarian sphere had caused "a strengthening of chauvinism," and "not only from above, but also from below." In his speech to the Ukrainian Communist Party Central Committee plenum, he said, "We are having chats about how they are shipping grain and sugar out to Moscow . . . . The question about Moscow, about the Soviet Union, the questions to which Volobuiev gave profoundly false, untruthful and abominable answers, today are being posed keenly by the kulak" (RGASPI 81/3/108/13). On 16 July 1928, the new general secretary of the Ukrainian Communist Party Central Committee Stanislav Kosior took up this topic at a meeting of activists of the Kharkiv Party organization. "In Ukraine, some people are whispering," he noted, "that grain is supposedly being shipped out to Moscow. Without a doubt, these are rumours of counterrevolutionary, Petliurist origin. It is clear that our enemies are hammering away along this line" ("Pidsumky lypnevykh").

In conditions of the onset of famine in 1928-29, "uncomfortable" questions were being posed, judging from the numerous denunciations in the Ukrainian Communist Party Central Committee information department and summaries of the GPU (secret police), such as "Where did the grain harvested in Ukraine go?", "How did it happen that the granary is left without grain?", and "Why is an agricultural republic suffering famine?" These matters were the subject of vigorous discussions by various strata of the Ukrainian population, frequently connected with the disadvantages of Ukraine being in the USSR and the benefits of the status of an independent state. In this context, mentions of the Ukrainian governments of the Central Rada and the Directory, and of their leaders—chiefly Symon Petliura, a figure that symbolized the idea of an independent Ukrainian state—became widespread. Already in February-March 1928, the security services recorded conversations in units of the Ukrainian Military District that were typical in this regard. Angered by the grain requisitions and the financial pressure on their parents, peasant soldiers openly said, "It would be better if Ukraine separated from Russia. We would live better; but now, we have to give the grain to Russia, and she sells it abroad. So it turns out that Ukraine is being treated like a cow for the milking" (RGVA 9/28/58/174 *verso*); "It would be better for the peasantry if Ukraine were independent. Then we would govern our country and our people ourselves;" "The USSR is agitating for the Soviet Union because it is afraid of losing Ukrainian bread" (RGVA 25899/2/430/387). At the same time, in conversations among themselves the soldiers said that "The Central Rada would never have insulted the peasantry like the Soviet government does," and spoke in defence of Petliura, whom the political officers invariably portrayed at political lessons as a "bandit," "pogromist," and "traitor to the interests of Ukraine." "Petliura's government truly fought for the interests of Ukraine, but now all orders come from Russia, which lives at the expense of Ukraine," said the peasants (RGVA 25899/2/430/405). "Petliura did not have time to fully reveal himself, and who knows what he would have been like if he had stayed in power" (RGVA 9/28/81/2); "If we had Petliura, there would be enough of everything in Ukraine"(RGVA 25899/2/430/540).

As the food supply situation became acute and hunger advanced, anti-imperial and anti-colonial attitudes continued to spread among the population, not only in the Ukrainian countryside but also among the intelligentsia in the cities, and some of the workers as well. In May 1928, workers in the enterprises of the Odesa region were heard saying, "The government is shipping grain abroad while we are starving," and "Moscow is eating white bread that it takes out of Ukraine" (TsDAHO 1/20/2775/17). According to information provided by the secretary of the Poltava regional Party committee, during a meeting of 1,200 railroad workers in the summer of 1928, "independentist, kulak attitudes" were voiced, such as "the Poltava region is Ukraine's grain centre, but you have shipped everything to Moscow and Leningrad, and they are eating white bread there, while we do not even have black bread" (TsDAHO 1/20/2775/88-89).

Similar attitudes were especially widespread in the villages in the summer of 1928 and in the winter and spring of 1929. In the village of Sukhany, Bohodukhiv district in the Kharkiv region, conversations were recorded among the poor peasants to the effect that "Ukraine is starving, while Moscow is provided with white bread." These attitudes were also expressed by some Soviet activists. During a lecture on the international position of the USSR, Komsomol members in the village of Vasylytsia of the Cherkasy region began shouting, "Why are they telling us about the threat from abroad when Moscow is suffocating us?" And they asked at the same time, "Why is there such a difference: Russia, which is not agricultural, has bread at 17 kopeks a kilo, while Ukraine pays 10 kopeks for only a pound [1 pound = 0.4095 kg]?" (TsDAHO 1/20/2989/6). In the village of Vodiane, Berestiv district in the Mariupol region, one of the local activists, a Party member, declared to the peasants: "Ukraine is a colony of Russia, from which it takes grain and taxes. They are squeezing the Ukrainians mercilessly" (TsDAHO 1/20/2989/11).

The attitudes of the more prosperous and middle layers of the peasantry in the village were even more radical. "How long will we remain under Russian rule?" heatedly asked one of the wealthy peasants in the village of Tarasivka of the Kupiansk district. "We have to separate from the Muscovites. Living with Russia is not good for us. We have a great deal of wealth, and Moscow takes everything" (TsDAHO 1/20/2989/25). Middle-level peasants from the village of Bubnova Slobidka in the Cherkasy region were reported to have angrily said the following: "The *katsaps* [derogatory term for Russians] ship out everything they take from us, and we Ukrainians are hungry and barefoot. This will not last long, everything will be turned upside-down" (TsDAHO 1/20/2989/26). The middle-level peasants in the village of Ksendzivka in the Uman region seconded them: "They are clearing our Ukraine of grain and shipping it to Russia. Russia is cheating Ukraine: it takes grain and sugar, but it does not give us manufactured goods, and furthermore it starves us to death" (TsDAHO 1/20/3315/26).

The prevalence of these attitudes was characterized as "noticeable," "not rare," and those that appear "most frequently" and are "widespread" in reports of the Ukrainian Communist Party Central Committee information division and representatives of the security services in numerous summaries of the GPU. The following example is typical. On 1 November 1928, at a meeting of the Ukrainian Communist Party Central Committee, the plenipotentiary for grain procurement, Chaika, having just returned from the Shepetivka region, related that among the conversations he had heard was "that all the grain goes to Moscow, that *they have turned Ukraine into a colony of Moscow*." Chaika added: "Quite a few comrades speak about *the broad dissemination* of this Petliurist agitation; *these conversations are fairly widespread*" (TsDAHO 1/1/309/25-63; 1/20/2769/8-46, emphasis in the original).

Negative political attitudes among various strata of the Ukrainian population connected with the topic of the exploitation of Ukraine's grain resources by the central government were also recorded in the ensuing years. Revelatory conversations were constant among the peasant youth in the Red Army. In a private conversation with soldiers in February 1931, one of the younger commanders of the 31st rifle division explained the reasons for the impoverished life of the republic's population as follows:

> If Ukraine were independent, then we would not have had to carry out collectivization. However much grain Ukraine gives to Russia, it will always be too little, and that is why here in Ukraine they brazenly seize the grain, regardless of the fact that we no longer have any, and give it to Russia—to those who are skinning us. (TsDAHO 1/20/3194/53)

A telling incident took place in Kharkiv on 26 February 1931, during the proceedings of the Thirteenth All-Ukrainian Congress of Soviets. A group of delegates and attendees at a forum of workers from Kharkiv factories (the Kharkiv locomotive works "Sickle and Hammer," among others) sent the presidium a resounding declaration containing a sharp criticism of the all-Union centre's policy toward Ukraine. The declaration essentially reflected anti-imperial and anti-colonial attitudes. It contained angry expressions against the ongoing "centralizing current," the extremely unequal division of wealth between the centre and the republic (they presented data indicating how in 1929 the Ukrainian SSR, with its population of 30 million, had the same budget as the region of Moscow, with its 5 million people), protesting against the limited powers of the Ukrainian government ("if it needs to do something, a sovereign republic does not bow down, yet we have to"). The declaration also pointed to the terrible conditions in the Ukrainian village ("barefoot, naked, hungry, humiliated, repressed, robbed a hundred times worse than they were robbed by the tsarist government, and worse than the greediest capitalist country robs its colonies"). The signatories drew a firm conclusion: "Russia is being built by the muscles of Ukrainian workers and peasants. Ukraine is collapsing" (TsDAHO 1/20/4171/10-19).

The continuing ruination of the Ukrainian countryside caused a further strengthening of negative political attitudes on the theme of Ukraine's colonial status. Masses of Ukrainian peasants went in search of bread to Moscow, Leningrad, Minsk, and other industrial centres better supplied with provisions than Ukraine. Conversations could be heard among various segments of the population about "Ukrainians begging" and noting that "for some reason, there is bread in Moscow, while in the Ukrainian cities it is practically impossible for the peasant to buy it." Party and government leaders, including Joseph Stalin, received letters of complaint. "I saw that in Russia a *pud* of bread costs 10 rubles, while in Ukraine it costs 80 *karbovantsi*. And there is none anyway, so everyone is going to Russia," wrote one Ukrainian peasant to Stalin (TsDAHO 1/20/5254/19). "I returned from the countryside two days ago and I saw all the misery there with my own eyes," wrote a rank-and-file Party worker from the Kyiv region to Stalin, adding that he himself was well fed in the Party dining-room. "It is painful to look at those unfortunate children and women perishing from hunger, waiting for their father to bring a loaf or two of bread from Moscow. For everyone is going to Moscow, Leningrad, and Minsk for bread" (TsDAHO 1/20/5254/12-13). Similar letters were addressed to the Ukrainian Party and government leadership. "Food supply is well organized in the Russian part of the USSR . . . the workers get white bread too, and there is no discussion about a lack of bread for the family," wrote one of the employees of the Liubotyn depot to Kosior. "National hatred is appearing in the Ukrainian workers' milieu . . . . Today you can easily say that 99 percent of the Ukrainian population has an anti-Soviet attitude" (TsDAHO 1/20/5406/4).

In the spring and summer of 1933, according to the observations of the secret service and Party workers, the degree of political protest in the Ukrainian countryside fell precipitously. The government's inaction in conditions of starvation, against the background of a Moscow-sanctioned information blockade, made a shocking impression on the populace and gave rise to a firm conviction among a part of it that the massive mortality of the Ukrainian population from hunger was no error in economic calculations but a purposeful act and predictable result of Ukraine's colonial status in the USSR. This was roughly the message of a letter from unknown residents of Poltava sent in August 1933 to the editors of the newspaper *Komunist* (*The Communist*): "The physical destruction of the Ukrainian nation, the exhaustion of its material and spiritual resources, is one of the most important points of the illegal program of Bolshevik centralism" (RGASPI 81/3/131/2).

We thus see that a significant part of Ukrainian society perceived Stalin's faminogenic policies as imperial, conditioned by Ukraine's colonial status, and connected the proximate causes of impoverishment and mass mortality from hunger with inequality and the exploitation of Ukrainian grain resources.

Did bearers of imperial consciousness exist in Ukraine? Certainly, but scholars have yet to elucidate its manifestations during the famines of 1928-29 and 1932-33. It is obvious, nevertheless, that among both the central Bolshevik elite and parts of the peripheral elite that ruled Ukraine, anti-Ukrainian attitudes were common, while a significant portion of the *nomenklatura* (Party specialist elite) did not know or use the Ukrainian language. Among those who did use it, fear of being declared nationalists reigned as purges were a constant.

Another matter that deserves attention is the ideological and propaganda backdrop that existed on the eve of the Ukrainian catastrophe. The conviction of bringing civilization to a backward or barbaric country as seen in the colonial policies and practices of Europeans in Africa and Asia, and of the English in Ireland was to some degree apparent in the Soviet empire. As demonstrated in the classic work of S. Ambirajan *Classical Political Economy and British Policy in India*, state policy during the Indian famines of the nineteenth century leaves no doubt that the ideology of the bureaucracy (racist, colonial, imbued with a Malthusian spirit) made its negative contribution to mass famine. Racial and political elements of English imperialism were clearly manifest in the Bengal famine of 1943. In *Churchill's Secret War*, Madhusree Mukerjee demonstrates how Churchill's contempt for Indians (he called the Indians "a beastly people with a beastly religion," and Mahatma Gandhi a "harmful subversive fanatic") informed his callousness in the face of the sufferings of the starving in Bengal (78). Elaborating on Sen's analysis, Mukerjee asserts that Churchill's failure to act to stem the growing famine was part of a strategy of maintaining British domination in India and was conditioned by his indifferent, hostile, and disdainful attitude to the Indians, their beliefs, and their leaders. If English propaganda depicted the Indians and Irish as uncouth, uneducated, and filthy barbarians who needed to be civilized, the Bolsheviks in their propaganda masked the national aspect under that of class. Their propaganda presented Russian culture as progressive, forward-looking, and revolutionary ("the language of the workers"), destined to defeat a regressive, backward Ukrainian peasant culture with its obsolete traditions (even its national musical instruments the "*kobza*" and "*bandura*") and its "bumpkin language." Through the lens of three of the most disastrous famines in modern history—the potato famine in Ireland, the famine in Bengal in 1943, and the string of famines that plagued Ethiopia in the 1970s and 1980s—Thomas Keneally shows how ideology, mindsets of governments, racial preconceptions, and administrative incompetence were, ultimately, more lethal than the initiating blights or crop failures.

Following from this, it is worth paying attention in Soviet propaganda to efforts at how certain categories of the population were depicted as potentially hostile to the government. In this context it is worth analyzing how the "image of the enemy" was constructed. In constructing the image of the dehumanized "kulak enemy" (the negative connotation of which was often intensified by applying the label "Petliurist"), the regime prepared the population psychologically for the annihilation of an entire social stratum. The role of this "struggle of cultures" in the Ukrainian Holodomor, however, demands further illumination from future scholars.

Conclusions

The interpretation of the Soviet Union as a nation-state (prominent from Soviet times and still dominant in the historiography of the Stalinist policies of famine creation), excludes *a priori* the imperial essence of the Soviet Union, causing methodological limitations. In this article I have sought to demonstrate the applicability of models of dependence and imperialism to our understanding of the dynamics and consequences of the policy of collectivization of agriculture, and of famine at the end of the 1920s and first part of the 1930s, focusing on Soviet Ukraine.

The Stalinist faminogenic policies can be regarded as a means of consolidating the Soviet empire, which was secured by violence. Along with this, the appropriation of the sovereignty of the Ukrainian SSR by the central government, the clear asymmetry of relations along the "centre-periphery" axis, Moscow's total control over food resources (including determination of grain deliveries and distribution), the ongoing exploitation of Ukrainian economic resources against the backdrop of depriving the regional *nomenklatura* of even minimal liquid resources—together with the anti-Ukrainian terror—caused the Ukrainian famine of 1928-29 and may have been a critical factor in the onset of the Holodomor.

The degree of assimilation of an imperial mentality by the central and peripheral administrative elites remains an open question. Archival documents clearly indicate, however, that the Stalinist faminogenic policies were interpreted by parts of various strata of Ukrainian society (the peripheral elite, the peasants, the intelligentsia) as a manifestation of Moscow's imperial rule and Ukraine's colonial dependence. Documents also show that the central government monitored and repressed those who expressed such attitudes.

The study of Stalinist famine-creation and of the tragedy of the Holodomor in the context of imperialism/colonialism is only beginning. In this, there is a similarity with Ireland, whose historians did not initially speak of a colonial factor in the Great Irish Famine. As the economic historian Cormac O'Grada pointed out at the beginning of the 1990s, the Gorta Mor of 1845-50— causing a million deaths and two million to leave their native land—was at first attributed to natural cataclysms, leaving London's economic policies unmentioned or excused.

To summarize, I consider the Holodomor a genocide, a concept much questioned in the cases of Bengal and Ireland. In this regard, I am in absolute solidarity with the view of the American scholar Mark von Hagen that as was the cases of famine in Ireland in 1845-50 or in Bengal in 1943, imperialism was a factor in causing the Holodomor. Moreover, in the USSR the state and party dictatorship under Stalin provided the context and environment in which the ruling elites and their bureaucratic machines reached new—in essence the highest—levels of imperialism/colonialism (von Hagen).[18]

Works Cited

5 s'ezd Sovetov. Biulleten' 17, zasedanie dvenadtsatoe, 27 May 1929.

Al'terman, A. Ia. "Problema tovarnosti zernovogo khoziaistva Ukrainy s sotsial'no-ekonomicheskoi tochki zreniia." *Khoziaistvo Ukrainy*, no. 6, 1928, pp. 101-110.

Ambirajan, S. *Classical Political Economy and British Policy in India*. Cambridge UP, 1978.

Anisimov, Ie. V. "Istoricheskie korni imperskogo myshleniia v Rossii." *Slavic Research Center Winter Symposium Socio-Cultural Dimensions of the Changes in the Slavic-Eurasian World*, 1996, http://src-h.slav.hokudai.ac.jp/sympo/Proceed97/Anisimov.html. Accessed 26 Feb. 2020.

Applebaum, Anne. *Red Famine: Stalin's War on Ukraine*. Doubleday, 2017.

Arkhireis'kyi, D. V. *Diial'nist' voiennykh narad Ukrainy v 1920-1924 rokakh (na materialakh pivdennykh hubernii)*. 2000. Dnipropetrovs'kyi derzhavnyi universytet, PhD dissertation (Dysertatsiia na zdobuttia nauk. stupenia kand. ist. nauk).

Baratov. *Na iug! Na iug!* Gosudarstvennoe izdatel'stvo, 1919.

Batalov, O. A. *Imperiia iak typ sotsial'no-istorychnoi orhanizatsii*. 2010. KhNU imeni V. N. Karazina, PhD dissertation (Avtoreferat dys. na zdobuttia nauk. stupenia kand. filosof. nauk).

Bohan, S. M. *Povstans'kyi rukh v Odes'kii hubernii u 1920-1923 rokakh*. 2003. Odes'kyi natsional'nyi universytet im. I. I. Mechnikova, PhD dissertation (Dysertatsiia na zdobuttia nauk. stupenia kand. ist. nauk).

Borisov, V. I., et al. *Prodovol'stvennaia politika na Iuge Rossii v period pervoi mirovoi voiny i revolutsii (1914-1918): monografiia*. 1997.

Borodaev, et al. "Proty burzhuazno-natsionalistychnoho shkidnytstva v s.-h. nautsi." *Bil'shovyk Ukrainy*, no. 11, 1933, pp. 116-24.

Borys, Jurij. *The Sovietization of Ukraine 1917-1923: The Communist Doctrine and Practice of National Self-Determination*. Revised ed., Canadian Institute of Ukrainian Studies, 1980.

[18] Holodomor Research and Education Centre in Ukraine, archive, 2017.

Cameron, Sarah. *The Hungry Steppe: Famine, Violence, and the Making of Soviet Kazakhstan*. Cornell UP, 2018.

Chernov, M. "Pytannia khlibnoho eksportu Ukrainy." *Visti VUTsVK*, 5 Jan. 1928.

Davies, R. W., and Stephen G. Wheatcroft. *The Years of Hunger: Soviet Agriculture, 1931-1933*. 1st ed., Palgrave Macmillan, 2004. The Industrialisation of Soviet Russia 5. Available online: https://eastsidemarxism.files.wordpress.com/2017/04/r-w-davies-stephen-g-wheatcroft-the-industrialisation-of-soviet-russia-volume-5-the-years-of-hunger-soviet-agriculture-1931-1933.pdf. Accessed 26 Feb. 2020.

Den, V. E. *Polozheniie Rossii v mirovom khoziaistve. Analiz russkogo eksporta do voiny: statisticheskii ocherk*. Severo-zapadnoe promyshlennoe biuro V.S.N.Kh. 1922.

Doyle, Michael W. *Empires*. Cornell UP, 1986.

Dyrektoriia, Rada Narodnykh Ministriv Ukrain'skoi Narodnoi Respubliky 1918-1920: *Dokumenty i materialy*. Vyd-vo Oleny Telihy, 2006. 2 vols.

Edgar, Adrienne Lynn. *Tribal Nation: The Making of Soviet Turkmenistan*. Princeton UP, 2004.

Etkind, Alexander. *Internal Colonization: Russia's Imperial Experience*. Polity, 2011.

Ezhegodnik khlebooborota za 1931-32, 1932-33 i predvaritel'nye itogi zagotovok 1933 g. (tablitsy). Komitet po zagotovkam s.-kh. Produktov pri SNK SSSR, 1934.

Frumkin, M. I. *Narodnoe khoziaistvo i vneshniaia torgovlia SSSR*. Gosizdat, 1926.

Graziosi, Andrea. "The Soviet 1931-1933 Famines and the Ukrainian Holodomor: Is a New Interpretation Possible, and What Would Its Consequences Be?" *Harvard Ukrainian Studies*, vol. 27, no. 1/4, 2004-05, pp. 97-115. DOI: 10.2307/41036863

Hirsch, Francine. *Empire of Nations: Ethnographic Knowledge and the Making of the Soviet Union*. Cornell UP, 2005. Culture and Society after Socialism.

Hosking, Geoffrey. *Rulers and Victims: The Russians in the Soviet Union*. Belknap Press, 2006.

Hrynevych, Liudmyla. *Holod 1928-1929 rr. u radians'kii Ukraini*. Instytut istorii Ukrainy NAN Ukrainy, 2013.

Hrynevych, V., et al. *Istoriia ukrains'koho viis'ka: 1917-1995*. Compiled by Ia. Dashkevych, Vydavnytstvo "Svit," 1996.

Hunczak, Taras, editor. *The Ukraine 1917-1921: A Study in Revolution*. Harvard Ukrainian Research Institute, 1977.

Iakovenko, I. G. "Ot imperii k natsional'nomu gosudarstvu (Popytka kontseptualizatsii protsessa)." *Polis*, no. 6 (36), 1996, pp. 117-28.

Iefimenko, Hennadii. *Vzaiemovidnosyny Kremlia ta Radian'skoi Ukrainy: Ekonomichnyi aspekt (1917-1919 pp.)*. Instytut istorii Ukrainy NAN Ukrainy, 2008.

Isakov, P. M. *Selian'skyi povstans'kyi rukh na Livoberezhnii Ukraini (berezen' 1919-lystopad 1921 rr.)*. 2001. NAN Ukrainy / Instytut istorii Ukrainy, PhD dissertation (Dysertatsiia na zdobuttia nauk. stupenia kand. ist. nauk).

Kak lomali NEP. Stenogrammy plenumov TsK VKP(b) 1928-1929 gg. V 5-ti tomakh. Vol. 3: *Plenum TsK VKP(b) 16-24 noiabria 1928 g.* Mezhdunarodnyi fond "Demokratiia," 2000.

Kappeler, Andreas. *Rosiia iak polietnichna imperiia*. Vyd-vo Katolyts'koho Ukrains'koho universytetu, 2005.

---. *The Russian Empire: A Multi-Ethnic History*. Routledge, 2001. Available online: https://www.taylorfrancis.com/books/9781315736792. Accessed 26 Feb. 2020.

Kaspe, Sviatoslav. *Imperiia i modernizatsiia. Obshchaia model' i rossiiskaia spetsifika*. ROSSPEN, 2001.

Keneally, Thomas. *Three Famines: Starvation and Politics*. Random House/Knopf Australia, 2010.

Khalid, Adeeb. *Making Uzbekistan: Nation, Empire, and Revolution in the Early USSR*. Cornell UP, 2015.

Kindler, Robert. *Stalin's Nomads. Power and Famine in Kazakhstan*. Pittsburgh UP, 2018.

Kondrashin, V. *Khlebozagotovitel'naia politika v gody pervoi piatiletki i ee rezul'taty (1929-1933 gg.)*. Politicheskaia entsiklopedia, 2014.

Kononenko, K. *Ukraina i Rosiia: Sotsiial'no-ekonomichni pidstavy ukrains'koi natsional'noi idei*. 1965.

Kontrol'nye tsifry narodnogo khoziaistva USSR na 1928-29 god. Izd-vo Gosplana USSR, 1928.

Kosheleva, L. et al., editors. *Pis'ma I. V. Stalina V. M. Molotovu. 1925-1936 gg. (Sbornik dokumentov)*. Rossiia molodaia, 1996.

Krasnosilets'kyi, D. P. *Antybil'shovyts'kyi rukh selian v Pravoberezhnii chastyni USRR u 1920-1924 rokakh*. KhNU, 2009.

Kulchytsky, Stanislav. *The Famine of 1932-1933 in Ukraine: An Anatomy of the Holodomor*. CIUS P, 2018.

Kul'chyts'kyi, S. *Chervonyi vyklyk. Istoriia komunizmu v Ukraini vid ioho narodzhennia do zahybeli*. Tempora, 2013. 3 vols.

Lenin, V. I. *Povne zibrannia tvoriv*. Vol. 50, Vydavnytstvo politychnoi literatury Ukrainy, 1975.

Lieven, Dominic. *Empire: The Russian Empire and Its Rivals*. Yale UP, 2001.

Mace, James E. *Communism and the Dilemmas of National Liberation: National Communism in Soviet Ukraine, 1918-1933*. Harvard Ukrainian Research Institute, 1983. Harvard Series in Ukrainian Studies.

Makuch, Andrij, and Frank E. Sysyn, editors. *Contextualizing the Holodomor: The Impact of Thirty Years of Ukrainian Famine Studies*. CIUS P, 2015.

Malynovs'kyi, B. V. *Ahrarna polityka Avstro-Uhorshchyny ta Nimechchyny v Ukraini, 1918 r.* 2001. Dnipropetrovs'kyi natsional'nyi universytet, PhD dissertation (Avtoreferat dys. na zdobuttia nauk. stupenia kand. ist. nauk).

Marcus, David. "Famine Crimes in International Law." *The American Journal of International Law*, vol. 97, no. 2, April 2003, pp. 245-81. DOI: 10.2307/3100102

Marochko, V. "Sprava 'Kontrrevoliutsiinoi shkidnyts'koi orhanizatsii v sil's'komu hospodarstvi USRR': mekhanizm i naslidky teroru." *Z arkhiviv VUChK-GPU-NKVD-KGB*, no. 1/2 (6/7), 1998, pp. 96-104.

Martin, Terry. *The Affirmative Action Empire: Nations and Nationalism in the Soviet Union, 1923-1939*. Cornell UP, 2001. Wilder House Series in Politics, History and Culture.

Motyl, Alexander J. *Imperial Ends: The Decay, Collapse, and Revival of Empires*. Columbia UP, 2001.

Motyl', Oleksandr (Alexander J. Motyl). "SRSR iak Rosiis'ka imperiia. Chym bula radians'ka Ukraina?" *Tyzhden'*, no. 46 (263), 15 Nov. 2012, https://tyzhden.ua/History/65141. Accessed 26 Feb. 2020.

Mukerjee, Madhusree. *Churchill's Secret War: The British Empire and the Ravaging of India during World War II*. Basic Books, 2010.

Mytsiuk, O. *Pro avtonomiiu Ukrainy v federatyvnii Rosii*. Druk. V. Levitans'koho, 1917.

Narodnoe khoziaistvo Ukrainy v 1921 g. Otchet Ukrainskogo Ekonomicheskogo Soveta Sovetu Truda i Oborony. 4-ia gosudarstvennaia tipografiia, 1922.

"Na Ukraini zahotovleno 260,2 mil. pudiv khliba. Richnyi plan zahotivel' vykonano na 98,2%." *Visti VUTsVK*, 4 July 1928.

"Na zahal'nu dopovid' pro piatyrichnyi plan narodnoho hospodarstva Ukrainy: postanovy XI Vseukrains'koho z''izdu rad robitnychykh, selians'kykh i chervonoarmiis'kykh deputativ, 15 travnia 1929 r." *Visti VUIVK*, 12 June 1929.

Ó Gráda, Cormac. *The Great Irish Famine*. Cambridge UP, 1995.

"O piatiletnem plane razvitiia narodnogo khoziaistva: postanovlenie V s''ezda Sovetov SSSR. 28 maia 1929 g." *Sobranie zakonov i rasporiazhenii*. Otdel 1, no. 35, 1929, p. 311.

Piatiletnii plan narodno-khoziaistvennogo stroitel'stva SSSR. Vol. 3, Izdatel'stvo "Planovoe khoziaistvo," 1930.

"Pidsumky lypnevykh plenumiv TsK VKP(b) ta TsK LKSMU: dopovid' heneral'noho sekretaria TsK KP(b)U tov. St. Kosiora na zborakh aktyvu Kharkivs'koi partorhanizatsii 16 lypnia 1928 r." *Komunist*, 18 July 1928.

Plazova, T. I. *Ukrains'kyi Partyzans'ko-Povstans'kyi Shtab ta ioho uchast' v orhanizatsii antybil'shovyts'koi borot'by v Ukraini (1920-1921 rr.)*. 2005. Natsional'nyi universytet "L'vivs'ka politekhnika," PhD dissertation (Dysertatsiia na zdobuttia nauk. stupenia kand. ist. nauk).

Popov, F. "Problemy ahrarnoi perenaselenosti ta shliakhy rozvytku narodn'oho hospodarstva USRR." *BIl'shovyk Ukrainy*, nos. 21-22, 1928, pp. 64-76.

Problemy rekonstruktsii narodnogo khoziaistva SSSR na piatiletie: piatiletnii perspektivnyi plan na V s"ezde Gosplanov. Planovoe khoziaistvo, Gosplan SSSR, 1929.

Rafalovs'kyi, Ie. P. *Prodovol'cha polityka uriadiv Ukrains'koi Derzhavy het'mana Petra Skoropads'koho*. 2007. Natsional'nyi pedahohichnyi universytet im. M. P. Drahomanova, PhD dissertation (Avtoreferat dys. na zdobuttia nauk. stupenia kand. ist. nauk).

Reshetar, John S. *The Ukrainian Revolution, 1917-1920: A Study in Nationalism*. Princeton UP, 1952.

Rudnytskyi, Omelian, et al. "Demography of a Man-Made Human Catastrophe: The Case of Massive Famine in Ukraine 1932-1933." *Canadian Studies in Population*, vol. 42, no. 1-2, 2015, pp. 53-80. DOI: 10.25336/P6FC7G

Sahni, Kalpana. *Crucifying the Orient. Russian Orientalism and the Colonization of Caucasus and Central Asia*. White Orchid Press, 1997.

Sen, Amartya. *Poverty and Famines: An Essay on Entitlement and Deprivation*. Oxford UP, 1981.

S"ezdy Sovetov Soiuza Sovetskikh Sotsialisticheskikh Respublik. Sbornik dokumentov. 1922-1936 gg. Compiled by D. A. Gaidukov et al., 1960.

Shevchenko, A. M. *Zovnishnia torhivlia portiv na Pivdni Ukrainy (druha polovyna XIX-pochatok XX st.)*. 2008. Izmail's'kyi derzhavnyi humanitarnyi instytut, PhD dissertation (Dys. na zdobuttia nauk. stupenia kand. ist. nauk).

Slezkine, Yuri. *Arctic Mirrors: Russia and the Small Peoples of the North*. Cornell UP, 1996.

Sobranie zakonov i rasporiazhenii. Otdel 1, no. 29 and no. 35, 1929.

Soloveichik, V. M. (V. M. Soloveichyk) "Osnovnye voprosy 5-letnego plana rekonstruktsii sel'skoho khoziaistva USRR." *Khoziaistvo Ukrainy*, no. 10, 1928, pp. 25-43.

"Sovershenno sekretno": Lubianka—Stalinu o polozhenii v strane (1922-1934 gg). Sbornik dokumentov v 10 tomakh. Vol. 7: *1927,* Institut Rossiiskoi istorii RAN, 2004.

Sovetskaia derevnia glazami VChK-OGPU-NKVD. Dokumenty i materialy v 4-kh tomakh. Vol. 2: *1923-29*. ROSSPEN, 2000.

Sprava 'Ukrains'koi filii Trudovoi selians'koi partii." Holovna redkolehiia "Reabilitovani istorieiu," 2010.

Stebnitskii, P. Ia. (Petro Stebnyts'kyi). *Ukraina v ekonomike Rossii.* 8-ia Gosudarstvennaia tipografiia, 1918. Stehnii, P. A. *Selians'ki povstannia v Pravoberezhnii chastyni USRR u 1921-1923 rr. (na materialakh petliurivs'koho rukhu).* 2000. Kremenchuts'kyi derzhavnyi politekhnichnyi instytut, PhD dissertation (Dysertatsiia na zdobuttia nauk. stupenia kand. ist. nauk).

Suni, Ronald (Ronald Suny). "Dialektika imperii: Rossiia i Sovetskii Soiuz." *Novaia imperskaia istoriia postsovetskogo prostranstva*, edited by I. Gerasimov et al., Kazan, "Tsentr Issledovanii Natsionalizma i Imperii," 2004, pp. 163-96.

Tauger, Mark B. "Grain Crisis or Famine? The Ukrainian State Commission for Aid to Crop-Failure Victims and the Ukrainian Famine of 1928-1929." *Provincial Landscapes: Local Dimensions of Soviet Power, 1917-1953*, edited by D. J. Raleigh, U of Pittsburgh P, 2001, pp. 146-70.

Tishkov, Valerii. "Chto est' Rossiia i rossiiskii narod." *Pro et Contra*, May-June 2007, pp. 21-41.

Thompson, Ewa. *Imperial Knowledge: Russian Literature and Colonialism.* Greenwood, 2000.

Thompstone, Stuart Ross. *The Organisation and Financing of Russian Foreign Trade before 1914.* 1991. University of London, PhD dissertation.

Ukrains'ka Tsentral'na rada: *Dokumenty i materialy.* Vol. 1: *4 bereznia–9 hrudnia 1917 r.* Naukova dumka, 1996.

---. Vol. 2: *10 hrudnia 1917 r.–29 kvitnia 1918 r.* Naukova dumka, 1997.

Vasyl'iev, V. *Politychne kerivnytstvo URSR i SRSR: dynamika vidnosyn "tsentr-subtsentr vlady" (1917-1938 rr.).* Instytut istorii Ukrainy NAN Ukrainy, 2014.

V. I. Lenin pro Ukrainu. Part II: *1917-1922.* Politvydav Ukrainy, 1969.

Vishnevskii, A. A. *Serp i rubl'. Konservativnaia modernizatsiia v SSSR.* OGI, 1998.

Vol'f, M. B., and G. A. Mebus. *Statisticheskii spravochnik po ekonomicheskoi geografii SSSR i drugikh gosudarstv.* Gosudarstvennoe izdatel'stvo, 1926.

Volobuiev, M. "Do problemy ukrains'koi ekonomiky." *Dokumenty ukrains'koho komunizmu,* 1962, pp. 132-230.

---. "Lyst do zhurnalu 'Bil'shovyk Ukrainy.'" *Bil'shovyk Ukrainy*, nos. 21-22, 1928, pp. 147-48.

von Hagen, Mark. "Holodomor i Holokost iak 'naivyshchi stadii' kolonializmu." Institute of the History of Ukraine / National Academy of Sciences of Ukraine, 23 Sept. 2015. Holodomor Research and Education Centre in Ukraine, Audiovisual Archive of the Holodomor Era. Public lecture.

Zbirnyk uzakonen' ta rozporiadzhen'. Viddil pershyi, no. 143, art. 99, 1929.

Archives

DAKhO State Archive of the Kharkiv Oblast (cited by *fond/opys/odynytsia zberihannia/arkush*)

RGASPI Russian State Archive of Social-Political History (cited by *fond/opis'/delo/list)*

RGVA Russian State Military Archive (cited by *fond/opis'/delo/list*)

TsA FSB RF Central Archive of the Federal Security Service of the Russian Federation (cited by *fond/opis'/delo/list*)

TsDAHO Central State Archive of Civic Associations of Ukraine (cited by *fond/opys/sprava/arkush*)

TsDAVO Central State Archive of Higher Organs of Government and Administration (cited by *fond/opys/sprava/arkush*)

Internal Colonialism, Alien Rule, and Famine in Ireland and Ukraine

Michael Hechter
Arizona State University

Abstract: The Irish famine of the mid nineteenth century and the Ukrainian famine of the twentieth century have been the subject of large and quite contentious literatures. Whereas many popular explanations of the Irish famine attribute it to the English government's infatuation with laissez-faire economic doctrines, by contrast the Ukrainian famine has often been ascribed to Stalin's resentment of Ukraine's resistance to the Soviet revolution. This essay suggests that despite their many differences, during these years both Ireland and Ukraine can be considered to have been internal colonies of their respective empires. The key implication of this conception is that these appalling famines arose from a common underlying cause: namely, the inferior political status of these regions relative to that of the core regions of these states. One of the defining characteristics of internal colonies is that they often suffer from alien rule. Alien rulers are typically indifferent to the welfare of the residents of the culturally distinctive regions within their borders. Due to this indifference, both the British and Soviet central rulers cast a blind eye to the fate of the Irish and Ukrainian peasants

Keywords: Ireland, Ukraine, famine, internal colonialism, alien rule.

Although the differences between Ireland and Ukraine are vast, their histories have something important in common: both were once dependent peripheries in imperial states. An insular Celtic tribal society with an overwhelmingly Catholic population, Ireland was conquered in the seventeenth century by Oliver Cromwell. The Cromwellian Settlement expropriated much of Ireland's land, giving it to Cromwell's Protestant financiers and the soldiers of his New Model Army as recompense for their support in the English Civil War. Thereafter, England instituted the Penal Laws (not rescinded until 1829), which among other things denied Catholics many civil rights and prohibited them from holding office anywhere in Great Britain. As the great Irish political theorist

---

* I wish to thank the participants of the conference, Communism and Hunger: The Soviet, Kazakh, Ukrainian, and Chinese Famines in Comparative Perspective at the University of Toronto (26-27 September 2014), where I presented an earlier draft of this present paper, and especially Marta Baziuk, Andrea Graziosi, and Frank Sysyn for inviting me to the conference. I also thank Anthony Garnaut for his advice.

Edmund Burke—a member of the Protestant Ascendancy—characterized them, these laws were "a machine of wise and elaborate contrivance, as well fitted for the oppression, impoverishment and degradation of a people, and the debasement in them of human nature itself, as ever proceeded from the perverted ingenuity of man" (Mitchel, *The Last Conquest* 10).

Whereas modern Ireland had been governed by only one alien ruler, modern Ukraine was divided between the Habsburg and Russian Empires, and after 1917 suffered periods of German, Soviet (Russian), Polish, and Czechoslovakian control (von Hagen). Beyond the fact of subjection to alien rule, Ukraine shares other parallels with the Irish experience. For example, Ukrainian culture was disparaged, and the Ukrainian language was suppressed in Romanov Russia.

The experiences of Ireland and Ukraine also mirrored, in part, that of the Western European overseas colonies, while the characteristics of the colonies also diverged substantially.[1] Each colony was geographically, culturally, and politically unique. Traditionally, the literature on colonial societies was built on the basis of ethnographic studies of the various cultural groups—or "tribes"—about which the colonial powers sought intelligence, the better to control them. Some of these ethnographies—by the likes of E. E. Evans-Pritchard, Bronisław Malinowski, and Alfred Radcliffe Brown—remain classics of modern social science.

Following arguments made after World War II by Max Gluckman and Georges Balandier, however, a new emphasis began to emerge in the postwar colonial literature, which stressed commonalities rather than differences (see Cooper 3-32).[2] In Balandier's view, these territories all faced a set of conditions that he termed "the colonial situation," which consisted of the following:

- The domination imposed by a foreign minority, racially (or ethnically) and culturally different, acting in the name of a racial (or ethnic) and cultural superiority, dogmatically affirmed, and imposing itself on an indigenous population constituting a numerical majority but inferior to the dominant group from a material point of view;
- A domination linking radically different civilizations into some form of relationship;

[1] In fact, this variation even occurred *within* each of the colonies (cf. Lawrence).

[2] Somewhat later, the British colonial officer J. S. Furnivall popularized the concept of "the plural society," which he considered a necessary outcome of European overseas colonialism (see Lee for an introduction and discussion of the subsequent literature).

- An industrialized society with a powerful economy and fast tempo of life imposing itself on a non-industrialized society with a "backward" economy in which the pace of living is much slower;
- The antagonistic relationship between these two societies resulting from the subservient role to which the colonial people are subjected as "instruments" of the colonial power; and
- The need, in maintaining this domination, to resort not only to force but also to a system of pseudo-justification and stereotyped behaviors. (54-55)

More than two decades later, I published *Internal Colonialism*, a study of the roots of nationalism in the Celtic Fringe of the United Kingdom (Hechter). The book argued that many aspects of Balandier's colonial situation antedated the rise of many overseas colonies. Indeed, something quite analogous had happened to the culturally distinct peripheries of the metropoles themselves—such as the United Kingdom, France and Spain—in the course of state-building. Christian attempts to rid the Iberian Peninsula of Muslims and Jews, the *Reconquistá*, began in eighth-century Asturias and continued over the course of at least seven hundred years, culminating in the Spanish Inquisition. Just as England had conquered Wales in 1536, added Scotland with the Treaty of Union in 1707, and incorporated Ireland in 1801, the Île de France had gradually extended its rule into Burgundy, Occitania, and Brittany over the centuries. For many Western European countries, state building necessarily entailed internal colonialism (see Bartlett for other European examples).[3]

I did not invent the term "internal colonialism": its earliest use was by Russian populists to describe the exploitation of peasants by urban classes. Later it was adopted by Antonio Gramsci, Vladimir Lenin, Ievgenii Preobrazhenskii, and Nikolai Bukharin to characterize the persisting underdevelopment of certain Russian and Italian regions. This usage was even more capacious than my own because it concerned the expansion of central state capacity into peripheral regions that shared a common culture with the core. In contrast, I reserved the term for states that extended their control over *culturally distinct* peripheries.

What then does the internal colonial situation consist of? *Internal Colonialism* presented two separate but related arguments (Hechter). The first, which is the focus of this paper, was couched at the level of *regions.*

[3] Likewise, Perdue can be read as the story of the establishment of internal colonialism in China, as the Qing Dynasty—ironically, ethnically Manchu rather than Han—extended its rule westward to Xingiang. See also Biran.

This argument holds that the lack of political sovereignty characteristic of internal colonies limited their economic welfare and threatened their cultural integrity. Whereas many internal colonies have been economically disadvantaged, there are exceptions such as Scotland and Catalonia, two territories that have been economically advanced. Nonetheless, even economically advanced peripheries can be considered internal colonies when the policies that govern these territories are decided in a larger political arena, one in which the periphery is destined to play only a minor role at best. The peripheral population, therefore, is denied the privilege and responsibility of determining its own political fate.

The second argument, an elaboration on one of the themes highlighted by Balandier, focused on individuals rather than regions and holds that culturally distinct identities remain salient among the members of groups that are subject to a cultural division of labour, regardless of increased interregional contact or industrialization. Due to the scarcity of data on the stratification of cultural groups, there was very little empirical support for this argument (my article on the cultural division of labour was an exception [Hechter, "Group Formation"]), but happily that situation recently has changed. New empirical analyses of inter-group conflict and civil war (some carried out under the rubric of "horizontal inequalities") have lent considerable support to the argument (see Stewart; Cederman et al.; Siroky and Hechter, "Ethnicity, Class, and Civil War").

In addition to the Celtic Fringe, which was the focus of *Internal Colonialism*, this type of analysis has been applied, at least informally, to a variety of cases (Stone), including Brittany (Reece) and Corsica in France (Siroky et al., "Containing Nationalism"); Estonia (Mettam and Williams) and Central Asia (Loring) in the USSR; Xingiang in China (Gladney; see also Sautman for a skeptical view); Quebec in Canada (McRoberts; Pettinicchio); Catalonia in Spain (McPhee); Palestine in Israel (Zureik); Alaska (Dryzek and Young), Native American reservations (Palmer and Rundstrom) and Appalachia in the USA (Lewis et al.); the Central Highlands of Vietnam (Evans); and the Torres Strait Islands in Australia and Eastern Viti Levu in Fiji (Durutalo). The argument as a whole fits some of these cases better than others (Hind; Chávez; Hechter, "Internal Colonialism Revisited").

In the remainder of this essay I will consider whether the internal colonial thesis can shed any light on two of the defining events in modern Irish and Ukrainian history: their famines. I make no claim to contribute to the large and contentious historiography on the causes of these disasters, but I do want to suggest that alien rule, a defining attribute of the internal colonial theory, is at least partially responsible for them.

Ireland's status as an internal colony played a critical role in the Great Famine of 1845-50. Whereas the ostensible culprit in the Irish famine was the arrival of potato blight ("*Phytophthora infestans*") to the British Isles and the Continent, the actual causes of the famine are a good deal more complicated. The key factor affecting the food supply was the extreme dependence of the Irish peasantry on the potato (Ó Gráda, *The Great Irish Famine*). This dependence, in turn, was exacerbated by the small size of Irish peasant plots.[4] The potato was the only subsistence crop that could be produced in the peasants' miniscule plots. The arrival of blight effectively destroyed the main food supply for millions of Irish peasants, but this did not necessarily cause starvation. Ireland was a major producer of grain and beef for the British market, and the British government could have acted to divert some of the food destined for export, but it did not.

The reasons why the government failed to alleviate the suffering of the Irish peasants remain the subject of vigorous and partisan controversy.[5] Among the factors that have been held responsible for the failure to relieve starvation are the hegemony of economic liberalism (*laissez-faire*) in England, which inveighed against nearly any government interference in commodity and labour markets; the pervasive anti-Irish racism of the British elite;[6] and fear of Irish nationalism, which previously had encouraged Britain's continental enemies to plan to invade Ireland and use it as a beachhead for a subsequent invasion of Britain.[7]

Just as in the Irish case, there is a good deal of debate about the causes of the Holodomor (the 1932-33 Famine in Ukraine). What is not in doubt, however, is that no biological agent was involved; the famine was an

---

[4] The extreme inequality in Irish landholding has its own history, one that I cannot rehearse here (see Solow).

[5] At the same time, it is important not to underestimate the challenges that the potato famine posed to the English rulers: "To have met the potato famine with anything like a complete success would have been a Herculean task for any government. The total failure of the food of a nation was . . . a fact new in history; such being the case, no machinery existed extensive enough to neutralize its effects, nor was there extant any plan upon which such machinery could be modeled. Great allowance must be therefore made for the shortcomings of the Government, in a crisis so new and so terrible; but after making the most liberal concessions on this head, it must be admitted that Lord John Russell and his colleagues were painfully unequal to the situation. They either could not or would not use all the appliances within their reach, to save the Irish people" (O'Rourke 65).

[6] Thus, the nineteenth-century Cambridge historian Charles Kingsley commented in a letter dated 4 July 1860, on his trip to Ireland: "But I am haunted by the human chimpanzees I saw along that hundred miles of horrible country. I don't believe they are our fault. I believe there are not only many more of them than of old, but they are happier, better, more comfortably fed and lodged under our rule than they ever were. But to see white chimpanzees is dreadful: if they were black, one would not feel it so much, but their skins, except where tanned by exposure, are as white as ours" (Curtis 84).

[7] However, by midcentury the fear of a continental invasion had receded; otherwise, as argued later in this essay, it might have spurred more compassionate policies.

entirely man-made affair caused by official Soviet policy (Plokhy 254). Some Ukrainian writers view it as a genocide instituted by Stalin to punish Ukrainians for anti-Soviet, counter-revolutionary, and nationalist sentiments, whereas others believe that rather than targeted at Ukraine, the Famine was a result of policies designed to maximize grain production for export throughout the USSR and beyond in order to finance rapid industrialization. More specifically, several factors have been suggested as causes of the 1932-33 Famine:

- The rapid introduction of collectivization in Ukraine compared to other regions;
- The high grain quotas placed upon Ukraine;
- The closure of the borders of Ukraine and the North Caucasus to prevent the migration of starving peasants;
- Moscow's unresponsiveness to information concerning the imminence of famine provided by Ukrainian officials in 1932;
- Stalin's suspicions of the Ukrainian peasantry and his fear of "losing Ukraine";
- Draconian measures taken by the Extraordinary Commission in Ukraine in 1932, confiscating grain as well as meat and vegetables, thereby contributing to a food shortage;
- The relative absence of starvation in Russia and Belarus; and
- The assault on the Ukrainian nation, indicated by terror and deportations, the purge of cultural and national leaders, and the cessation of the policy of Ukrainization. (Marples 36)

I have neither the competence nor the inclination to weigh in on debates about whether the Holodomor qualifies as a genocide. What is indisputable in the case of both famines, however, is that the policies of both core states led to continued export from these food-producing regions rather than diversion of food to their starving peasants. This outcome is fully in line with Amartya Sen's influential analysis of the general causes of famine. For Sen, the ultimate causes of famines lie not in the insufficiency of food in a given territory but in the "entitlements" that affect its distribution. Sen regards each individual in the economy as having an endowment consisting of land, labour, and other resources. Each bundle of resources can be transformed into a set of entitlements via exchange. Starvation happens when individuals cannot command the commodity bundles that could keep them alive.[8] This can occur when their endowment collapses (due, for example, to the potato blight in Ireland or to the state's requisitioning of grain and other staples in the USSR), or when the value of their product falls precipitously. For Sen, therefore, the ultimate causes of famine are intrinsically social and political.

In a study of a number of Victorian famines associated with the onset of El Niño conditions, Mike Davis likewise concludes that social and political factors were responsible for famine rather than destructive environmental shocks that hamper food production. For Davis, the real culprits in these environmentally induced famines were capitalists in thrall to the liberal doctrines of *laissez-faire*. In his view, these powerful actors were fanatically opposed to state policies that might have distributed food to the starving, preferring to let the invisible hand have its way—a position not so dissimilar to that currently held by many Republican legislators in the United States with respect to health care, among other issues.

The fly in the ointment, however, is that the great famines of the twentieth century—the Holodomor and other Soviet famines, the 1958-61 famine in Maoist China, Cambodian starvation in the 1970s, and the continuing death from hunger in North Korea—have occurred in command economies, not liberal capitalist ones (Carney). If famines have occurred under both liberal capitalist and state socialist regimes, then neither of these ideologies can be either necessary or sufficient to cause famine. This is not to deny the obvious point that in each case, ideology was used to justify, if not to initiate, the policies that led to starvation. In the Irish case, blaming the popularity of *laissez-faire* for the state's refusal to intervene in the market is an old trope that was first enunciated in John Mitchel's *The Last Conquest of Ireland (Perhaps)*, published in 1860, and later by James Connolly, the principal theorist of Irish nationalism and one of the victims of the Easter Rising.[9] In the USSR, both Stalin's (ostensibly Marxian) commitment to the collectivization of agriculture and his desire to punish

[8] In market economies, such as nineteenth-century Ireland, individuals' exchange entitlements included (1) their ability to find employment (at a given wage and length of time); (2) their ability to sell their non-labour assets; (3) what they could produce from their own labour power and endowments; (4) the cost of attaining resources and the value of the products they could sell; (5) the welfare benefits they were entitled to, and (6) the taxes they had to pay.

[9] Whereas Connolly's views derived from a Marxist analysis, Mitchel's were animated by antipathy to liberalism in all its forms. After escaping to the USA to avoid arrest in Ireland, Mitchel became a strong advocate of the Confederacy and a defender of slavery.

what he considered to be the counter-revolutionary Ukrainians have been presented as justifications for the harsh Soviet policies.[10]

Despite the continuing controversies about the causes of these two famines—much of it politically motivated[11]—the hard truth is that in both cases, alien rulers in London and Moscow refused to suspend the export of grain and other foodstuffs and supply it to starving farmers in culturally distinct peripheries.[12] United Kingdom Prime Minister Tony Blair admitted as much in his 1997 apology to the Irish people:

> That one million people should have died in what was then part of the richest and most powerful nation in the world is something that still causes pain as we reflect on it today. Those who governed in London at the time failed their people through standing by while a crop failure turned into a massive human tragedy. As a consequence, these famines led to massive loss of life and widespread emigration. (Marks)

One implication that can be drawn from these histories is that had Ireland and Ukraine been self-governing rather than subject to alien rule, their political leaders might have taken more steps to relieve the suffering. Unlike alien rulers, native ones generally have greater incentives to be responsive to the grievances of their constituents. In both London and Moscow there was not much sympathy for the fate of the ethnically and linguistically distinct Irish and Ukrainians, and neither periphery had the political capacity required to exercise decisive influence in their respective cores.

---

[10] "Soviets, among them also the Soviets in the national republics, held the real executive power in their hands and linked the party to state apparatus. As long as the Kremlin had full control over these institutions there was no danger of the disintegration of the Soviet Union. If this control were to shift to the regional structures of the Party, for example in case of a crisis in the center, then this threat would become very real indeed. On the grounds of that strong national (non-Soviet) inclination towards traditions of statehood, the Kremlin judged Ukraine to pose the greatest risk" (Kulchytskyi 28).

[11] Some of the politicization is evident in memorials to the famines. Little notice was taken of the centenary of the Irish famine in 1945. "Ireland in 1945 was a country of ration books, looking anxiously at European neighbours menaced by food shortage. It was no time to expend resources on memorialising Famine. By 1995 Ireland was at possibly the most energizing stage of an upward economic trajectory, the eventual unhappy downturn of which was more than a decade away. Ironically, this brave new Ireland was founded on the embrace of an economic strategy that was a latter-day mutant of the political economy once excoriated for turning the failure of the potato crop in the 1840s into a famine. There was little advertence to this irony" (Comerford 67).

[12] Unlike the British state, the USSR did provide some food relief to Ukraine, but it was far from sufficient to prevent mass starvation (Kulchytskyi 28).

The modifier "might" in the preceding paragraph expresses an important caveat, however. Native rulers may be more *motivated* to alleviate famine and stimulate peripheral economic growth than their alien counterparts, but their capacity to do so hinges on the actual *policies* that they enact. If they adopt unsuitable or ill-advised policies, they may do no better than some alien rulers and might even do worse. Take Ireland, for example. Although the leaders of the newly formed Republic clearly sought to promote economic growth following independence in 1922, their antipathy to free trade and foreign direct investment hampered their ability to deliver it. Only after the government liberalized trade and investment policies in the 1990s—a full seven decades after the birth of the Republic—did Irish economic fortunes begin to shoot up (Ó Gráda, *A Rocky Road*).

Rather than viewing these two famines as solely the outcome of ideological commitments to economic liberalism or the malevolent ill will of core state rulers like Stalin, they can also be regarded as tragic by-products of alien rule. There is an overwhelming scholarly consensus that in the best of circumstances alien rule promotes indifference about the welfare of members of peripheral groups; more frequently, it is nakedly exploitative. The reason for alien rulers' exploitative policies lies in their motivations to control or annex these territories in the first place. No one seriously believes that these motivations are altruistic (despite high-flown justifications like the famous French *mission civilisatrice*). Whatever they may say, alien rulers never seek to control or annex territories to make life better for their culturally distinct inhabitants. Instead, they do so for their own instrumental purposes: to help prop up their regimes, to loot resources of land and labour, to provide foodstuffs for their core populations, to open markets for their goods, to foster military expansionism, to increase security, and so forth. Since the whole point of alien rule is to profit the core regime, it can be no surprise that alien rulers could care less about providing good governance to the populations they have expended blood and treasure to conquer.[13]

Yet the historical record also reveals that in a minority of cases alien rulers do manage to provide good governance to their subjects (Hechter, *Alien Rule*). The Genoese Republic's *podesteria* resolved incipient inter-clan conflict and delivered substantially higher economic growth to the city-state for over a century. Similarly, the Chinese Maritime Customs Service (CMCS), a proto-state providing a panoply of public goods in China, propped up a shaky Qing regime and the subsequent republic from the mid-

[13] And their efforts to profit from their colonies extended to all sectors of economic life, including the manipulation of currency systems (Narsey).

nineteenth century to 1949. Lavish American aid and counsel during the postwar occupations of Japan and Germany helped to establish successful and prosperous democracies in these two countries. Finally, as the recent demonstrations against Beijing's interference in the politics of Hong Kong reveal, many people in Hong Kong would prefer alien rule by the British to native rule by Beijing.

If alien rule can have such variable effects, then it is crucial to understand the conditions under which it promotes favourable outcomes. Since this is a question that has hardly ever been asked before, few studies bear upon it. My starting point is to assume that a good part of the answer lies in what the economists refer to as incentive compatibility. A policy is incentive compatible if each party can attain their best outcome merely by acting on the basis of their own true preferences. With respect to core-periphery interaction, the simplest implication is that an optimal policy is one that promotes the welfare of both parties.

At a first approximation, welfare in this sense encapsulates all the state-provided public goods desired by the inhabitants of each region. Take public education as an example of one relevant domain. Whereas residents of the core prefer their children to be educated in the dominant language (English in the United Kingdom; Russian in Ukraine), residents of the periphery may prefer education in their native language (Gaelic in Ireland, Ukrainian in Ukraine). An incentive-compatible policy in this realm, therefore, would give to each region the kind of language instruction that its inhabitants prefer. This outcome is likely to occur when fair and effective governance in the periphery also promotes the welfare of rulers in the core. This raises an obvious question: when do alien rulers profit from promoting good governance in the periphery? Two evident benefits are security and economic growth. If a peripheral territory is valuable to the core and can credibly threaten to secede from it, then cores have an incentive to make concessions—such as enacting good governance—to keep it in the fold (Siroky et al., "Center-Periphery"; Dzutsati).[14] Likewise, if providing good

[14] In general, rulers are likely to offer concessions that increase local autonomy to territories under their control in circumstances where both parties profit. This form of control goes under the umbrella term of "indirect rule" (Mamdani; Hechter, *Containing Nationalism*; Gerring et al.; Naseemullah and Staniland; Siroky et al., "Containing Nationalism"). This principle even came into play during Nazi rule in occupied Europe. In Denmark, for example, the Germans struck a co-operative agreement that allowed the Danes to retain their own government in return for access to Danish food production, airfields, and other goods. This desire to maintain a low-cost form of occupation was largely responsible for saving the lives of a huge proportion of the Danish Jewish population, even after Hitler demanded that they be sent to concentration camps (Lidegaard; see also Futselaar).

governance in the periphery enhances core economic development, then this will also motivate core rulers to promote peripheral welfare. Absent these kinds of inducements, alien rulers have little reason to govern the periphery either effectively or fairly.

What implications does this analysis have for understanding the Irish and Ukrainian famines? Since internal colonies are potential sites for the development of secessionist movements, central authorities are likely to adopt more repressive policies in the periphery than in the core of the state. During the Napoleonic Wars, the British government dreaded the prospect of a French invasion of Ireland—and the French indeed had mounted unsuccessful invasions in 1796 and 1798 to support the rebellious United Irishmen—but by the mid-nineteenth century this concern had waned. In 1932 Stalin, however, did express fear that Ukraine might be ripe for secession, and this might have exacerbated Soviet policy in the Holodomor (Klid and Motyl 239-40). Yet each of these peripheries continued to produce grain and other critical foodstuffs for their alien rulers despite the massive starvation and social dislocation faced by their inhabitants. As a result, both alien rulers could ignore the massive human costs of their policies with relative impunity.

And so they did.

Works Cited

Balandier, Georges. "The Colonial Situation: A Theoretical Approach." *Social Change: The Colonial Situation*, edited by I. Wallerstein, John Wiley & Sons, 1966, pp. 34-61.

Bartlett, Robert. *The Making of Europe: Conquest, Colonization and Cultural Change, 950-1350.* Penguin, 1994.

Biran, Michal. "Periods of Non-Han Rule." *A Companion to Chinese History*, edited by Michael Szonyi, Wiley Blackwell, 2017, pp. 129-42. Wiley-Blackwell Companions to History.

Carney, Judith A. Review of *Late Victorian Holocausts,* by Mike Davis. *Annals of the Association of American Geographers*, vol. 92, no. 1, 2002, pp. 173-75.

Cederman, Lars-Erik, et al. *Inequality, Grievances, and Civil War.* Cambridge UP, 2013.

Chávez, John R. "Aliens in Their Native Lands: The Persistence of Internal Colonial Theory." *Journal of World History*, vol. 22, no. 4, 2011, pp. 785-809.

Comerford, Vincent. "Grievance, Scourge or Shame? The Complexity of Attitudes to Ireland's Great Famine." *Holodomor and Gorta Mór:*

Histories, Memories and Representations of Famine in Ukraine and Ireland, edited by Christian Noack et al., Anthem Press, 2012, pp. 51-73.

Connolly, James. *Labour in Irish History*. Andesite Press, 2017.

Cooper, Frederick. *Colonialism in Question: Theory, Knowledge, History*. California UP, 2005.

Curtis, L. Perry Jr. *Anglo-Saxons and Celts: A Study of Anti-Irish Prejudice in Victorian England.* Conference on British Studies at the University of Bridgeport, distributed by New York UP, 1968. Studies in British History and Culture 2.

Davis, Mike. *Late Victorian Holocausts: El Niño Famines and the Making of the Third World*. Verso, 2001.

Dryzek, John, and Oran Young. "Internal Colonialism in the Circumpolar North: The Case of Alaska." *Development and Change*, vol. 16, no. 1, 1985, pp. 123-45. DOI: 10.1111/j.1467-7660.1985.tb00204.x

Durutalo, Simione. *Internal Colonialism and Unequal Regional Development: The Case of Western Viti Levu, Fiji*. 1985. The University of the South Pacific, PhD dissertation.

Dzutsati, Valery. *Divide and Retreat: Redistribution, Cultural Differences, and International Security as Determinants of Secessionist Violence*. 2017. Arizona State University, PhD dissertation.

Evans, Grant. "Internal Colonialism in the Central Highlands of Vietnam." *Sojourn: Journal of Social Issues in Southeast Asia*, vol. 7, no. 2, 1992, pp. 274-304.

Futselaar, Ralf. *Lard, Lice, and Longevity: The Standard of Living in Occupied Denmark and the Netherlands, 1940-1945*. Aksant, 2008.

Gerring, John, et al. "An Institutional Theory of Direct and Indirect Rule." *World Politics*, vol. 63, no. 3, 2011, pp. 377-433. DOI: 10.1017/S0043887111000104

Gladney, Dru C. "Internal Colonialism and the Uyghur Nationality: Chinese Nationalism and Its Subaltern Subjects." *Cahiers d'Études sur la Méditerranée Orientale et le Monde Turco-Iranien*, vol. 25, 1998, http://journals.openedition.org/cemoti/48. DOI: 10.4000/cemoti.48

Gluckman, Max. "Malinowski's 'Functional' Analysis of Social Change." *Social Change: The Colonial Situation*, edited by I. Wallerstein, John Wiley & Sons, 1966, pp. 25-33.

Hechter, Michael. *Alien Rule*. Cambridge UP, 2013.

---. *Containing Nationalism.* Oxford UP, 2000.

---. "Group Formation and the Cultural Division of Labor." *American Journal of Sociology*, vol. 84, no. 2, 1978, pp. 293-318. DOI: 10.1086/226785

---. *Internal Colonialism: The Celtic Fringe in British National Development, 1536-1966*. U of California P, 1975.

---. "Internal Colonialism Revisited." *New Nationalisms of the Developed West: Toward Explanation*, edited by Edward A. Tiryakian and Ronald Rogowski, George Allen & Unwin, 1985, pp. 17-26.

Hind, Robert J. "The Internal Colonial Concept." *Comparative Studies in Society and History*, vol. 26, no. 3, 1984, pp. 543-68. DOI: 10.1017/S0010417500011130

Klid, Bohdan, and Alexander J. Motyl. *The Holomodor Reader: A Sourcebook on the Famine of 1932-1933 in Ukraine.* Canadian Institute of Ukrainian Studies P, 2012.

Kulchytskyi, Stanislav V. "Holodomor in Ukraine 1932-1933: An Interpretation of Facts." *Holodomor and Gorta Mór: Histories, Memories and Representations of Famine in Ukraine and Ireland*, edited by Christian Noack et al., Anthem Press, 2012, pp. 19-34.

Lawrence, Adria. *Imperial Rule and the Politics of Nationalism: Anti-Colonial Protest in the French Empire*. Cambridge UP, 2014.

Lee, Hock Guan. "Furnivall's Plural Society and Leach's Political Systems of Highland Burma." *Sojourn: Journal of Social Issues in Southeast Asia*, vol. 24, no. 1, 2009, pp. 32-46. DOI: 10.1355/sj24-1c

Lewis, Helen Matthews, et al. *Colonialism in Modern America: The Appalachian Case*. Appalachian Consortium Press, 1978.

Lidegaard, Bo. *Countrymen: The Untold Story of How Denmark's Jews Escaped the Nazis, of the Courage of Their Fellow Danes—and of the Extraordinary Role of the SS*. Translated from Danish by Robert Maass, Alfred A. Knopf, 2013.

Loring, Benjamin. "'Colonizers with Party Cards': Soviet Internal Colonialism in Central Asia." *Kritika: Explorations in Russian and Eurasian History*, vol. 15, no. 1, 2014, pp. 77-102. DOI: 10.1353/kri.2014.0012

Mamdani, Mahmood. *Citizen and Subject: Contemporary Africa and the Legacy of Colonialism*. Princeton UP, 1996.

Marks, Kathie. "Blair Issues Apology for Irish Potato Famine." *The Independent*, 2 June 1997.

Marples, David R. "Ethnic Issues in the Famine of 1932-1933 in Ukraine." *Holodomor and Gorta Mór: Histories, Memories and Representations of Famine in Ukraine and Ireland*, edited by Christian Noack et al., Anthem Press, 2012, pp. 35-50.

McPhee, Peter. "A Case-Study of Internal Colonization: The Francisation of Northern Catalonia." *Review*, vol. 3, no. 3, 1980, pp. 398-428.

McRoberts, Kenneth. *Quebec: Social Change and Political Crisis*. McClelland and Stewart, 1980.

Mettam, Colin W., and Stephen Wyn Williams. "Internal Colonialism and Cultural Divisions of Labour in the Soviet Republic of Estonia." *Nations and Nationalism*, vol. 4, 1998, pp. 363-88. DOI: 10.1111/j.1354-5078.1998.00363.x

Mitchel, John. *Jail Journal*. The Citizen, 1854.

---. *The Last Conquest of Ireland (Perhaps)*. Edited by Patrick Maume, U College Dublin P, 2005.

Narsey, Wadan. *British Imperialism and the Making of Colonial Currency Systems*. Palgrave Macmillan, 2016.

Naseemullah, A., and P. Staniland. "Indirect Rule and Varieties of Governance." *Governance: An International Journal of Policy, Administration, and Institutions*, vol. 29, no. 1, 2016, pp. 13-30. DOI: 10.1111/gove.12129

Ó Gráda, Cormac. *The Great Irish Famine*. Macmillan, 1989.

---. *A Rocky Road: The Irish Economy since the 1920s*. Manchester UP, 1997.

O'Rourke, John. *The History of the Great Irish Famine of 1847, with Notices of Earlier Irish Famines*. McGlashan and Gill / James Duffy and Sons, 1875.

Palmer, Mark, and Robert Rundstrom. "GIS, Internal Colonialism, and the US Bureau of Indian Affairs." *Annals of the Association of American Geographers*, vol. 103, no. 5, 2013, pp. 1142-59. DOI: 10.1080/00045608.2012.720233

Perdue, Peter C. *China Marches West: The Qing Conquest of Central Eurasia*. Belknap Press, 2005.

Pettinicchio, David. "Migration and Ethnic Nationalism: Anglophone Exit and the 'Decolonisation' of Québec." *Nations and Nationalism*, vol. 18, no. 4, 2012, pp. 719-43. DOI: 10.1111/j.1469-8129.2011.00513.x

Plokhy, Serhii. *The Gates of Europe: A History of Ukraine*. Basic Books, 2015.

Reece, J. "Internal Colonialism: The Case of Brittany." *Ethnic and Racial Studies*, vol. 2, no. 3, 1979, pp. 275-92. DOI: 10.1080/01419870.1979.9993269

Sautman, Barry. "Is Xingiang an Internal Colony?" *Inner Asia*, vol. 2, no. 2, 2000, pp. 239-71.

Sen, Amartya. *Poverty and Famines: An Essay on Entitlement and Deprivation*. Cambridge UP, 1981.

Siroky, David S., et al. "Center-Periphery Bargaining in the Age of Democracy." *Swiss Political Science Review*, vol. 22, no. 4, 2016, pp. 439-53. DOI: 10.1111/spsr.12235

Siroky, David S. et al. "Containing Nationalism: Culture, Economics and Indirect Rule in Corsica," *Comparative Political Studies*, 2020. DOI: 10.1177/0010414020957671

Siroky, David S., and Michael Hechter. "Ethnicity, Class, and Civil War: The Role of Hierarchy, Segmentation, and Cross-Cutting Cleavages." *Civil Wars*, vol. 18, no. 1, 2016, pp. 91-107. DOI: 10.1080/13698249.2016.1145178

Solow, Barbara. *The Land Question and the Irish Economy*. Harvard UP, 1971.

Stewart, Frances. *Horizontal Inequalities and Conflict: Understanding Group Violence in Multiethnic Societies*. Palgrave, 2008.

Stone, John, editor. *Internal Colonialism in Comparative Perspective*. Special issue of *Ethnic and Racial Studies*, vol. 2, no. 3, 1979.

von Hagen, Mark. *War in a European Borderland: Occupations and Occupation Plans in Galicia and Ukraine, 1914-1918*. Washington UP, 2007. Donald W. Treadgold Studies on Russia, East Europe, and Central Asia.

Zureik, Elia T. *The Palestinians in Israel: A Study in Internal Colonialism*. Routledge & Kegan Paul, 1979.

Was the Great Irish Famine a Colonial Famine?

Peter Gray
Queen's University Belfast

Abstract: This article reviews the historical debate on the colonial causation and dimensions of the Great Irish Famine of 1845-50. It does so by briefly reviewing the evolution of the colonial relationship between Great Britain and Ireland before focusing on a number of specific fields of debate relating to the coloniality of the Irish famine. These include the economic structures and dynamics developing over the century before 1845 and the vulnerability of Irish society, the vector of the potato blight and its impact on food availability, and, most extensively, the motivations for and characteristics of British state response to the catastrophe. The variant interpretations of these factors in the nationalist, revisionist, post-revisionist, and post-colonial historiography are reviewed. The author concludes by drawing on his own primary research to suggest that, while shaped by colonial stereotypes and a preoccupation with social engineering, the British state and public response to the Irish crisis was varied and not intentionally genocidal, although ultimately subordinating humanitarianism to perceived British national interest. Critical British contemporaries drew negative parallels between the neglect of Ireland and the prioritization of imperial expansion overseas, while Irish nationalists concluded that the mortality of the famine demonstrated the bankruptcy of the British-Irish Union of 1800.

Keywords: Ireland, Britain, Union, potato, Trevelyan, providence.

At first sight, this might appear a rather redundant question—not least in the context of a volume dedicated to exploring the comparative colonial contexts of modern famines. Nevertheless, in the case of the Great Irish Famine of the 1840s, it is a necessary question to pose, not least as the historical literature on the subject, and the historiographical frames of reference to which it relates, are to some extent conflicted on the subject. My purpose in this paper is not to provide a simple yes or no answer, but to investigate the ways in which the Irish famine experience of the nineteenth century can be construed as "colonial" and what the limitations of this interpretation might be.

It is, of course, unquestionable that Ireland had a long-standing colonial relationship with its nearest neighbour, initially the kingdom of England, which sought to extend its authority over the neighbouring island from the late twelfth century, and later the new composite state of Great Britain, which emerged in the early seventeenth century through the union of the crowns of England and Scotland, and was consolidated as the United

Kingdom of Great Britain in 1707. A geographically constrained medieval English colony on the east coast of Ireland was massively expanded and transformed by a series of wars, suppressed rebellions, land confiscations, and legal consolidation between the 1530s and 1690s. These wars occurred in the context of the European wars of religion and sometimes took the form of an overt Protestant crusade against the perceived threat of "Catholic power" in Ireland and the risk this might pose to the British state. This process resulted not only in the projection of imperial authority from London over the whole island, but the substantive (if never universal) replacement of both the Catholic indigenous and old-colonial landowning elite by a "new English" and emphatically Protestant ascendancy of landowners, reinforced in the early eighteenth century by a series of penal laws intended to induce further conversions from the old elites and keep Catholicism permanently subordinated politically and socially. To provide a garrison against insurrection and revive an economy devastated by war and depopulation, plantations of English and Scottish Protestant settlers were attempted in several regions, although this only proved successful in terms of producing a demographic majority in the north-eastern counties of Ulster, closest to Scotland.[1]

A number of Irish historians, Nicholas Canny most prominently, have drawn parallels between this early modern re-conquest and colonization of Ireland and the British Atlantic colonial expansion that paralleled it. Similarly, from the late seventeenth century, the Irish economy was formally subordinated to an English (later British) mercantilist system that restricted its ability to export certain products (such as woollens) and its entitlement to trade directly with colonies within the empire. While these commercial restrictions did not ultimately inhibit the massive growth of Ireland's two major export commodities in the eighteenth century-manufactured linen (exempt from legislative impediments) and animal products—and later grain crops, they were a source of political resentment in contemporary Ireland and of much debate in subsequent economic history.

While thus apparently colonial in its political and economic relations with Great Britain, and in its internal social structures, there were at the same time certain ambiguities. Over the course of the eighteenth century, a significant section of the landed Protestant elite came to articulate a "patriotic" opposition to British policies that assumed or sought to enforce Ireland's continuing colonial and mercantile inferiority: political and quasi-military mobilization against such grievances from the late 1770s led to a

[1] See recent surveys of the period from 1540 to 1800 by Jane Ohlmeyer and Ultán Gillen in Bourke and McBride (21-73).

staged withdrawal from direct policy subordination by the British government (although informal political control over the Irish parliament was reasserted from the mid-1780s). Unlike the American "patriots," their Irish counterparts rejected the "colonial" construction of Ireland's constitutional position and insisted that it was in fact an ancient "sister kingdom" of Great Britain, with its parliament (also of medieval origin) ideally embodying that status. This assertion of Ireland's non-colonial character in the eighteenth century was polemical and directed against explicitly colonial policy from London. It was carried forward into the nineteenth-century Irish nationalist tradition, combining with older Catholic traditions that also constructed Ireland as an ancient European kingdom, now seeking the restoration of its rightful constitutional autonomy through "Repeal of the Union" or "Home Rule." At the same time, some modern Irish historians have given it some justification, with Sean Connolly, for example, arguing that eighteenth-century Ireland fitted better into a European "*ancien régime*" frame of reference (with parallels with central and eastern Europe) than that of classic colonialism (Connolly).

The constitutional relationship between the two countries changed fundamentally in 1800, with the passage of the Irish Act of Union, abolishing the separate Irish Parliament and transferring its representation to the newly enlarged Parliament of the United Kingdom of Great Britain and Ireland. Ireland thus became officially an integral part of the metropolitan state (the only part of the British Empire to be thus incorporated). Following the Union, it lost its separate currency and exchequer, but retained a subordinate government at Dublin Castle, which continued to be appointed by Westminster, and its own legal administration. Initially excluded from representation in the Union parliament and from major offices under the Crown, after a major political mobilization led by the charismatic lawyer-politician Daniel O'Connell, Irish Catholics were politically "emancipated" in 1829, albeit within the constraints of high property qualifications for both the franchise and admission to parliament.

Constitutionally, then, Ireland by the 1840s was a hybrid entity, a "kingdom" united with and having representation in the imperial centre, but retaining the structural legacies of its previous colonial subordination. It also featured a large and well-organized nationalist movement, which rejected the legitimacy of the Union, resented the economic and religious privileges of the descendants of the settler elite, and demanded the restoration of political autonomy under a more representative franchise. Attempts by British liberals to integrate the Catholic elite into the British body politic in the 1830s and 1840s (at the expense of some alienation of the Protestant landed elite) were of limited success, while the great bulk of the peasant population remained disaffected or at best indifferent toward the state as well as the landlord class (Geoghegan). As I have argued elsewhere, much of the public debate about Ireland's "colonial" status in this period centred on the continuing existence of the office of lord lieutenant or "viceroy" as head of the Irish government ("'Ireland's Last Fetter'"). Paradoxically, it was British radicals and in 1850 the governing Whig party that sought its abolition as a colonial vestige symbolizing Ireland's incomplete incorporation into the British body politic, while Catholic nationalists defended it as an emblem of separate historic statehood (Gray, "'Ireland's Last Fetter'"). Tellingly, despite these rather abstract controversies, the ultimate decision to retain it rested on security considerations: the necessity of retaining a British authority figure in Dublin with military powers reflected a degree of colonial anxiety on the part of the establishment about the legitimacy of British rule and the challenges posed by revolutionary nationalist movements and agrarian rebellion (Gray, "'Ireland's Last Fetter'").

Thus, sketching the nature of the colonial (perhaps better described as quasi-colonial) nature of Irish-British constitutional relationships in this period is of limited value. The question of the relationship between colonialism and the famine needs to be refined—and to do so I will divide it up into the following areas for investigation: the socio-economic structures in existence in 1845; trigger mechanisms of famine in Ireland; and the determinants of state response—to what extent did these embody "colonial" mentalities and calculations and to what extent other ideological and pragmatic forces? Finally, I will explore the colonial impact and reactions to Irish famine in the wider British empire.

There remains a debate within Irish economic history about the extent to which the legacies of aggressive colonial economic policies, especially of the seventeenth and eighteenth centuries, created continuing socio-economic structures that rendered Ireland particularly vulnerable to famine. While older nationalist readings attributed all weaknesses in the economy to colonialism or the denial of national autonomy or independence, "revisionist" economic historians in Ireland in the 1960s and after set out to challenge this. Louis Cullen, in his general economic history of modern Ireland published in 1972, questioned this nationalist determinism, drawing attention to growth sectors in the pre-famine Irish economy and the country's ability to exploit colonial opportunities (such as the transatlantic provision trade and later the export market in linens). Even for the period after the economic shocks brought on by the end of inflated wartime conditions from 1814-15, these historians would stress the variegated nature of the pre-famine economy, not only in the successful industrialization of the north-east, but the modernization and commercialization of agriculture in the east and around Dublin (Cullen). One member of this revisionist group, Liam Kennedy, has been the most outspoken in rejecting the validity of any colonial or post-colonial frame of reference for interpreting the modern Irish past. Kennedy observed that evidence for such a relationship, especially as it related to economic history, was at best elusive, "despite the length of the Irish-English connection and the wealth of historical materials" (109). This rather sweeping rejection appears to have been part of a wider reaction to the dominant place acquired by the 1990s of often rather reductionist post-colonial models in Irish literary and cultural studies and their application to contemporary political controversies, especially relating to the Northern Irish conflict (see Howe).

The more econometrically minded historians who have dominated Irish economic history since the 1980s, most prominently Joel Mokyr and Cormac Ó Gráda, have differed from the revisionists in robustly rejecting any neo-Malthusian reading of Irish vulnerability in the early nineteenth century, but have nevertheless tended to avoid overt colonial models of explanation for the underlying causes of famine. Mokyr's seminal monograph *Why Ireland Starved* restricts its frame of reference to the half century before 1845. He stresses such factors as entrepreneurial failure, the collapse of proto-industrialization due to factory-based competition, and limited capital formation in Ireland as causes of economic weakness, exacerbated by Ireland's status as a "small open economy" by the middle decades of the century. However, Mokyr downplays the role of government economic policies in bringing this about. His point of comparison is not the British Empire, but the experience of another European country—the Netherlands (Mokyr). Ó Gráda, for his part, characterizes the Irish agricultural economy as underdeveloped in contrast to England and lowland Scotland, but not in comparison to most of central, eastern and southern Europe (indeed Ireland's indices for literacy, urbanization, and industrial employment were above European averages for the early 1840s). His argument tends to stress the contingency of Irish socio-economic vulnerability in the period (and its concentration in certain districts and among the labouring poor) rather than identifying any elements of inevitability arising from either population pressure or colonialism. At the same time, both Ó Gráda and Mokyr would, to a much greater extent than the revisionists, identify state failure in response to the famine crisis as a serious causal factor in explaining mass excess mortality, and both are open to investigating the applicability of Amartya Sen's theory of entitlement-related vulnerability to the Irish case.

Two groups of scholars have more recently sought to revive a more colonial mode of explanation for famine causation in Ireland. Firstly, there is a group of Irish historical geographers, including David Nally, whose recent book *Human Encumbrances* attempts to apply the Foucauldian notion of colonial biopolitics to famine causation and response in 1840s Ireland. The eminent geographer William J. Smyth at University College Cork, central to the team that produced the core sections of the *Atlas of the Great Irish Famine* in 2012, stresses "*longue durée*" structures of colonial governance in explaining the events of 1845-50. In the *Atlas*, both Smyth and Nally trace long-term weaknesses in the economy to the early modern colonial period, the devastation of war, and the reconstruction of Ireland as an extractive agrarian producer, tied to English demand (Smyth; Nally, "The Colonial Dimensions"). Both the established economic historians and political historians of British governance of 1840s Ireland might quibble with the tendency towards reductionism and an assumption that certain policy agendas were inherently "colonial" in these interpretations, but they are welcome in doing much to re-introduce the debate about the colonial back into the historiography of the Great Famine. The other group seeking to do so, although perhaps without the same degree of critical impact, are the cluster of Marxist-leaning economists, sociologists, and literary critics associated with Terrence McDonough, who contributed to the provocatively titled collection *Was Ireland a Colony?* in 2005. The economic discussion in this book offers a much more negative picture of economic development than that of the mainstream economic historians, utilizing dependency theory and Marxist analysis to stress the continuing post-mercantilist subordination of the Irish economy to the British and the continuation of feudal social relations as characteristic of the Irish countryside (McDonough).

I turn now to the trigger mechanisms leading to the onset and continuation of famine conditions in 1840s Ireland. The central role of the potato blight ("*Phytophthora infestans*") in devastating the subsistence crop of the rural poor, directly or indirectly over five consecutive harvests from 1845 to 49, is not contested by those posing nationalist or post-colonial critiques of the dominant economic narrative. For econometric historians, this was the exogenous shock, essentially unforeseeable and unpredictable, that threw a vulnerable economic system and impoverished social groups within it into a catastrophic crisis. The scale of the blight's impact on agricultural production and calorific availability was stressed initially by Austin Bourke in a series of publications from the 1970s, and most tellingly by the American economic historian Peter Solar in his 1989 article "The Great Famine Was No Ordinary Subsistence Crisis," which makes a strong case for a real food availability decline crisis, at least in 1845-47.

Identifying a clearly colonial dimension to this epiphenomenon is difficult, beyond highlighting the structural factor of the acute levels of potato dependency potentially consequent on the subordination of the Irish agrarian economy to British demand for imported grain. If the potato arrived in Ireland through colonial exchanges (it was allegedly first introduced by Sir Walter Raleigh on the estate granted to him as part of the sixteenth-century plantation of Munster), it was not until the later eighteenth century, and as a consequence of the rapid and under-capitalized boom in grain cash-cropping for export, that it began to acquire a dangerously high level of dominance in the diet of labourers and poor peasants. However, the fatal blight that arrived from the Americas in 1845 came as the consequence of global capitalist exchanges in seed potatoes (arriving in Ireland via Belgium and England) rather than through any mechanism specific to Ireland.

Instead of contesting the blight as the harbinger of famine, both nationalists and those seeking to trace a colonial interpretation of causation for mass mortality and associated radical social restructuring, have focused on government response to the crisis triggered by the blight, rather than on the disease itself. At its most extreme, as articulated by the exiled revolutionary nationalist John Mitchel in 1860 (and echoed by his followers ever since), "The Almighty, indeed, sent the potato blight, but the English created the famine" (219). This "Mitchelite" interpretation posited both a genocidal intent on the part of the British government and a mechanism for bringing it about—the forced export of the alleged "superabundance" of other foodstuffs produced in Ireland that, if retained, would have been sufficient to prevent a famine threatened by potato failure (see Donnelly). Although it remains resilient in popular historical writing to the present, the economic case for this was undermined through painstaking analysis of export/import patterns and the calorific value of foodstuffs available in Ireland by Solar (see also Coogan). This does not, however, preclude an investigation into the ideological preoccupations underpinning food policy in the later 1840s, or the possibility that some greater retention of the export surplus (if this had been accompanied by an effective distribution policy) could not have made a significant difference in mortality rates, especially in the "hunger winter" of 1846-47.

Within more solidly grounded historical writing, the debate over famine policy, its motivations, and its consequences continues to veer between, on one side, the argument for a coherent and rigorously pursued ideological agenda of "colonial biopolitics," as proposed by Nally in *Human Encumbrances* and supported from a more nationalist perspective by Christine Kinealy, and, on the other side, neo-liberal apologias for the government and its operatives offered by Robin Haines in her tome on the Treasury administrator Charles Trevelyan. More recently, the latter position has been enhanced by an attribution of government failure as almost entirely due to the external constraints set by the London money markets in a period of fiscal crisis, as argued by Charles Read.

Rather than give a detailed analysis of the literature on this complex and contested field, I will summarize my own conclusions on the subject, with particular emphasis on the question to what extent policy can be seen as "colonial" and in what ways. Firstly, and perhaps most importantly, it should be recalled that the government in office for most of the Famine period, that of Whig party leader Lord John Russell, was weak (with a minority of votes in parliament), internally factionalized, and buffeted by external crises, including not just the potato blight, but a British fiscal and industrial crisis in 1847, and the European revolutions of 1848. This weakness rendered the administration particularly susceptible to shifts in articulated public opinion, especially in the metropolis, and voiced through the major London newspapers. While at certain times the press and middle-class public could express a remarkable degree of humanitarian concern for the plight of famine-sufferers in Ireland (as manifest in the large amounts collected for charitable relief in early 1847), at other times—and increasingly as the famine lengthened—this could degenerate into antagonistic and racialized stereotyping and an insistence that "natural causes" should take their effect in Ireland. The conflicting responses and swings of opinion are worthy of attention, but fundamentally the collapse of sympathy for Ireland and the Irish was grounded in long-standing prejudices in England that rendered it too easy to "other" the Irish and deny any common "British" characteristics or entitlements to them as citizens of what was (after 1800) nominally a United Kingdom (Gray, "The Great British Famine"). As the prime minister himself observed following the UK general election of August 1847, it was "very difficult to please England, Scotland and Ireland at the same time—we have in the opinion of Great Britain done too much for Ireland and have lost elections for doing so. In Ireland the reverse."[2]

In addition to the hostile effusions toward the "barbarous" Irish from organs such as the London *Times*, there were clearly ideological preoccupations evident within the administration, if by no means shared, or shared with equal intensity, by all ministers and administrators. *Laissez-faire* ideas had paramountcy, if checked in some policy areas and at some times by arguments that exceptional circumstances prevailed in Ireland that should permit some limited deviance from "orthodox" political economy. In itself, *laissez-faire* was not an inherently colonialist position (a similar non-interventionist policy had been adopted in England and

[2] Russell to Clarendon, 2 Aug. 1847, Bodleiean Library, Oxford, Clar. dep. Ir., box 43.

Scotland in response to the acute unemployment crisis and hunger, albeit not famine, of 1842-43), although it might be argued it was deployed as such if used in a discriminatory fashion against Ireland or with inadequate consideration for its inapplicability to Irish conditions.

Although evident in *Times* leading articles and in some (although, interestingly, not all) treatments of the Irish crisis in the political caricatures of the satirical journal *Punch*, overtly racialized language was rarely employed in governmental public and private discourses in the 1840s. In one of the few extant occasions in which such language was used, the lord lieutenant of Ireland, Lord Clarendon, wrote to the prime minister in August 1847 making an explicit colonial parallel: "Esquimaux and New Zealanders [i.e. Maoris] are more thrifty and industrious than these people who deserve to be left to their fate instead of the hardworking people of England being taxed for their support."[3] Despite this outburst, however, Clarendon's subsequent interventions were to demand increased relief spending in Ireland, which bore almost no fruit, and to denounce the mean-spiritedness of Treasury policy. His warnings in late 1848 that "the religion and charity of John Bull [i.e. England] will in the end revolt" against the deadly consequences of inaction, led him to endorse Irish fury against "C[harles] Wood and Trevelyan who sit coolly watching and applauding what they call 'the operation of natural causes.'"[4] In the wake of the failure of his proposed scheme of "remedial measures" to provide employment schemes and assisted emigration in Ireland, the prime minister could only lament that in his opinion it was less the "crude Trevelyanism" of the Treasury than the hostility to further aid expenditure lying "deep in the breasts of the British people" that ruled out further interventions.[5]

Russell was personally a weak premier, and it seems clear that the centre of gravity in Irish famine policy from 1846 lay principally with the Treasury, headed administratively by Charles Edward Trevelyan (the "*bête noire*" of so much popular historiography of the Irish Famine) and his political superior, the Chancellor of the Exchequer, Sir Charles Wood. The private and public correspondence and publications of both (and their allies) indicate a strong ideological drive that combined with elements of pragmatism to shape policy. To what extent was this "Trevelyanism" lamented by Clarendon colonialist in character? Trevelyan, who had previously served in British India, was himself certainly conscious of the existence of racialized prejudice concerning Ireland in much of British

---

[3] Clarendon to Russell, 10 Aug. 1847, Bodleiean Library, Oxford, Clarendon letterbooks.

[4] Clarendon to Russell, 6 Dec. 1848, Bodleiean Library, Oxford, Clarendon letterbook 3.

[5] Russell to Clarendon, 8 Dec. 1848, 24 Feb. 1849, Bodleiean Library, Oxford, Clar. Dep. Ir., box 43, box 26.

public opinion. However, he disliked the *Times'* attacks on the racial deficiencies of the "Celts" and confided that, given his Cornish ancestry,

I myself boast to be of Celtic origin; I have always regarded with peculiar interest the Celtic branch of our national family. However superior the German race may be in some points, I would not have Ireland Anglo-Saxon if I could; and it has always appeared to me, that in the infinitely varied distribution of the rich gifts of Providence, the Celtic race has no reason to complain of its share.[6]

At the same time, he regularly and vehemently denounced the "defective part of the national character" of Ireland as the root social cause of the famine there. This he connected not to the Gaelic/Celtic origins of the bulk of the peasantry nor to the Catholicism of the majority, but to a spirit of dependency on the state and reluctance to engage in self-help that infected society as a whole. While the peasant needed to be educated in work discipline, the principal target of Trevelyan's invective, and arguably of the policy instruments he advocated and sought to control, were the "nobility and gentry" of Ireland, the class he held to be morally and practically responsible for the underdeveloped and socially backward state of Irish society and, hence, of its fatal potato dependency. This target group (accepted as such by much of British liberal opinion in the 1840s) was, of course, overwhelmingly British and "Anglo-Saxon" in origin. A deeply religious man, Trevelyan sincerely believed that divine providence had intervened through the potato blight to bring a "blessing" to Ireland by revealing the corruption of its social and moral constitution and initiating a "social revolution" that would see the landowners either shoulder their legitimate burden of the costs of relief and reconstruction or be swept away themselves through bankruptcy and "free trade in land."[7]

This was the repeated refrain of his relentlessly "optimistic" apologia for government policy in Ireland, published as *The Irish Crisis* in early 1848 (a text which was approved by the government, but is, in my opinion, unquestionably Trevelyan's own in tone and argument). The concluding section, setting out his conviction that the era of Ireland's previous colonial subjection to Britain was past and that the famine was achieving the final social assimilation of the two societies under the Union, is worth quoting at length:

Our humble but sincere conviction is, that the appointed time of Ireland's regeneration is at last come. For several centuries we were in a

---

[6] Trevelyan to S. Spring Rice, 10 Nov. 1846, Bodleiean Library, Oxford, Trevelyan letterbooks, vol. 9.

[7] See Trevelyan to Monteagle, 9 Oct. 1846, NLI, Monteagle Papers, Ms 13,397; Gray, "Ideology and the Famine."

state of open warfare with the native Irish, who were treated as foreign enemies, and were not admitted to the privileges and civilizing influences of the English law, even when they most desired it . . . . Now, thank God, we are in a different position; and although many waves of disturbance must pass over us before that troubled sea can entirely subside, and time must be allowed for morbid habits to place to a more healthy action, England and Ireland are, with one great exception, subject to equal laws; and so far as the maladies of Ireland are traceable to political causes, nearly every practical remedy has been applied. The deep and inveterate root of social evil remained, and this has been laid bare by a direct stroke of an all-wise and all-merciful Providence, as if this part of the case were beyond the unassisted power of man . . . . God grant that the generation to which this great opportunity has been offered may rightly perform its part, and that we may not relax our efforts until Ireland fully participates in the social health and physical prosperity of Great Britain, which will be the true consummation of their union! (Trevelyan 199-201)

Trevelyan's opinions were delusional both respecting the likely political consequences of the famine and in seeking to impose a utopian liberal social transformation on a country prostrated by the destruction of the staple food of over half its population. The policy he endorsed involved a transfer of responsibility for mass mortality from the state to the recalcitrant landlord class, while at the same time permitting that class to uproot from the soil hundreds of thousands of the "surplus population" of peasants through land clearances in the latter stages of the famine. Obsessed with imposing his vision of reconstructing Irish society in the name of national integration (I have elsewhere characterized the dominant policy as amounting to an attempted "capitalist cultural revolution"), Trevelyan and the government he served permitted hundreds of thousands who might have been saved by more interventionist relief policy, to die from neglect (Gray, *Famine, Land, and Politics* 331).

In conclusion, we return to the question to what extent was the Irish Famine "colonial"? In terms of policy, the question was posed most starkly at the time by the conservative and later nationalist Irish politician Isaac Butt: had the famine occurred at Cornwall rather than Cork, would the government have responded in similar fashion ("The Famine in the Land")? His conclusion that Ireland was being denied the benefits of the Union led him to question the value of the British connection (Butt, *The Rate in Aid*). However, as a counterfactual, no definitive answer can be given. On the one hand, government policy toward the contemporaneous potato famine in the Scottish Highlands and Islands differed little from Irish policy. On the other hand, the smaller scale of the crisis, the proportionately much greater and long-lasting charitable transfers from industrial to impoverished rural districts, and the ability and willingness of Scottish landowners to comply with government demands that they feed, employ, and (more typically) assist to emigrate their cottar tenants, led to a quite different outcome in terms of mortality (Devine). The spirit of the 1834 new English poor law, with its emphasis on less eligibility, was not dissimilar to the Irish poor law in intent and sparked widespread social resistance in northern working-class districts.

However, what rendered Ireland different was the continuing colonial context in which policy was enacted and the continuing legacy of the deep social structures created by previous colonial practice (too readily dismissed as redundant by Trevelyan and his allies). British working-class radicals (the Chartists) sought entry into the British political nation on equal terms; Irish nationalists (whether constitutionalist or revolutionary) rejected the legitimacy of Ireland's incorporation into the Union and regarded it as emblematic of the country's continuing subordination. Whether, as has often been claimed, a self-governing Ireland would inevitably have dealt more effectively with the famine crisis is an open question (the policies of self-governing Netherlands in the 1840s and autonomous Finland when faced with devastating famine in 1867-68 raise serious doubts about this) (Gray, "Famine Relief"; Newby).

However, in this governing context, and given the continuing use of British military force under viceregal authority to repress both revolutionary nationalist threats and agrarian social violence in the later 1840s, state policy could not but be construed as colonial in nature. Had that policy been benign (and there were indeed some episodes of humanitarian response, most notably in the brief episode of relief via state famine kitchens, which fed over three millions daily in summer 1847), this might have passed unnoticed. However, when the policies of the latter stages of the famine were denounced by one of the government's senior poor-law administrators as amounting to "one of extermination," it is inevitable that they should have been so inscribed in Irish memory.[8] We might leave the last word to that official, Edward Twisleton, who in evidence to a parliamentary committee in 1849 lamented that the county had failed to spare itself "the deep disgrace of permitting any of our miserable fellow subjects . . . to die of starvation." Referring to the expense and bloodshed involved in the contemporaneous expansion of Britain's Indian domains, he pointed to the humanitarian failure in Ireland and concluded, "of how much less permanent importance is the conquest of

---

[8] Clarendon to Russell, 12 Mar. 1849, Bodleiean Library, Oxford, Clarendon Letterbook 5.

Scinde or the Punjaub for the greatness of the Empire!"[9] The British state's abject failure to deploy its full resources to alleviate Irish famine (and, later, Indian famines of 1866, 1876-79, 1896-99, 1899-1900 and 1943-44) thus was due in part to colonial stereotyping and attempted social engineering, but unlike a number of twentieth-century cases, was not genocidal in intent.

Works Cited

Bourke, Austin. *The Visitation of God? The Potato Blight and the Great Irish Famine.* Lilliput Press, 1993.

Bourke, Richard, and Ian McBride, editors. *The Princeton History of Modern Ireland.* Princeton UP, 2016.

Butt, Isaac. "The Famine in the Land. What Has Been Done and What Is to Be Done." *Dublin University Magazine,* vol. 29, April 1847, pp. 501-40.

---. *The Rate in Aid: A Letter to the Right Honourable The Earl of Roden.* McGlashan, 1849.

Canny, Nicholas. *Kingdom and Colony: Ireland in the Atlantic World, 1560-1800.* Johns Hopkins UP, 1988.

Connolly, Sean J. *Religion, Law and Power: The Making of Protestant Ireland, 1660*-1760. Clarendon Press, 1992.

Coogan, Tim Pat. *The Famine Plot: England's Role in Ireland's Greatest Tragedy.* St. Martin's Press, 2012.

Cullen, Louis M. *An Economic History of Ireland since 1600.* B. T. Batsford, 1972.

Devine, T. M. *The Great Highland Famine: Hunger, Emigration, and the Scottish Highlands in the Nineteenth Century.* John Donald, 1988.

Donnelly, James. "The Construction of the Memory of the Famine in Ireland and the Irish Diaspora, 1850-1900." *Éire-Ireland,* vol. 31, no. 1, 1996, pp. 26-61. DOI: 10.1353/eir.1996.0002

Geoghegan, Patrick M. "The Impact of O'Connell, 1815-1850." *The Cambridge History of Ireland,* vol. III, *1730-1880,* edited by James Kelly, Cambridge UP, 2018, pp. 102-27.

Gray, Peter. *Famine, Land, and Politics: British Government and Irish Society, 1843-50.* Irish Academic P, 1999.

[9] Edward Twisleton's evidence, *Second report of the select committee of the house of lords, appointed to inquire into the operation of the Irish poor law,* HC 1849 (228), xvi, 717; Twisleton to Clarendon, 10 Mar. 1849, Bodleiean Library, Oxford, Clar. Dep. Ir., box 29.

---. "Famine Relief Policy in Comparative Perspective: Ireland, Scotland, and North-Western Europe, 1845-1849." *Éire-Ireland*, vol. 32, no. 1, 1997, pp. 86-108.

---. "'The Great British Famine of 1845 to 1850'? Ireland, the UK and Peripherality in Famine Relief and Philanthropy." *Famines in European Economic History: The Last Great European Famines Reconsidered*, edited by D. Curran et al., Routledge, 2015, pp. 83-96.

---. "Ideology and the Famine." *The Great Irish Famine: The Thomas Davis Lectures*, edited by Cathal Póirtéir, Mercier Press, 1995, pp. 86-103.

---. "'Ireland's Last Fetter Struck Off': The Lord Lieutenancy Debate, 1800-67." *Was Ireland a Colony? Economics, Politics, and Culture in Nineteenth-Century Ireland*, edited by T. McDonough, Irish Academic P, 2005, pp. 87-101.

Haines, Robin. *Charles Trevelyan and the Great Irish Famine*. Four Courts Press, 2004.

Howe, Stephen. *Ireland and Empire: Colonial Legacies in Irish History and Culture*. Oxford UP, 2000.

Kennedy, Liam. "Colonial and Post-Colonial Models." *Oxford Companion to Irish History*, edited by S. J. Connolly, Oxford UP, 2002, p. 109.

Kinealy, Christine. *A Death-Dealing Famine: The Great Hunger in Ireland*. Pluto Press, 1997.

McDonough, Terrence, editor. *Was Ireland a Colony? Economics, Politics and Culture in Nineteenth-Century Ireland*. Irish Academic P, 2005.

Mitchel, John. *The Last Conquest of Ireland (Perhaps)*. Cameron Ferguson, 1860.

Mokyr, Joel. *Why Ireland Starved: A Quantitative and Analytical History of the Irish Economy, 1800-50*. Allen & Unwin, 1983.

Nally, David P. "The Colonial Dimensions of the Great Irish Famine." *Atlas of the Great Irish Famine*, edited by J. Crowley et al., Cork UP, 2012, pp. 64-74.

---. *Human Encumbrances: Political Violence and the Great Irish Famine*. Notre Dame UP, 2011.

Newby, Andrew. "'Neither Do These Tenants or Their Children Emigrate': Famine and Transatlantic Emigration from Finland in the Nineteenth Century." *Atlantic Studies*, vol. 11, no. 3, 2014, pp. 382-402. DOI: 10.1080/14788810.2014.899116

Ó Gráda, Cormac. *The Great Irish Famine*. Cambridge UP, 1995.

Read, Charles. "Laissez-faire, the Irish Famine, and British Financial Crisis." *Economic History Review*, vol. 69, no. 2, 2016, pp. 411-34. DOI: 10.1111/ehr.12274

Smyth, William J. "The Longue Durée: Imperial Britain and Colonial Ireland." *Atlas of the Great Irish Famine*, edited by J. Crowley et al., Cork UP, 2012, pp. 46-63.

Solar, Peter. "The Great Famine Was No Ordinary Subsistence Crisis." *Famine: The Irish Experience, 900-1900*, edited by E. Margaret Crawford, John Donald, 1989, pp. 112-29.

Trevelyan, Charles. *The Irish Crisis*. Longman, Brown, Green & Longmans, 1848.

The 1958-62 Chinese Famine and Its Impact on Ethnic Minorities

Lucien Bianco
L'École des Hautes Études en Sciences Sociales

Abstract: China underwent its most murderous famine between 1958 and 1962. Although a demographic transition from the countryside to the cities was in its early stage and gross domestic product (GDP) per capita was among the lowest in the world, objective conditions were far less decisive than Chinese Communist Party (CCP) policies in bringing about the famine. A development strategy copied on the Soviet model favoured quick industrialization at the expense of rural dwellers. Such novelties as people's communes, communal canteens, and backyard furnaces further aggravated the famine. Though ethnic minorities represented only 6 percent of China's population, compared to forty-seven percent in the Soviet Union, Soviet nationality policies heavily influenced those of China. Initially mild, especially for Tibetans, Chinese nationality policies became more authoritarian with the advent of the Great Leap Forward in 1958. Qinghai Tibetans resisted the closure of many monasteries; then the same policies, and famine itself, caused a more important rebellion in 1959 in Xizang (Tibet). Repression and the flight of the Dalai Lama to northern India coincided with the end of Tibet's special status in China.

Internal colonialism did not, however, aggravate the impact of famine on national minorities in China. Their rate of population growth between the first two censuses (1953 and 1982) exceeded that of Han Chinese. Among the provinces most severely affected by famine, only Qinghai was largely inhabited by ethnic minorities. Within Qinghai the same pattern prevailed as in Han populated provinces: the highest toll in famine deaths was concentrated in easily accessible grain surplus areas. The overwhelming majority of victims of the Chinese famine were Han peasants. At most, 5 percent were members of ethnic minorities, compared to eighty percent of victims in the Soviet Union in the period between 1930 and 1933.

Keywords: famine, China, national minorities, Tibetans, Qinghai.

I. The Famine in China

The most murderous famine in human history killed between 20 and 40 million people in China between 1958 and 1962.[1] Although the most murderous in absolute terms, it killed fewer people in

[1] Estimates of excess mortality vary between 15 and 46 million, the most frequent being in the 30-36 million range. See, among others, Yang, *Tombstone* 427-30.

proportion to the total population than did the Khmer famines in Cambodia between 1975 and 1979 (Ó Gráda 24), and many fewer than the 1930-33 famine in Kazakhstan and the 1932-33 Holodomor in Ukraine (Rudnytskyi et al.). The overall proportion of famine deaths in the Soviet Union in 1930-33 was slightly less, given that China's population in 1958 was roughly four times that of the USSR in the early 1930s (Bianco 125).[2]

During the worst years of the Chinese famine (1959-61), some starving people extended their lives by a few weeks—or hastened their deaths—by eating anything at hand—by cutting up carrion flesh, fishing dead rats out of cesspits, or eating a mixture of earth and weeds called "Guanyin's earth" (after the goddess of mercy) that filled their stomachs before blocking their intestines completely, because it could be neither digested nor evacuated. Others ate flesh from dead bodies found along the roadside. Nor did people refrain from eating members of their own families who had died at home. Sometimes they even killed them. Children were not allowed to go out for fear they could be killed; there were cases where mothers strangled, cut up, and boiled their own children, some having lost their minds. Rather than eating their own children, people would exchange their children with children of their neighbours, each surviving thanks to the other's offspring. In one district in Anhui, an especially badly hit province, this was not a rare practice and was called "*yi zi er chi*" ("exchanging children for eating").[3]

Pretexts and Valid Excuses for Famine

The Chinese Communists first hid the famine and later referred to 1959-61 as the "three bad years," using natural disasters as an explanation for the death toll. Some regions of the country did suffer from bad weather in 1959 and 1961, and others experienced a drought in 1960, but one author (Jisheng Yang) found that within a 27-year period (1956-83), eleven years of bad weather conditions and even natural disasters affected more regions than in 1959-60 without causing famine, or even a noteworthy drop in cereal production (*Tombstone* 452-56). What is true is that agriculture was vulnerable to vagaries in the weather—agricultural production, being highly unstable because it depended on rainfall, was unreliable enough for the government to be able to blame the famine on natural causes.

Another excuse for the death toll pointed to Nikita Khrushchev, who recalled the Soviet experts in China in the summer of 1960. Putting aside the fact that Mao Zedong, Chairman of the People's Republic of China (PRC),

---

[2] See my comparison of the Soviet and Chinese famines in Bianco 125-66.

[3] The expression "exchanging children for eating" had been in use for centuries, so much so that it may have been more often spoken than actually implemented.

had done everything possible to provoke that recall, it had practically no impact on agricultural production. There were indeed very few agronomists among the Soviet specialists, and Khrushchev had twice offered to send help but was haughtily turned down (Dikötter 111).

The one argument that would have carried some weight was not mentioned by Chinese propaganda, namely, a demographic transition that was still in its early stages, with fertility rates at high levels and mortality rates falling rapidly. Mortality was falling far more quickly in China than it had during the first decade of the Soviet rule, if only because the fight against infectious diseases worldwide was far more effective in the 1950s than in the 1920s. Apart from China's chronological advantage, the Chinese regime in fact contributed to the fall in mortality rates during the eight years preceding the disaster of the Great Leap Forward (Banister 56). Against the background of this spectacular fall in mortality rates, the famine appears even more deadly, for had mortality remained at pre-1949 levels, quite a few of those who died of hunger would not have survived until 1958. Given that the birth rate did not begin to decline noticeably until the 1970s, the natural population increase was very rapid during the first phase of the demographic transition, at between 2 and 2.5 percent per year between 1954 and 1957 (Banister 352).

Furthermore, urbanization in China was proceeding more quickly than population growth. It started from very low levels, with an urban population in 1957 of fifteen percent, and rose by more than 8 percent in 1958, and by fifteen percent in 1959. In that year alone, China's urban population increased by 16.5 million (from 107.2 million to 123.7 million), a record that was surpassed the following year (Banister 330-31; Lardy 369). That rapid urbanization was less due to natural growth, which was slower in the cities than in the countryside, than to a hasty rural exodus triggered by break-neck industrialization. Most of the migrants were young peasants. Given the surfeit of rural labourers, the migrants easily could have been replaced in the fields had the Great Leap Forward (GLF) not mobilized the workforce for enormous hydroelectric projects and small backyard furnaces.

This rapid urbanization was the corollary to an unrealistic development strategy, but development as such was an inevitable course. The slow start to the demographic transition went hand in hand with economic underdevelopment. In 1949 China's gross domestic product (GDP) per capita was among the lowest in the world and remained so until the eve of the fateful GLF (Wemheuer 27, 270n4). A classic study entitled *China: Land of Famine* published by Walter Mallory in 1926 rightly implied that famine had long been endemic in China. A famine had killed some ten million people in the north and the northwest of the country between 1928 and 1930, and there were famines in 1920-21 (in north China) and 1943 (in Henan province) (Lillian Li 304). However, each of these famines paled in comparison to the awful famine that had hit imperial China between 1876 and 1879.

FAMINE IN CHINA: FROM THE GREAT TURNING POINT TO THE GREAT LEAP FORWARD

Modernization and Development Strategy

Mao loved to praise the virtues of "negative examples," mercilessly pointing them out from among the ever-criticized class enemies in order to educate the heirs of the 1911 Chinese revolution that overthrew China's last imperial dynasty (the Qing dynasty) and established the Republic of China (ROC). But did he learn any lessons from the negative example provided by the tragedy of 1931-33? Apparently he did, because in 1958 he inaugurated a "Chinese way" that departed from the model he had unswervingly followed until that point. This claim to originality would have been praiseworthy had the new model corrected the aberrations of the original, but it did not.

Mao criticized the Stalinist development strategy and altered his own, but his corrections did not factor in a famine that was distant in both time and space and about which he knew very little. The first Chinese Five-Year Plan (1953-57) can be credited with accelerated industrial construction, but it also confirmed that it was no longer possible to continue neglecting agriculture. That sector had received only 7 percent of the plan's total investment, compared with 46.5 percent for heavy industry. The emphasis on expensive technology had drawn abundantly on the country's meagre capital resources but very little on the over-abundant workforce. It was in part to remedy that imbalance that the Great Leap Forward was concocted during the winter of 1957-58.

Unfortunately, the necessary readjustments in agriculture and the consumer industries were not accomplished at the expense of heavy industry. If industry had benefitted disproportionately in the past, it benefitted still more in 1958, obtaining 57 percent of the total investment versus 46.5 percent. In 1959 that investment reached an historic record of 43.4 percent of the country's gross domestic product. Steel, that symbol of modernity and power, demanded maximum effort, as witnessed by the cascade of quotas that followed one after the other in the space of a few months: from 6.2 million tonnes (annual production) in February 1958, already a sixteen percent increase over the 5.35 million tonnes produced in 1957, to eleven and then twelve million tonnes, as reported in three speeches Mao made in early September of that year (MacFarquhar 89-90).

As in the USSR a generation earlier, the rural economy and rural societies in China paid the price of an accelerated industrialization program; in both countries a similar development strategy led to excessive monetary transfers from agriculture to heavy industry. In some respects, the GLF was an exaggerated reproduction of the first Soviet Five-Year Plan (1928-32). Production targets that were already "teleological" during the first Soviet Plan became more so during the Chinese GLF (Graziosi, *Histoire* 76-77). In both Soviet Union and China, a direct cause of famine was excessive and ruthless grain requisitioning from producers that continued well after the famine had started.

Famine Aggravated by Novelties

In China, an overambitious industrialization strategy was made more dangerous by novelties that the party experimented with and often forcibly imposed. A huge increase in the production of steel was to come in part from small backyard furnaces, which between seventy and ninety million peasants (sources differ)—mostly peasant women—were busy stoking, using rudimentary techniques. To keep those furnaces going, the local communist cadres seized saucepans, stoves, scissors, knives, spades, pickaxes, bicycles, iron railings, door knockers, and temple bells to produce such mediocre steel that nine-tenths had to be thrown away as scrap (Yang, *Tombstone* 28, 177; *Stèles* 309).

Having lost their kitchen utensils, people could no longer cook in their own homes. Everyone ate in the communal canteens, which served free food provided by the newly created People's Communes. Canteens wasted food as a result of sloppy management, privileges, and corruption. According to one student of the famine, canteens may have been responsible for one third of the total number of deaths from starvation (Yang, *Tombstone* 191).

During China's First Five-Year Plan (1953-57), agricultural cooperatives became responsible for agricultural production following collectivization. The far larger People's Commune, created on the scale of the massive projects it was supposed to undertake, was charged with speeding up social evolution and carrying out a veritable transition from a family framework to a community one. Was the commune the social counterpart of the economic Great Leap Forward? This was hoped a little and claimed a great deal. Preaching by example, many People's Communes in Henan province (where the first commune was founded) ceased to distribute work points (which enabled working members to buy necessities) because everything was supposedly free—not only food, but clothing, education, medical care, weddings, and funerals. Without going that far, other communes abolished private plots, which were deemed as useless as personal pots and pans, given the impending advent of "each according to his need." Propaganda even hinted that the arrival of the Communist society was just around the corner. "Dizzy with success" or not, China was proceeding faster than the Soviet model—within a few months, ninety-nine percent of the peasants had become members of People's Communes.

Mobilized in almost military fashion, commune members went to work in squads. The peasants were "soldiers on the agricultural front." This metaphor betrayed the true ambition of the GLF, which was less social than economic: the mobilization of the masses to industrialize the nation and to forge workers out of peasant foot soldiers. In a matter of weeks, some sixty million villagers were packed off to water projects near and far, small and large. In no time they had built numerous dams and dug countless irrigation ditches, all with the most rudimentary tools, working day and night in shifts to the sound of martial music blaring from loudspeakers. But since the projects were designed by peasants rather than engineers, and built from earth, corn cobs, and bamboo rather than cement, many of the constructs washed away in the first floods. Many of the dams and reservoirs that survived reduced the yields they were supposed to improve with irrigation, for in their haste to get the job done quickly, cadres of peasants often dispensed with provisions for drainage. As a result of subsequent evaporation, salts built up in the reservoir water and intensified the salinity of the soil during irrigation.

The mobilization of a female labour force, now "liberated" from domestic tasks thanks to communal canteens, did little to offset the shortage of labour that was a consequence of those projects and the rural furnaces. In addition, there was an exodus to the cities, which boosted the workforce in modern industry from just over nine million in 1957 to more than twenty-five million in 1958. Chairman Mao ordered the mechanization of agriculture, but such fast-track industrialization could not be carried out at the drop of a hat. In the meantime, sickles, spades, and pickaxes would have been welcome, but they had been melted down in the furnaces. As a result of the labour shortage, a portion of the bumper harvest of 1958 began to rot in the fields. The GLF had achieved the seemingly impossible feat of creating a workforce shortage among the largest peasantry in the world.

Blatant Lies

Credit for the excellent harvest of 1958, the best since the Revolution of 1949, was attributed to the People's Communes and the GLF rather than to good weather. According to regional reports, 450 million tonnes of cereals were brought in that year, but Mao decided to be cautious and announced a harvest of 375 million tonnes. In the absence of reliable statistics, the official production figures for 1958 were thus decided by Chairman Mao, and it was on that basis that the 1959 production target was set at 525 million tonnes, while land to be sown was reduced by ten percent and land to be sown with cereals was reduced by thirteen percent. The leaders were now grappling with a thorny issue: what should they do with the surplus rice and wheat? Mao suggested that the peasants work in the morning and devote the rest of the day to educating themselves. In fact, at 197.6 million tonnes, compared with 195 million in 1957, the good harvest of 1958 exceeded that of the previous year by only1.33 percent. With less land sown and less favourable weather conditions, the 1959 harvest fell to 170 million tonnes. People were growing disillusioned even before they heard these poor results. By spring, in canteens where people had eaten their fill the previous fall, some foodstuffs were already running low. Matters grew worse after the harvest, for on the basis of those inflated harvest forecasts, grain procurement reached record levels, far above all the other excessive levies in Mao's lifetime: 67.4 million tonnes, nearly twenty million of which would later have to be returned to the starving peasants (Ash 970).

While not the sole cause, this pernicious process of wrong decisions made on the basis of blatant lies considerably aggravated the famine. The leadership had set an example for outrageous exaggeration that others followed, exhorting the populace: "Let's achieve the second Five-Year Plan in two years." The Communist Party cadres were under such pressure that they were "tempted to inflate figures at every level" (Xue Muqiao, in charge of statistics, was fired in 1959 because of his opposition to the compilation of deceptive local progress statistics at the sacrifice of national statistics, as suggested by Choh-Ming Li 111-12). The leaders were then taken in by the lies for which they, first and foremost, were to blame. The accumulation of successive lies at each level of the administrative hierarchy resulted in seriously distorted national figures. The production figures became so fantastic that the increase in cereal procurement quotas appeared reasonable. Unrelenting competition between cadres impelled them to try harder to surpass their neighbours, to launch satellites ever higher in the skies. In this case, the Sputnik-level accomplishments were to be previously unheard of yields,[4] not to mention agricultural products prodigious in their size and volume: sixty-kilo pumpkins, one-pound ears of corn, wheat growing so densely that it could bear the weight of three children, and so on (Teiwes and Sun 123). In 1958 the convoy transporting Mao to the centre of

[4] Becker, *La grande famine* 176. MacFarquhar 127 ("sputnik" fields: Deng Xiaoping himself believed a peasant who claimed to have harvested 35 tonnes of rice on one *mu* of land, in other words, on 660 square meters).

the Xushui model commune in Hubei province passed turnips, cabbages, carrots, and other vegetables piled up along the roadside for more than a *li* (a third of a mile). Mao was told in all seriousness that the peasants had thrown them there, not knowing what to do with such excess. The commune's Party secretary confirmed this, saying: "Here everybody eats five meals a day for free" (Teiwes and Sun 123). In the words of Mao's personal doctor, "The whole of China was a theatre, and everyone redoubled their efforts at exaggeration to please Mao" (Zhisui Li 302).[5]

LATE AWAKENING, LUSHAN, AND POST-LUSHAN RELAPSE

Late Awakening

Despite this spectacle, Mao was not duped for long by the fantastical reports that came to him from the provinces. During the winter of 1958-59, it became clear that notwithstanding the good harvest, grain procurement deliveries were below forecast and there was a risk of food shortages in the cities, where populations had risen considerably. In collusion with the local cadres, the peasants had held back a portion of the harvest. Some provincial leaders wanted to lead a merciless anti-concealment campaign, but Mao declared his sympathy with those peasants driven to this kind of passive resistance by overzealous levies: "I now support conservatism. I stand on the side of right deviation. I am against egalitarianism and left adventurism" (speech on 5 March 1959, qtd. in Dikötter 86). As early as December 1958 Mao warned that the advent of Communism would have to wait.

One sign of the changing times was the (provisional) return of Chen Yun (1905-95). Chen, a member of the Permanent Committee of the Politburo and fifth in line in terms of power in the regime, was in charge of the economy and the only leader who had opposed the GLF strategy from the start, which had led to him being shunted aside. In the spring of 1959, he visited Henan, the vanguard province for utopian political activism, but he did not believe a single word or number of the fairy tales spun by the regional leaders. Mao himself gave the following instructions to the party cadres in a letter dated 29 April 1959: "Fixing production targets must be based on realities . . . . State exactly how much you have harvested and refrain from making false statements that are contrary to facts" (MacFarquhar 171). In June, without batting an eye, Mao seems to have accepted Chen Yun's proposal to reduce the steel production quota for 1959.

[5] See also Becker, *La grande famine* 110, 121-22, 176. A trick photograph published in *China Pictorial* in 1958 and reproduced in Manning and Wemheuer (55) shows not three but four children standing on rice plants, the stool beneath them artfully concealed.

Lushan (July-August, 1959)

Overall, a good half year, from November 1958 to June 1959, was devoted to "consolidation," the standard euphemism for retreat. At the end of June, 1959, when Mao went to Lushan (Jiangxi province) to preside over the leadership's summer meeting, he appeared resolved to confirm his rejection of exaggerations, illusions, and imbalances, as symbolized by Chen Yun's return to favour. Another leader, Marshal Peng Dehuai, Minister of Defence, had also made some enquiries in four provinces and drawn the same conclusions as Chen. Peng was the son of a poor peasant himself, something quite unusual in the Party leadership, and had seen famine as a child; it had killed several of his brothers. So, Peng plucked up his courage and went to see Mao in Lushan to persuade him to go still further in correcting his GLF strategy. Thwarted in making his case face-to-face because Mao was asleep (even more than Stalin, Mao was a night owl, who slept part of the day and imposed his rhythm on his entourage), Peng spent that night writing a letter to him. There was nothing really original in that letter, which expressed the unspoken opinions of the majority in the Party leadership, but Peng committed the crime of "*lèse-majesté*" by attempting to show what lessons could be drawn from the GLF experience—the prerogative of the Party leader. After criticizing the irresponsible slogans Mao had launched earlier, Peng attributed the left-wing errors of the past twelve months to "petit-bourgeois fanaticism" in terms resembling those used by Lenin to denounce left-wing Communism as "an infantile disorder" (Teiwes and Sun 202-12; MacFarquhar 212-16; Yang, *Tombstone* 355-60; Union Research Institute 7-13).

That was more than Mao could take. He could criticize himself, but for someone else to criticize him was intolerable. Mao chose to interpret that private letter, written to urge him to pursue a retreat he had already begun, as a political attack. The majority of the leaders were as surprised as Peng by the ferocious assault that followed, but then sided with Mao in criticizing Peng. Mao gave them no choice: they could either support the president or follow the militaristic "plotter" Peng. The army remained silent, but just to make sure, Mao sent an ultimatum to his generals, stating: "If you take Peng's side, I will place myself at the head of the peasants and lead guerrilla warfare against you" (MacFarquhar 222). The Plenary Session of the Central Committee met on 2 August 1959 and condemned the right-wing opportunism of the anti-Party clique headed by Peng Dehuai. The warning was clear: anyone criticizing the GLF would be considered part of that clique of reprobates.

Post-Lushan Relapse and Hecatomb (Late 1959 to Late 1961)

Lushan was not only one of the regime's turning points; it was *the* turning point for the famine. "Had the leadership reversed course in the summer of

1959 at Lushan, the number of victims claimed by famine might have been counted in the millions, and not in tens of millions" (Dikötter 103).[6] Frank Dikötter's assessment illustrates a bitter truth: Peng's courage relaunched and aggravated the famine. The torrent of denunciations of right-wing opportunists and Peng's henchmen discouraged local cadres and provincial leaders from carrying out the adjustments they had begun earlier in the year. Anyone wanting to avoid being labelled a right-wing opportunist had to be careful not to challenge the validity of the People's Communes or the communal canteens. It was less dangerous to err on the left than to err on the right. At the end of 1959, the canteens were feeding four hundred million people, or more than seventy-two percent of the members of People's Communes (and nearly ninety-eight percent in Henan, one of the provinces in which the famine was most devastating). Again, a lethal frenzy had been launched but of a different magnitude than during the first phase of the GLF.

The 1962 harvest, while not as good as harvests from 1952 to 1959, was better than in the two previous years and helped to put an end to the carnage. A more decisive factor in stopping the famine, however, was the two measures that helped to reduce grain procurement quotas in the countryside, namely, increasing cereal imports and sending some twenty million recent arrivals to the cities back to their villages (Wemheuer 142-47). While no one knows the exact number and year by year distribution of excess death, all agree that most people that had died from famine had died following the summer 1959 meeting of the Chinese Communist Party (CCP) leaders in Lushan, especially in 1960, a year about as lethal as the four years 1958, 1959, 1961, and 1962 taken together.

Table 1 compiles two estimates of the number of "abnormal" deaths. While their divergences illustrate our enduring ignorance, both estimates show that most deaths occurred from 1959 to 1961. Yang in *Tombstone* readily admits that his figures are based on much underestimated provincial data.

---

[6] Yang suggests that as a result of Lushan, the number of dead from starvation may have tripled, from twelve to thirty-six million (*Tombstone* 350).

Table 1. *Years versus "Abnormal" deaths (high and low estimates), according to Che Li 46-52; Yang, Tombstone 415; Yang, Stèles 501.*

1958	921,000	720,000
1959	4,819,000	4,750,000
1960	17,002,000	11,090,000
1961	8,476,000	3,000,000
1962	3,350,000	420,000
Total	**34,568,000**	**20,980,000**

II. Red China As an Empire

Ethnic Minorities and Internal Colonialism

The Early 1950s

Whereas ethnic minorities represented almost half (forty-seven percent) of the population of the Soviet Union in 1930, they comprised only six percent of the Chinese population in 1958. In the Soviet Union, minorities were officially distributed among fifty-five national minorities (although in reality there were more), which together amounted to less than one third (twenty-one percent) of the single Ukrainian nationality among the whole USSR population.

Though the question of dealing with ethnic minorities was therefore much less important for the Chinese than for the Soviet communists, the policies of these two governments were quite similar with respect to nationalities. The attitude of the CCP toward ethnic minorities was heavily influenced by the early policies of the USSR. Instead of republics and autonomous regions, the CCP merely established "autonomous regions." The Communist Party cadres for the autonomous regions were recruited from among the minorities, but as a rule, ultimate power rested with the Han secretary of the region's CCP Committee (Wemheuer 161-64).

Furthermore, Tibet, which had enjoyed independence from 1913 to 1951, was granted a special status. The CCP abstained from promoting social revolution in Tibet and did not interfere in the exploitation by monasteries of their estates. Inner Mongolia benefitted as well from the early tolerant policy of "indigenization," but became from 1949 the recipient of massive Han migration. The "Hanization" of the province followed. By the time of the 2000 census, Han represented seventy-eight percent of the population of Inner Mongolia. All other minorities were allowed a fair degree of self-rule between 1949 and 1957.

The GLF Turning Point

As in many other respects, the Great Leap Forward (GLF) was a turning point in policies toward minorities. While not established everywhere, People's Communes brought sudden and dramatic changes to most minority regions. Campaigns against local nationalism and well-known indigenous personalities were soon launched. Han cadres imbued with a spirit of "*dahan zhuyi*" ("great Hanism") endeavoured to "help their little brothers" by inciting them to get rid of religious superstitions and backward customs. At first, Tibet was exempted from such activist policies, but the exemption was limited to the autonomous region of central Tibet, Xizang.[7] Many monasteries were closed in 1958 in Qinghai, where land and livestock were forcibly collectivized. An overambitious campaign to sedentarize nomads and turn grasslands into agricultural land was launched, reminiscent of the policy imposed a generation earlier on Kazakhstan (Wemheuer 170). It brought disastrous results, although less disastrous than in Kazakhstan. A huge number of cattle died here: their numbers decreased from fifteen million in 1957 to 10.8 million in 1958 and to 9.3 million in 1960. The erstwhile nomads went hungry, and many Tibetans fled to Xizang (central Tibet).[8] In Qinghai an important uprising linked to hunger involved more than one hundred thousand people. About half that number was arrested, as were many nomads who had fled the famine and were treated as "bandit rebels." Conflicts about collectivization, sedentarization, and the closure of monasteries had thus been turned into a rebellion against Han colonizers.

By the next spring, an even more important uprising, indeed the most serious armed rebellion ever suffered by the People's Republic of China (PRC), erupted in Xizang. It was suppressed by the People's Liberation Army in a matter of weeks, but in the meantime, mass demonstrations in Lhasa and the flight of the Dalai Lama to northern India had inaugurated a new era in Han-Tibetan relations. Tibet was no longer to be spared, and thereafter Beijing representatives in Lhasa directly ruled Xizang, like any other province. The end of Tibet's special status removed any remaining doubt about the internal colonialism promoted and maintained by the CCP as part of its Red Empire.

---

[7] A majority of Tibetans lived outside central Tibet, in the surrounding provinces to the east of Xizang, mostly throughout Qinghai province but also in western Sichuan, south-western Gansu, and northern Yunnan provinces.

[8] Some sixty thousand Tibetans, including a minority from Gansu, Sichuan, and Yunnan provinces, fled to central Tibet in 1960 (Wemheuer 299n64).

Empire and Excess Famine Deaths

Natural Increase in Starvation Rates and Death Rates among Han and Minority Populations

A first rough indication in the rate of starvation in China is provided by the censuses of 1953 and 1982. In that twenty-nine-year span, the Han population grew at a rate of 1.9 percent per year, and the ethnic minorities grew at a rate of 2.2 percent per year. The latter rate obscures great discrepancies, which ranged from a low 1.2 percent for Tibetans (caused more by the flight to India of tens of thousands of Tibetans than by repression and excess famine deaths), to 2.4 percent for Hui and Miao, to 2.9 percent for Mongols (Aubin 303-04).

We know that the famine was less devastating among the ethnic minorities of Xizang, Xinjiang, and Inner Mongolia (where death rates remained under 2 percent even in 1960, the worst year) than in China as a whole. By contrast, autonomous minority counties in Yunnan recorded a high death rate of 2.62 percent in 1960, and the entire Guangxi Zhuang minority autonomous region endured the even higher rate of 2.94 percent (however, such higher rates remain well below those then affecting hundreds of millions of Han). In Guangxi and Yunnan, the leading cadres were mostly Han, who strictly implemented Beijing's murderous policies (Yang, *Tombstone* 397).

Factors Aggravating Famine

A key factor in an excess of unnatural deaths stems from the activist zeal demonstrated by some regional leaders in implementing Maoist radical policies. This was particularly the case in mostly Han-populated provinces, such as Anhui and Henan, where the famine was especially severe.

A second factor in large parts of the western periphery of China, largely inhabited by ethnic minorities, was the problem of delivering surplus grain to grain-deficit areas such as Xizang. The famine in Ukraine in the 1930s was caused by an opposite situation. Ukraine was a grain-surplus area, required to provide excessive amounts of grain to the state.

The third factor is more complex but might have been the most important. In the China of 1958, as in the USSR in the 1930s, cities received the lion's share of the food. However, the industrial crop-growing areas adjacent to the main urban areas, as well as old industrial areas such as the northeast, were also given a food priority. Besides these privileged areas, the minority regions of western and northern China also belonged to the less severely afflicted famine areas, if only because they produced less grain and were harder to reach; thus, procurement quotas were set low or were non-existent. As a rule, the areas most afflicted by severe famine were those surplus areas relatively well served by modern transport, and these areas were for the most part predominantly Han-populated (Garnaut 315-48; see especially 317-18).

Highest Provincial Death Rates

According to the most complete study of the Great Leap Forward famine, the rate of "unnatural" deaths during the famine was highest in Sichuan, Anhui, Gansu, Henan, Shandong, Qinghai, and Hunan provinces (Yang, *Tombstone* 394). With the exception of Qinghai, all provinces on this list were populated mainly (and some of them almost exclusively) by Han. The first and third provinces (Sichuan and Gansu) had some minorities (mostly Tibetan) in their western peripheries, but on the whole, Han and Tibetans suffered alike in Sichuan, Gansu, and Qinghai (Wemheuer 205). Qinghai province, which ranks sixth in terms of people lost to this famine, was the only one that was at the time mainly inhabited by ethnic, namely Tibetan, minorities.

Qinghai, the Most Severely Affected Minority Area in the Chinese Famine of 1958 to 1962

Unlike Ukraine in the 1930s, Qinghai in the 1950s, although a grain-deficit area, was able to import grain between 1953 and 1964 (Wemheuer 172). In 1960, during the acme of the famine crisis, Qinghai ranked fifth, not sixth, among the worst-affected provinces.[9] Official figures (underestimates) counted 102,900 unnatural deaths from 1958 to 1962, a high percentage for a total population of 2,440,000 inhabitants.

[9] The highest mortality rates among China's twenty-eight provinces in 1960, the worst year of the famine, were as follows, per thousand: Anhui, 68.58; Sichuan, 53.97; Guizhou, 52.33; Gansu, 41.03; Qinghai: 40.73; Henan, 39.60 (Yang, *Tombstone* 394, *Stèles* 455). By contrast, the three largest cities and the northeast of China experienced the lowest mortality rates, per thousand: Shanghai, 6.8; Beijing, 9.2; Inner Mongolia, 9.5; Jilin, 10.1; Tianjin, 10.3; Heilongjiang, 10.5; Liaoning: 11.5 (Dali L. Yang, *Calamity* 38).

Figure 1. Qinghai province[10]

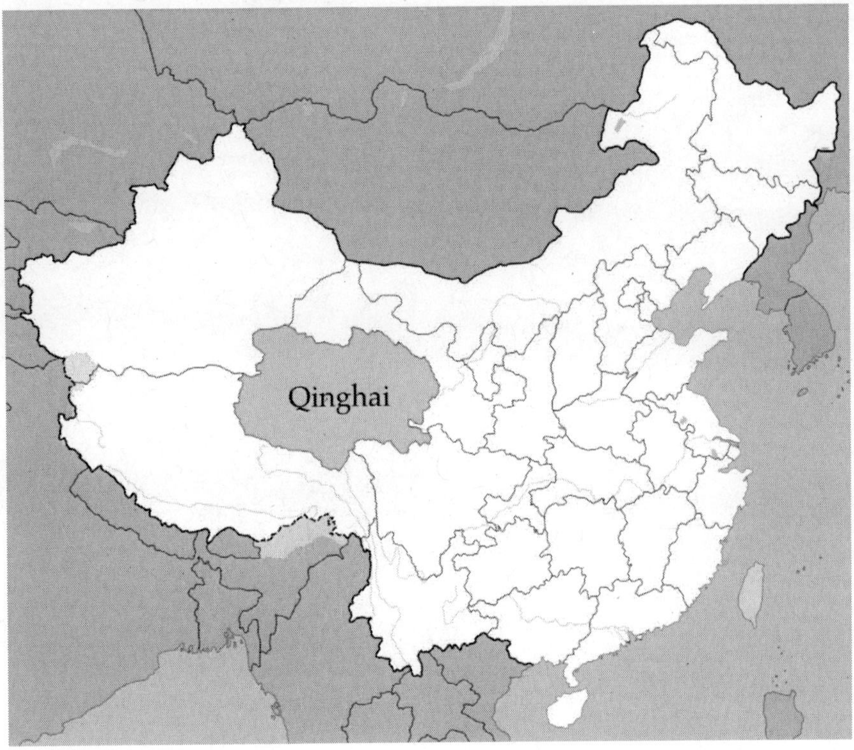

[10] "La province du Qinghai (en rouge) sur le territoire de la Chine," *Wikipedia,* https://fr.wikipedia.org/wiki/Qinghai#/media/Fichier:China_Qinghai.svg. Accessed 8 Jan. 2021.

Figure 2. Map (close-up) of Xining area, in eastern Qinghai[11]

Figure 3. Map: From Xining to Minhe, near the border with Gansu province[12]

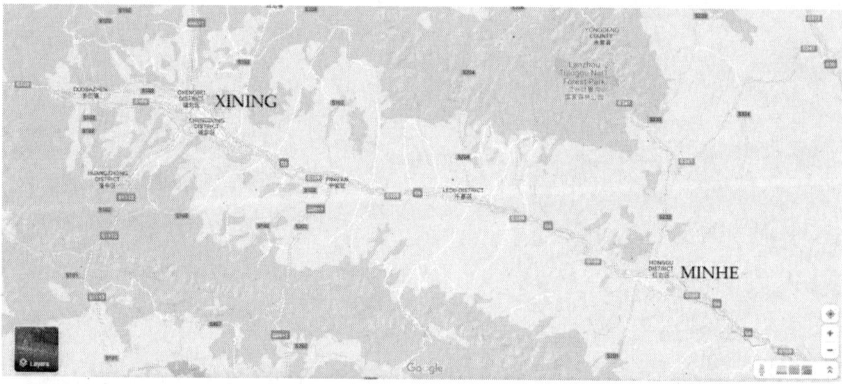

[11] *Zhonghua Renmin Gongheguo fen sheng dituji* (*Provincial Atlas of the People's Republic of China*) 28.
[12] Google Maps, https://www.google.com/maps/@36.4631395,102.079269,10.25z?hl=fr. Accessed 8 Jan. 2021.

Figures 1, 2, and 3 depict the causal connection between modern transport and famine in Qinghai, with grain surplus areas located in the eastern, relatively accessible part of the province, being especially hard hit. This was indeed the case for Minhe county, located on the border with Gansu province, halfway between Lanzhou and Xining, respective capitals of Gansu and Qinghai provinces. Minhe county, renowned as a grain and fruit provider for the entire province, may have lost as many as twenty-five percent of its population between 1958 and 1960. More than 1 in 8 inhabitants of Huangzhong, another rich county, situated ten miles west of Xining, starved to death in 1960. Both Minhe and Huangzhong counties were sites of notorious cases of cannibalism, as well as especially harsh repression of dissenters, including people who dared to utter the mildest criticisms of authorities (Yang, *Stèles* 455-58).[13]

Some Qinghai Tibetans did indeed suffer an awful fate during the famine, but so did many more Han inhabitants of Sichuan, Anhui, Henan, and Shandong provinces. The worst case of mishandling the famine may have been the refusal to distribute the contents of silos located near the border between Henan and Hubei provinces to starving inhabitants of both provinces, almost all Han people.

In China as a whole, Han peasants constituted the overwhelming majority of the famine victims, and multi-ethnic borderlands such as Tibet, Xinjiang, and Inner Mongolia were "spared the worst of the famine" (Graziosi, "Stalin's and Mao's Famines" 93; Garnaut 337). Deaths from starvation among ethnic minorities amounted to some five percent of the total number of excess deaths, compared to eighty percent of the 1931-33 famine victims in Soviet Union, who happened to be Ukrainians, Kazakhs, or other non-Russians. Within China, we can merely compare the five percent of excess deaths among ethnic minorities to the six percent within China's total population. In other words, the great Chinese Famine did not kill, proportionally, more minority than Han people.

[13] As far as I know, none of these criticisms and complaints referred to religious matters. As a whole, religion in Tibetan or Hui inhabited areas contributed almost nothing to the severity of famine, much less than the causes mentioned above, of which the availability of modern transport to convey surplus production was the most influential.

Works Cited

Ash, Robert. "Squeezing the Peasants: Grain Extraction, Food Consumption and Rural Living Standards in Mao's China." *The China Quarterly*, vol. 188, Dec. 2006, pp. 959-98. DOI: 10.1017/S0305741006000518

Aubin, Françoise. "Une Chine multinationale." *La Chine au XXe siècle, De 1949 à aujourd'hui,* edited by Marie-Claire Bergère et al., vol. 2, Fayard, 1990, pp. 287-304.

Banister, Judith. *China's Changing Population*. Stanford UP, 1987.

Becker, Jasper. *Hungry Ghosts, China's Secret Famine*. John Murray, 1996.

---. *La grande famine de Mao*. Editions Dagorno, 1998.

Bianco, Lucien. *Stalin and Mao: A Comparison of the Russian and Chinese Revolutions*. The Chinese UP, 2018.

Dikötter, Frank. *Mao's Great Famine. The History of China's Most Devastating Catastrophe, 1958-1962*. Bloomsbury, 2010.

Garnaut, Anthony. "The Geography of the Great Leap Famine." *Modern China*, vol. 40, no. 3, 2014, pp. 315-48. DOI: 10.1177/0097700413507425

Graziosi, Andrea. *Histoire de l'URSS*. Nouvelle Clio, 2010.

---. "Stalin's and Mao's Famines: Similarities and Differences." *Communism and Hunger: The Ukrainian, Chinese, Kazakh, and Soviet Famines in Comparative Perspective,* edited by Andrea Graziosi and Frank E. Sysyn, Canadian Institute of Ukrainian Studies P, 2016, pp. 83-101.

Lardy, Nicolas R. "Chapter 8: The Chinese Economy under Stress, 1958-1965." *Cambridge History of China*, edited by Roderick MacFarquhar and John K. Fairbank, vol. 14: *The People's Republic*, Cambridge UP, 1987, pp. 360-97.

Li, Che. "Dajihuang niandai fei zhengchang siwang de ling yizhong jisuan" ["A New Estimate of the Number of Abnormal Deaths at the Time of the Great Famine"]. *Yanhuang Chunqiu*, vol. 7, 2012, pp. 46-52.

Li, Choh-Ming. *The Statistical System of Communist China*. U of California P, 1962.

Li, Lillian. *Fighting Famine in North China*. Stanford UP, 2007.

Li, Zhisui. *La vie privée du Président Mao.* Plon, 1994.

MacFarquhar, Roderick. *The Origins of the Cultural Revolution.* Vol. 2: *The Great Leap Forward, 1958-1960,* Columbia UP, 1983.

Mallory, Walter H. *China: Land of Famine*. American Geographic Society, 1926.

Manning, Kimberley Ens, and Felix Wemheuer, editors. *Eating Bitterness: New Perspectives on China's Great Leap Forward and Famine*. UBC Press, 2011.

Ó Gráda, Cormac. *Famine, A Short History*, Princeton UP, 2009.

Rudnytskyi, O., et al. "Demography of a Man-Made Human Catastrophe: The Case of Massive Famine in Ukraine 1932-1933." *Canadian Studies in Population*, vol. 42, no. 1-2, 2015, pp. 53-80. DOI: 10.25336/P6FC7G

Teiwes, Frederick C., and Warren Sun. *China's Road to Disaster: Mao, Central Politicians, and Provincial Leaders in the Unfolding of the Great Leap Forward, 1955-1959*. M.E. Sharpe, 1999.

Union Research Institute. *The Case of Peng Teh-Huai, 1959-1968*. Union Press, 1968.

Wemheuer, Felix. *Famine Politics in Maoist China and the Soviet Union*. Yale UP, 2014.

Yang, Dali L. *Calamity and Reform in China. State, Rural Society, and Institutional Change since the Great Leap Famine*. Stanford UP, 1996.

---. *Stèles. La Grande Famine en Chine, 1958-1961.* Translated into French by Louis Vincenolles and Sylvie Gentil, Ed. du Seuil, 2012.

---. *Tombstone: The Great Chinese Famine, 1958-1962.* Translated into English by Stacy Mosher and Guo Han, Farrar, Straus and Giroux, 2012.

Zhonghua Renmin Gongheguo fen sheng dituji (Provincial Atlas of the People's Republic of China), Beijing, Ditu (Editions: "Geographical Maps"), 1977.

Raphaël Lemkin, Genocide, Colonialism, Famine, and Ukraine

Douglas Irvin-Erickson
George Mason University

Abstract: Many words have been used to name and describe the Great Ukrainian Famine of 1932-33, including "famine" and "catastrophe," "the Holodomor," and now "genocide." Was the famine genocide? Was the famine part of a genocide? Is the word genocide an exaggeration? Is naming the famine a genocide part of an attempt to dramatize events for political purposes today? Is the refusal to call the famine a genocide an act of genocide denial? This article argues that, though more than seven decades have passed and the Soviet Union has come and gone, questions about genocide in Ukraine remain intertwined in the discourses and narratives surrounding conflicts over Ukraine's economic, political, social, and cultural position between the European Union and the Russian Federation. Given the implications of this word—"genocide"—within the context of current conflicts over Ukrainian history and identity and even sovereignty, it is important to reflect on how this concept has been used and applied. This paper analyzes conflict in Ukraine in the 1930s using Raphaël Lemkin's definition of genocide, as opposed to the legal definition established by the UN Genocide Convention, and discusses the conceptual strengths of Lemkin's definition of genocide in terms of understanding a wide-spectrum of oppressive, repressive, and violent processes of empire-building and colonization that occurred in Ukraine, and which culminated in the Holodomor.

Keywords: Ukrainian famine, Holodomor, genocide, empire, Raphaël Lemkin.

INTRODUCTION[1]

Over the last eighty years, there have been many words used to name and describe the Great Ukrainian Famine of 1932-33. Throughout the 1930s, foreign language newspapers used the terms "famine" and "catastrophe," and the event came to be known later as "the Holodomor." The rise of new terminologies in international law—such as terror, crimes against nations, crimes against humanity, and genocide—expanded the lexicon for describing the famine in Ukraine in scholarly and popular

---

[1] This paper was delivered in Kyiv, Ukraine, on 5 June 2017, at the conference hall of the Ukrainian House. Portions of the paper draw on my biography of Raphaël Lemkin, published by the University of Pennsylvania Press, and my article on Lemkin (Irvin-Erickson, *Raphaël Lemkin and the Concept of Genocide*; Irvin-Erickson, "Genocide, the 'Family of Mind'").

discourses. Perhaps the most contentious of these appellations has proven to be "genocide."

Was the famine genocide? Was the famine part of a genocide? Is the word "genocide" an exaggeration? Is naming the famine a genocide part of an attempt to dramatize events for political purposes today? Is the refusal to call the famine a genocide an act of genocide denial? These questions generate intense scholarly controversy and mobilize political action amongst activists on all sides (see Naimark). Even though more than seven decades have passed and the Soviet Union has come and gone, questions about genocide in Ukraine remain intertwined in the discourses and narratives surrounding conflicts over Ukraine's economic, political, social, and cultural position between the European Union and the Russian Federation, and the armed conflict that began with the Russian invasion of Ukraine and annexation of Crimea in 2014 (see Irvin-Erickson, "Genocide Discourses").

Given the implications of this word—"genocide"—within the context of current conflicts over Ukrainian history and identity and even sovereignty, it is important to reflect on how this concept has been used and applied. The word "genocide" was coined by the Polish Jewish jurist Raphaël Lemkin late in the winter of 1941-42 and first appeared in print in Lemkin's magnum opus *Axis Rule in Occupied Europe*. In *Axis Rule,* which was fundamentally about the German occupation of Poland (see Rabinbach), Lemkin did not intend to establish a typology of what all genocides were, nor did he maintain that the case of genocide perpetrated by Germany under Nazi rule in the 1930s and 1940s was the prototypical case of genocide. Rather, he saw the Holocaust as one of many genocides across history.

Indeed, Lemkin's thinking on genocide was inspired by the social and intellectual milieu in which he was born. He was raised in a Jewish family on a farm in imperial Russia, in a region he described as "historically known as Lithuania," which became part of independent Poland, passed into Soviet hands, and is now part of Belarus (Lemkin, *Autobiography*). Growing up in a multi-cultural, multi-ethnic, and multi-religious milieu, Lemkin, like many of his peers, was raised speaking Russian, Yiddish, and Polish as first languages. He became fluent in Hebrew and German in early childhood, as well as in local dialects of Russian and Belarusian, and by early adulthood, had added French, English, Spanish, and Italian to his repertoire. Lemkin understood what it felt like to be a minority in an oppressive nation-state, where belonging and basic citizenship rights, including the right to life, were awarded by states to individuals according to their national identity—and where state policies were often set towards the goal of eradicating entire identity-based social groups, erasing not just the individuals but also their cultural imprints. Lemkin understood, acutely, the value of human diversity but also that human societies did not automatically value diversity. Instead, cosmopolitan sensibilities had to be created and defended. He believed, therefore, that it was necessary to safeguard the institutions and values that allow individuals to be free to express their own subjective identities, to be curious about others' identities and cultures, and to integrate the contributions and identities of others into their own (see Bronner). It was this dynamism between the ideas and cultures of national groups, Lemkin believed, that allowed human creativity to flourish, enriching the lives of individuals and world civilization as a whole. Genocide, Lemkin thought, is intended to destroy such a world: to stamp out differences in the name of creating homogeneous communities where individuals who hold different identities are repressed, marginalized, exiled, or even killed, and to restrict the participation in public life of individuals who belong to subaltern or minority groups.

Lemkin did not classify the famine in Ukraine as a genocide. Rather, he saw the famine as the most brutal stage of a genocide. Indeed, for Lemkin, genocide was about destroying what he called the national patterns of the oppressed, what we might today call their social identities. Thus, for Lemkin, the Soviet genocide against the Ukrainian nation began long before the first individuals were killed. Famine is a particularly effective means of committing genocide, Lemkin believed, not only because of the large number of individual deaths it achieves but because hunger and starvation shatter the social bonds between families, friends, and communities. In Lemkin's mind, what makes starvation such an effective tool for destroying social groups is that hunger pits members of a social group into competition for survival, ensuring that the bonds of trust, friendship, and love that hold a social group together, and which form the basic content of an individual's social identity, are shattered.

PART 1: LEMKIN ON GENOCIDE AND COLONIALISM

To understand Lemkin's thoughts on famine as a technique of genocide, it is necessary to first outline Lemkin's definition of "nation"—the entity he asserted that genocide destroyed. It is also worth noting what Lemkin thought perpetrators of genocide sought to gain by destroying nations"—genocide as a form of inter-group conflict and a fundamentally colonial act.[2]

---

[2] This line of inquiry, in which Lemkin conceptualized the Soviet genocide in Ukraine as a form of colonial conflict, can contribute to new directions in Soviet studies that employ the concepts of empire and colonization to understand the Soviet Union. See Annus; von Hagen.

Genocide, Lemkin wrote in *Axis Rule*, was "a coordinated plan of different actions aiming at the destruction of essential foundations of the life of national groups, with the aim of annihilating the groups themselves" (79). Lemkin conceived of genocide as having two phases: "One, the destruction of the national pattern of the oppressed group; the other, the imposition of the national pattern of the oppressor" (*Axis Rule* 79). "Directed against the national group as an entity," he wrote, "the actions involved" in committing genocide "are directed against individuals, not in their individual capacity, but as members of the national group" (Lemkin, *Axis Rule* 79). Lemkin thus interpreted the genocide perpetrated by Nazi Germany as a colonial project of transforming the demographics of Germany and the newly conquered regions of occupied Europe. "In line with this policy of imposing the German national pattern, particularly in the incorporated territories, the occupant has organized a system of colonization of these areas," Lemkin wrote (*Axis Rule* 83). As a consequence of this colonization, Lemkin concluded that "participation in economic life is thus dependent upon one's being German or being devoted to the cause of Germanism. Consequently, promoting a national ideology other than German is made difficult and dangerous" (*Axis Rule* 86).

Lemkin's was not an unprecedented analysis of the German occupation of Europe. Newspapers and political and popular discourses throughout Eastern Europe commonly referred to the German occupying army as a colonizing force.[3] Lemkin's ideas were also strikingly similar to those espoused by the theorist Otto Bauer, whom Lemkin identified as a major influence on his thinking. "Modern imperialism" does not seek a unified world, Bauer wrote in his classic book *The Question of Nationalities and Social Democracy* (published in 1907 and republished in 1924), but rather "encloses the economic zone of the individual country within a customs border" that opens up the less developed country as a sphere of investment and sales for the capitalists of the developed country (379). Modern imperialism, therefore, "does not dream of freedom, but prepares for war," Bauer contended, because the modern nation-state "does not believe in the possibility of uniting the whole of humanity in free and peaceful exchange" but "seeks to help its own land at the cost of the other by arming itself with tariffs, with navies, and with soldiers against other countries" (379). The primary goal of state militaries, Bauer argued, was not only to defeat other armies in battle but to eliminate national groups whose way of life hindered capitalist expansion into new markets. These violent processes of destroying nations as sociological entities were most pronounced in

[3] See, for example, Korostelina, for the Crimean Tatar discourse.

Eastern Europe and in European colonies, Bauer wrote. The armies that were raised by nation-states, Bauer continued,

> must be ready and willing to be used, today in African and tomorrow in India, today to exterminate a Negro tribe root and branch and tomorrow to struggle against the white soldiers of another nation. Today they must protect the owners of large gold mines against the rebellion of their foreign workers and tomorrow dispense bloody punishment to the Egyptian peasants for beating their arrogant conqueror. (390)

Yet it was not enough that the armies of nation states had to be willing to inflict such brutality. Bauer suggested that the citizens of nation states must "desire" to subjugate, enslave, and destroy entire nations of less developed others in the name of their nation. Thus, state elites exploit racism and national chauvinism to legitimize the attempt to destroy nations and national ways of life that impede the expansion of capitalist forms of social organization. Remarkably, Lemkin would argue that the Soviet regime under Stalin was conducting a similar program to eradicate entire national ways of life to advance their modernizing, economic program. Lemkin's definition of genocide clearly borrowed heavily from Bauer (see Irvin-Erickson, *Lemkin*).

Genocide as the Destruction of Nations

If genocide was the destruction of nations and national patterns, what was a nation according to Lemkin? Here again, Lemkin borrowed heavily from the Austro-Hungarian theorists and political figures Karl Renner and Otto Bauer.[4] Bauer had argued that modern nations were "communities of character" that developed out of "communities of fate" (7). For Bauer, nations were not derived territorially, as liberal nationalism professed, nor were they the closed off and organic entities that conservatives (and German Romantic theorists) believed them to be. For Bauer, national consciousness was "by no means synonymous with the love of one's own nation or the will for the political unity of the nation"—"national consciousness is to be understood as the simple recognition of membership in the nation" (120). This also meant that the content of national identity was always changing because both nationality and nations as social groups were products of the consciousness of individuals (Bauer 21). Thus for Bauer, nations were neither trans-historical nor primordial entities but

---

[4] See Renner, especially 30 and 39. Compare this to Lemkin's correspondences with Renner. Raphael Lemkin to Karl Renner, March 29, 1950, Raphael Lemkin Papers, American Jewish Association, Cincinnati, Ohio, United States. Box 1, Folder 15.

constantly changing as individuals themselves changed and as new "communities of fate" formed and developed into new "communities of character" (109). Consequently, national identity was not a zero-sum game, and national identities were not mutually exclusive. Lemkin would borrow these ideas explicitly in his late, unpublished writings on genocide and quietly announced this position in a footnote in *Axis Rule* (91n5).

In contrast to Lemkin's understanding of what nations were, developed from the social and political theory of Bauer and Renner, orthodox Marxist positions and transcendentalist or neo-Kantian liberal thinkers saw nations as categories, derived from either materialist or spiritual theories of history (Nimni 162). For Bauer and Renner, nations were historical processes rather than categories (Nimni 162-63). Bauer's definition of a nation as "a community of character formed out of a community of fate" does not locate the nation purely in the realm of psychological consciousness, where communal bonds are formed through abstract notions of solidarity, nor does it locate the nation within materialist thinking. At the same time, because nations existed within the consciousness of individuals who recognized the existence of nations, nations took on objective social characteristics. However, nations constantly reformed as new communities of fate formed and created new communities of character. Indeed, Bauer argued, nations could not be identified by empirical theorists who defined the essential characteristics of a nation in the abstract and then looked at the real world to see whether or not a given group constituted a nation (Nimni 161).

A nation, according to Lemkin, was above all a collection of individuals who thought of themselves as belonging to the same group, with the help of shared languages, arts, mythologies, folklores, collective histories, traditions, religions and even shared ancestry or a shared geographical location. Languages, lineages, pseudo-scientific theories of biology, religions, and geography—these only created the boundaries of national groups when people believed that these things mattered. Importantly, this principle meant that a given individual could belong to more than one nation at the same time since the criteria for establishing nations were not mutually exclusive. Individuals could enter into and out of certain "families of mind" throughout their lives or could express one identity at one time and another at another time, or multiple national identities at once. Within this conception, no individual could ever be fully representative of a nation; nor could any individual be reduced to a nation.

It was for this reason that Lemkin considered many different kinds of groups to be "nations," believed that nations were constituted by people's recognition that they were part of a nation, argued that nations were always changing their national character and that this dynamism enriched the lives of individuals, and felt that each individual could hold many different national identities throughout his or her life—oftentimes holding several at once. Lemkin even posited that under the rubric of "nations," various sociological groups could be included, such as "those who play cards, or those who engage in unlawful trade practices or in breaking up unions." Genocide, Lemkin reasoned, could be conducted against criminals because states often criminalized certain types of subjectivities and ethnic identities. After all, he argued, had not the Soviet Union conceived of counter-revolutionary forms of national consciousness as criminal?

What then for Lemkin was genocide? His definition was simple. Genocide was the destruction of nations, which entailed the destruction of the national patterns of the oppressed group and the imposition of the national patterns of the oppressor. This definition is remarkably different from the definition of genocide found in the UN Genocide Convention, which reads:

> **Article I**
> The Contracting Parties confirm that genocide, whether committed in time of peace or in time of war, is a crime under international law which they undertake to prevent and to punish.
>
> **Article II**
> In the present Convention, genocide means any of the following acts committed with intent to destroy, in whole or in part, a national, ethnical, racial or religious group, as such:
>
> (a) Killing members of the group;
> (b) Causing serious bodily or mental harm to members of the group;
> (c) Deliberately inflicting on the group conditions of life calculated to bring about its physical destruction in whole or in part;
> (d) Imposing measures intended to prevent births within the group;
> (e) Forcibly transferring children of the group to another group.
>
> **Article III**
> The following acts shall be punishable:
>
> (a) Genocide;
> (b) Conspiracy to commit genocide;
> (c) Direct and public incitement to commit genocide;
> (d) Attempt to commit genocide;
> (e) Complicity in genocide. (United Nations Convention)

A discussion of how the United Nations Genocide Convention of 1948 came to define genocide is beyond the scope of this paper, but it is an issue I consider at length in my book on Lemkin and the concept of genocide

(*Raphaël Lemkin*). Suffice it to say that Lemkin's ideas on genocide were largely rejected by the major powers at the UN, who did not want to outlaw attempts to destroy national patterns and whose delegates sought to preserve the right of their governments to oppress minorities within their own borders.[5]

For Lemkin, genocide was not necessarily an act of mass murder, though mass murder could be genocide if the act was committed with the intention of destroying a nation. Instead, genocide was about destroying a nation. If genocide was the destruction of nations and national patterns, then genocide for Lemkin was very much the destruction of "families of mind" as well as the destruction of social processes by which "communities of character" formed from "communities of fate." As such, in Lemkin's conceptualization, genocide could be achieved through direct and indirect violence or through forms of repression that could be called in today's parlance "structural violence" (see Galtung). In fact, under Lemkin's definition, genocide could be achieved without the death of a single individual—if the social processes of group formation of "families of mind" were targeted for destruction, leaving individual people alive but permanently altering their social identities and national patterns, making the social reproduction of the group impossible.

PART 2: LEMKIN ON THE SOVIETS

Lemkin coined the word genocide in 1941, but his thinking on the destruction of nations can be traced to the late 1920s. In 1926, at the age of 26, Lemkin published his first book, *Kodeks karny republik sowieckich* (*The Penal Code of the Soviet Republics*). When the book was released, he had just graduated with his doctorate in Law from Jan Kazimierz University in the capital of Galicia, Lviv (known as Lwów in interwar Poland). The book contained the first Polish translation of the Soviet penal code. In his commentary, Lemkin briefly addressed Stalin's nationalities policies while dealing mainly with the historical evolution of the Russian and Soviet penal codes. In 1928, the speaker of the Polish parliament, Wacław Makowski, wrote the introduction to Lemkin's next book, *Kodeks karny Rosji Sowieckiej 1927* (*The 1927 Criminal Code of Soviet Russia*). In his analysis of the 1927 penal code, Lemkin noted that the reforms made to the Soviet penal code after Lenin's death marked no substantive difference from the laws Lenin's party enacted in 1922. The only difference, he wrote, was that the new code drew on nineteenth-century Italian Positive legal theory to explicitly codify

[5] Weiss-Wendt makes it perfectly clear, for example, that the Soviet delegation had far more influence on the definition of genocide as it became codified in the law than Lemkin did.

"social protection" as the purpose of the law. This small but crucial observation would remain a central component of his study of genocide and the law; he saw genocide as legitimized through laws that allowed for the removal of ethnic and national minorities from society under slogans of social protection.

Lemkin's commentary on the Soviet penal code explicitly examined Lenin's policy of using Soviet law as a component of the dictatorship of the proletariat. The Soviet system conceived of the law as a form of social protection, Lemkin wrote, not simply a system to punish individual crimes ("Dzieje"; see also Kornat 98). The law, in this formulation, legitimized the arrest, suppression, oppression, and killing of people who had a social consciousness that was deemed criminal, Lemkin wrote. In the Soviet context this criminal social consciousness was called "enemy nationalism." The Soviet Union was solving its "nationalities problem" by legalizing the suppression, repression, and elimination of entire social groups who had forms of social consciousness that the ruling elites believed were threats to state power and could be a countervailing force to the revolution. The Soviet legal code, Lemkin wrote, was therefore not merely a tool for maintaining the gains of the proletarian revolution; the law was a means for educating the proletariat in the new social order and actively supported the creation of the new communist system by sanctioning the state violence and coercion necessary for the destruction and transformation of the bourgeoisie and national minorities into Soviet citizens ("Ustawodawstwo" 7; see also Kornat 98). The goal of this state-directed force was to create, destroy, and re-organize social relationships by managing the identity of Soviet populations in a way that was perceived as benefitting the Soviet revolutionary project or the state itself (Feierstein 1). From the ashes of the old bourgeois and peasant identities, a new social identity would be created as a matter of state policy—*Homo Sovieticus.* The new Soviet Man, as Stalin called this new social identity, would hold no allegiances to previous national identities but would demonstrate a consciousness amenable to the socialist program.

In the late 1920s Lemkin had not yet proposed the term genocide and would not coin the neologism until almost two decades later. Still, the origins of Lemkin's ideas can be traced to his early writings. What is striking is that Lemkin's focus was not on mass killing but rather on the way the social identities or national patterns of individuals and groups living in states was seen as a primary security concern for states and governments. By the time Lemkin published *Axis Rule*, he was ready to argue that the nature of armed conflict in the modern world had fundamentally changed. Warfare was no longer conducted between armies but between armies and populations. In his *History of Genocide*—an unfinished three-volume world history of genocide he was writing when he died—Lemkin traced the origins of this development in the colonial Spanish conquests in the Americas and the European conquests in South Asia and Africa. Modern warfare, he argued in *Axis Rule* and in his *History*, was defined by state (or state-like) actors using institutions, security forces, and armies to wage war against civilian populations, with the goal of transforming "the human element" of societies within the borders they sought to govern and rule (Irvin-Erickson, *Raphaël Lemkin* 77).

A second important development in Lemkin's ideas on genocide occurred in October 1933, when he authored a paper proposing the outlawing of the crimes of "barbarism" and "vandalism" under international humanitarian law at the League of Nations ("Akte der Barberei" 117-19). At that time, Lemkin wrote, his colleagues at the Association Internationale de Droit Pénal and many of his friends were discussing *Mein Kampf* and believed the German chancellor intended to carry out pogroms against Jews and institute a regime of biological national purity (*Totally Unofficial* 21). "Now was the time to outlaw the destruction of national, racial, and religious groups," Lemkin wrote, describing his sense of urgency to begin working with the Association (*Totally Unofficial* 22). Building on his works on the Soviet penal code, the proposal was Lemkin's first attempt to prevent the destruction of nations (Segesser and Gessler). He intended to deliver his paper at the Fifth Conference for the Unification of Penal Law in Madrid in 1933 (Lemkin, "Les Actes" 48-56).

Lemkin's paper listed five "new types of crimes," which he argued to be included as part of the laws of nations:

a) barbarity
b) vandalism
c) provoking catastrophes in international communication
d) disrupting international communication
e) spreading human, animal, or vegetable contagion.

In his text, Lemkin credited Vespasian V. Pella with creating the concepts of barbarity and vandalism, citing papers delivered by Pella and Henri Donnedieu de Vabres. Pella had used these concepts in his 1929 proposal to outlaw currency counterfeiting (Lewis 188).[6] Lemkin's writings gave the words theoretical content that Pella had not provided (see Jiménez de Asúa et al.). Scholars have shown that Lemkin's unique intellectual

[6] See League of Nations, *Proceedings of the International Conference for the Adoption of a Convention for the Suppression of Counterfeiting Currency, Geneva, April 9th to 20th, 1929* (Geneva), C.328.M.114.1929.II, pp. 52-55.

contribution was to apply the principles of universal jurisdiction to these new crimes, linking the legal conception of terrorism to the practice of state violence targeting national minorities. This was a direct response to the Nazi rise to power and SA (the so-called Brownshirts) terror unleashed against Jews in Germany, as well as Soviet terror (Kraft; also see Troebst).

Mark Lewis has suggested that Pella primarily wanted to use international law to protect the Versailles system of borders against the rising aggression of Hungarian and Italian nationalist movements and what he saw as a communist movement in the Soviet Union that would eventually threaten to engulf central European states. Lemkin, on the other hand, wanted to deal with the breakdown of the League of Nations system by expanding international criminal law to protect vulnerable minority populations from persecution and destruction, while extending international criminal law to cover crimes committed by state officials against their own populations in times of formal peace (Lewis 295; see also Müller; Troebst).

As he prepared for the conference in Madrid, Lemkin expected a "big fight" (*Totally Unofficial* 23). *Gazeta Warszawska* (*Warsaw Gazette*), an influential anti-Semitic Warsaw newspaper, came out against his paper in its 25 October 1933 issue after the conference. The newspaper accused Lemkin of acting in the interests of his Jewish race and not the Polish nation. At the time, Poland was seeking non-aggression pacts with both Stalin and Hitler. Wishing not to antagonize the two powers, the Polish government blocked Lemkin from leaving the country. In what appears to be a blatant case of antisemitism, Lemkin was denied travel documents and prevented from presenting his ideas.[7] Without his presence, his proposal to outlaw barbarity and vandalism was tabled without debate. Within weeks, Lemkin was forced to resign from his public posts.

In the paper Lemkin intended to deliver in Madrid, he articulated a need for international humanitarian law to prevent the purposeful destruction of works of culture that represented the specific genius of national and religious groups and to protect the physical and spiritual life of nations and people ("Les Actes"). He defined barbarism as the attempt to destroy ethnic, religious, or social collectivities. Lemkin also included in this category brutalities that strike at the lives and dignity of individuals as part of a campaign to exterminate the collectivity in which the victim is a member ("Les Actes"). A systematic and organized assault against whole populations, barbarism encompassed pogroms, massacres, mass rape, forced removal of populations, forced adoptions, and cruelties designed to

---

[7] Why Lemkin was prevented from going to Madrid is disputed. For varying accounts see Korey; Power; Szawłowski.

humiliate the victims, or even attempts to destroy the economic existence of the members of a collectivity in order to destroy the collectivity. Vandalism, Lemkin wrote, was an attack targeting a collectivity taking the form of a systematic and organized assault against the heritage or unique genius and achievements of a collectivity. Vandalism was the crime of destroying a group's cultural works, including libraries and art, but also their unique rituals, ceremonies, and beliefs. The cultural creations, arts, and traditions of each nation and culture contribute to the enrichment of all humanity, Lemkin reasoned, and therefore belong rightfully to all humanity ("Les Actes"). Lemkin insisted the two crimes were intertwined in the process of attacking the physical and spiritual existence of nations.[8]

Lemkin's crimes of "barbarism" and "vandalism" are almost identical in form to his descriptions of Soviet terror in his discussion of the Soviet penal code, as if Lemkin were attempting to create an international law in 1933 that would apply to the political and legal conditions in the USSR. Andrei Vyshinskii, the Procurator General of the Russian SFSR, recognized this immediately. Vyshinskii—who was the mastermind of Stalin's show trials, orchestrated Stalin's notorious great purge in 1937, and went on to serve as the Soviet Minister of Foreign Affairs—accused Lemkin of attempting to create international laws that specifically targeted the Soviet Union. A decade later, Vyshinskii would square off a second time against Lemkin at the United Nations. In 1933, however, the Russian prosecutor general would call Lemkin's barbarism and vandalism part of a larger plot that Lemkin had been spinning for years on behalf of the capitalist powers to ensnare the USSR in a web of international law that could threaten the vitality of the revolution.

Lemkin grouped laws on barbarity and vandalism together with laws against state terrorism, piracy, slavery, pornography, narcotics trade, counterfeiting money, disrupting international communication, and spreading human, animal, and vegetable contagions. Vyshinskii believed this grouping was a ruse and denounced Lemkin for inventing laws intended to target actions of the Soviet Union under the pretense of creating a neutral, apolitical body of unified international laws. In the introduction of a book by Aron Trainin covering the international movement for the unification of penal law, Vyshinskii wrote that the unification movement never mentioned actual struggles "with international crooks and charlatans of any stripe, not the fight with the bandits like Al Capone," but instead focused on abstract concepts like "terrorism" (4).[9] The

[8] Elsewhere, I have written about Lemkin's definition of nation. See Irvin-Erickson, "Genocide, the 'Family of Mind.'"

[9] I thank Gennadi Pobereżny for helping me translate this text.

concept of terrorism that these Western liberals claimed to be fighting, Vyshinskii continued, "turned into the central problem of the bourgeois unification movement" because it created the basis for limiting state sovereignty and "removing the state from its pedestal" (4). Vyshinskii went on to add that "no evasions and intricacies of such unifiers as Lemkin, who tried again to disguise the true purpose of the criminal interventionists with references to 'vandalism' and 'barbarism,' can mislead anybody," because "the true meaning of the unifiers' efforts is to legally and politically justify the right of the counter-revolutionary bourgeoisie to intervene in the internal affairs of any state, under the pretext that they are concerned for the fate of 'culture and civilization'" (4-5).

What was it that Vyshinskii found so objectionable in Lemkin's thinking? In the existing laws of nations, Lemkin wrote, there were three categories of humanitarian protections. The first category corresponded to attacks on individual rights and included laws against slavery and laws to prevent people from being treated as commodities. The second category of offences related to the individual and the collectivity, and essentially amounted to minority rights treaties that he believed were fully inadequate and morally fraught. The third category concerned the relationship between two or more collectivities and encompassed offences against the laws of nations that seek to protect peaceful relations between collectivities, such as outlawing propaganda intended to incite wars (Lemkin, "Les Actes"). In his proposal to outlaw barbarity and vandalism, Lemkin offered another type of violation—one that he believed was a hallmark of Soviet terror and the kinds of violence defining Nazi politics in Germany. This fourth category consisted of attacks committed against individuals with the intention of destroying a collectivity. In such cases, Lemkin wrote, the goal of the perpetrator is to harm an individual in a way that damaged the collectivity to which the individual belongs. These types of offences violate human rights, but also undermine the foundation of society (Lemkin, "Les Actes"). Yet in these matters, Lemkin believed, international law was silent precisely because the nature of armed conflict had changed with the rise of the horrors of colonial conflict in the nineteenth century and the advent of state security forces and armies across Europe that targeted their own civilians and treating minority populations as enemies of the state. As explained in *Axis Rule*, Lemkin intended to synthesize the ideas of "barbarism" and "vandalism" into the single conception of genocide.

PART 3: LEMKIN ON HUNGER AND GENOCIDE

If Lemkin defined genocide (and by extension "barbarism" and "vandalism") as the destruction of nations ("families of mind"), which involved the destruction or removal of the national pattern of the oppressed and the imposition of the national pattern of an oppressor—then it follows that Lemkin would be most concerned with acts that destroyed bonds of social solidarity that made group life and the social reproduction of groups possible. And indeed, this is precisely why Lemkin believed that in many cases, the destruction of libraries and the banning of folk traditions and religious customs could be acts of genocide, while large-scale acts of mass killing and massacres might not qualify as genocidal. What is so vicious about famine and hunger as a tool for committing genocide, Lemkin believed, is that this form of violence not only targeted large numbers of individuals but places the victims in competition with each other for their very survival. In turning the victims into enemies of one another, famine and hunger destroy the bonds of trust and solidarity within a society while inflicting permanent damage to the individual's sense of belonging and trust, which further serve to destroy the "family of mind."

In chapters 8 and 9 of *Axis Rule*, Lemkin noted that the first regulations against Jews issued across Europe were restrictions to their freedom of movement, property, and employment and the imposition of food rationing based on racial criteria. In Nazi-occupied Poland, Jews over the age of ten were required to wear a yellow Star of David on an armband, and laws were passed requiring all Jewish-owned enterprises and stores to have special signs visible to the public. Lemkin cited decrees such as a statewide ban on Jews using the Polish railroad, which accompanied new laws that physically removed Jews from public life and moved them into ghettos. In May 1941, a decree of the Führer implementing the 1935 Reich Nationality Code and the 1935 Act for the Protection of German Blood and German Honour in Poland concretized who would live and who would be consigned to die (Lemkin, *Axis Rule* 509). Lemkin established that these laws structured a set of interrelated developments that included racially motivated preferences in distributing food, the establishment of Jewish ghettos, the implementation of forced labour, and the development of concentration camps and extermination camps.

Lemkin argued in *Axis Rule* that Hitler and the Nazi Party had set out to commit genocide beginning in the 1930s, but the decision to kill the Jews and other victim groups *en masse* developed contingently as successive layers of laws and decrees and overlapping administrative structures shaped the political and social development of the genocide. He cited, for instance, Hermann Göring's 1941 order that people of German blood be given preference in access to foodstuffs (Lemkin, *Axis Rule* 87). Yet besides privileging Germans, the decree did not instruct the authorities on how to ration the food. Instead, the distribution of food corresponded to pre-existing administrative regulations. The dynamic consequence was that German nationals had retained one hundred percent of their dietary requirement of carbohydrates and ninety-seven percent of their protein needs across the occupied territories. Ethnic Czechs obtained ninety percent of their nutrition needs, followed in diminishing order by the Dutch, Belgians, Poles in the incorporated territory, and then Poles in the non-incorporated territories, who all were receiving around seventy percent of their nutrition needs. At the bottom of the list were ethnic Greeks, who obtained only thirty percent of their daily nutrition needs, and Jews, who were subsisting on only twenty percent of their daily food requirements. In the Warsaw ghettos—where the Nazis enforced strict control over the distribution of food and artificially inflated the price of grains—German nationals remained well fed, but anemia rose one hundred and thirteen percent amongst ethnic Poles, and four hundred and thirty-five percent among Jews (Lemkin, *Axis Rule* 88).

Lemkin saw this discrimination in access to food as an element of a larger pattern of endangering the health of "undesired national groups" (*Axis Rule* 88n2). The occupying administrations throughout Europe withheld firewood and medicine from non-Germans in winter. In Poland during the fall of 1940, Hermann Göring decreed that all citizens of the former Polish state who did not have German blood had to turn over their property to the German occupying authorities (Lemkin, *Axis Rule* 511-16). During the winter of 1940-41, low-level officials requisitioned warm clothing, blankets, and heating fuel from Jews (Lemkin, *Axis Rule* 88). The efforts to physically endanger the health of the Jews was bolstered by the conditions in the ghettos where they were forced to live in crowded, inadequate housing. There were laws mandating that Jews who left the ghetto looking for food or shelter could be executed (Lemkin, *Axis Rule* 75). Prohibited from leaving the ghetto, Jews were thereby "denied the use of public parks" and "denied the right of fresh air," which was "especially pernicious to the health of children," Lemkin wrote (*Axis Rule* 88).

In Lemkin's analysis, the various techniques of genocide were always intertwined—whether they were physical or non-physical, or whether they were acts of direct violence or indirect, structural, and cultural violence. As such, Lemkin certainly saw both the physical death and the deterioration of the physical health of the targeted victims as acts intended to destroy the victim group. However, he was far more concerned with the destruction of Jewish social institutions and the effect of this destruction on the social cohesion and physical well-being of the Jewish "nation," or the Jewish "family of mind." Forcing Jews into the ghettos, in Lemkin's analysis, had brought about a near total annihilation of Jewish social life. Crowding, hunger, poor sanitation, and a violent typhus epidemic led to a twenty percent death rate, the disintegration of social solidarity, and the end of customs, traditions, and rites. The Jewish Council, or Judenrat, he argued, was used to shatter the bonds of the Jewish nation, as council members carried out Nazi directives targeting fellow Jews and were instructed to select which neighbours were sent to death camps, lest they themselves be killed. The Jewish Councils, and the slow deprivation of food and basic resources needed to sustain life, meant that the victims were now in competition with each other for survival. Victims viewed fellow victims as their enemies in conflict, which achieved two things for the perpetrators. First, it redirected resistance away from the perpetrators, and second, in turning victims against each other, it accelerated the destruction of the victim group, both physically and sociologically.

It should be noted that it is not true that the Germans succeeded in reducing the Jews in ghettos to social-less beings (Corni). Still, many scholars have since substantiated what Lemkin gleaned from rumours and Nazi decrees: that waves of refugees, starvation, and disease did unravel social customs and cultural rituals, causing social cohesion and solidarity to break down in the Jewish ghettos across Europe (Goldberg 91-92). But this did not mean that Jewish social life or culture disintegrated in the ghettos. Lemkin knew there were resistance movements and armed uprisings (Norman Davies), but he did not know that many council members willingly accompanied their family members to the camps, refused to collaborate, or sabotaged Nazi plans (Trunk). He also did not know that underground support networks were set up to hide those most vulnerable to Nazi purges and to distribute contraband: food, fuel, and weapons (Gutman). Nevertheless, Lemkin believed that ghetto life had proven that the social, cultural, moral, and ultimately the physical and biological techniques of genocide could be orchestrated through very simple political and economic levers that deprived people of basic food and shelter. For this reason, Lemkin gave special attention to the laws governing economic life, for he believed they demonstrated that the seemingly disparate laws and decrees of the Axis rule actually formed an overlapping network orientated toward the destruction of national diversity. In this sense, the social and political aspect of ghetto life was not unique to the ghetto but a central facet of the broader genocide throughout the lands under Axis occupation. In the Netherlands, for instance, a provision to prevent Jews from opening bank accounts excluded them from the economy and undermined their social basis (Lemkin, *Axis Rule* 76). Across Europe, Lemkin demonstrated that Axis occupiers forbade Jews from being employed, prevented Jews from receiving state unemployment benefits, and made it illegal for Jews to receive money, food, and shelter from non-Jews. In the German-occupied Russian territories, Lemkin documented taxes that were put in place that essentially mandated that the salary paid to Jews would be entirely redirected to the state (*Axis Rule* 311). Even though these examples did not involve physically putting people in actual ghettos, the genocidal principle was the same, according to Lemkin. Jews were materially marginalized while the bonds of social solidarity were strained, with the goal of undermining the social basis of group life. In terms of hunger as a weapon of genocide, when life becomes a "daily fight literally for bread and physical survival," Lemkin wrote, "thinking in both general and national terms" becomes impossible as families, friends, neighbours, and communities begin to compete for food (*Axis Rule* 85). This destruction of group life, the shattering of these social bonds built on love and trust amongst family members and friends, cripples the ability of the victim group as a whole to fulfill the "cultural-spiritual requirements" of group life (Lemkin, *Axis Rule* 85). In such conditions, nations as families of mind could hardly exist. Hunger as a tactic for committing genocide not only killed people—it was a most effective means of destroying the national patterns of the targeted group.

PART 4: UKRAINE

In 1953, Lemkin spoke on the Ukrainian genocide at a commemoration of the Great Ukrainian Famine, known as the Holodomor (Luciuk; Serbyn, "Lemkin on Genocide"; Lemkin, *Soviet Genocide in the Ukraine*). Written two decades after the famine, the speech demonstrates the extent to which Lemkin's analysis of Soviet atrocities aligned with his early analysis of the Soviet terror, his work on barbarity and vandalism, and indeed his theory of genocide as the destruction of nations as "families of mind." The speech, delivered in 1953, should therefore be understood within the context of Lemkin's political and legal analysis of the Soviet regime that he developed in the early 1930s (Troebst).

In this speech, Lemkin considered Stalin's attempt to starve the peasantry as the most brutal attack against the Ukrainian nation. But the famine, for Lemkin, was the third stage in what he called a "four-pronged" genocide of the Ukrainian family of mind (Serbyn, "Ukrainian Famine"). "The first blow" of the genocide against the Ukrainian nation was "aimed at the intelligentsia, the national brain, so as to paralyze the rest of the body," he wrote (Lemkin, "Soviet Genocide" 3). Here, Lemkin was primarily addressing the Soviet targeting of individuals with violence and terror with the intention of destroying the social fabric of Ukrainian group life. "In 1920, 1926, and again in 1930-33, teachers, writers, artists, thinkers, [and] political leaders, were liquidated, imprisoned or deported . . . . 51,713 intellectuals were sent to Siberia in 1931 alone . . . . At least 114 major poets, writers and artists, the most prominent cultural leaders of the nation, have met the same fate" (Lemkin, "Soviet Genocide" 1; also see Serbyn, "Lemkin on Genocide of Nations" and Irvin-Erickson, "Genocide, the 'Family of Mind'"). What made these attacks genocidal was not that Stalin's regime killed so many people but that these individuals were killed with the purpose of destroying a distinctly Ukrainian "national pattern" or "family of mind."

A central concern for Lemkin in *Axis Rule* was the notion that the killing of individuals becomes genocide only when their killing contributes to the destruction of a group. He wrote that the object of genocide is to "annihilate the group themselves" through the "disintegration of the political and social institution of the culture, language, national feelings, religion, and the economic existence of national groups, and the destruction of the personal security, liberty, health, dignity, and even the lives of the individuals belonging to such groups" (Lemkin, *Axis Rule* 79). As discussed earlier, genocide could, in Lemkin's terms, be committed through what we might call indirect violence or structural violence, in addition to direct violence. In Lemkin's 1953 address during the commemoration of the Ukrainian famine, for example, he placed the Soviet genocide with the context of acts of the Soviet state intended to dismantle the functioning of the Ukrainian Orthodox and Ukrainian Catholic churches. This attempt to destroy the institution of the Ukrainian church—through arrests, forced conversion, disbanding, and killing—was the "second prong" of the genocide:

> Going along with this attack on the intelligentsia was an offensive against the churches, priests and hierarchy, the "soul" of Ukraine. Between 1926 and 1932, the Ukrainian Orthodox Autocephalous Church, its Metropolitan (Lypkivsky) and ten thousand clergy were liquidated. In 1945, when the Soviets established themselves in Western Ukraine, a similar fate was meted out to the Ukrainian Catholic Church. That Russification was the only issue involved is clearly demonstrated by the fact that before its liquidation, the Church was offered the opportunity to join the Russian Patriarch at Moscow, the Kremlin's political tool. (Lemkin, "Soviet Genocide" 3)

Simply "for the crime of being Ukrainian,"

> the Church itself was declared a society detrimental to the welfare of the Soviet state, its members were marked down in the Soviet police files as potential "enemies of the people." As a matter of fact, with the exception of 150,000 members in Slovakia, the Ukrainian Catholic Church has been officially liquidated, its hierarchy imprisoned, its clergy dispersed and deported. (Lemkin, "Soviet Genocide" 4)

Lemkin considered the Soviet assault on the Ukrainian clergy and intellectuals as genocidal because they are "attacks on the Soul" of the people that will continue to have a serious effect on the Brain of Ukraine, for it is the families of the clergy that have traditionally supplied a large part of the intellectuals, while the priests themselves have been the leaders of the villages, their wives the heads of the charitable organizations. The religious orders ran schools and took care of much of the organized charities. (Lemkin, "Soviet Genocide" 4)

Lemkin's language of genocide as targeting the "soul" and the "brain" of a national group has been criticized as archaic and illiberal and has been interpreted to mean that he believed "that the murder of a poet is morally worse than the murder of a janitor, because the 'brain' without the 'body' cannot function" (Jones 11). While this is certainly a valid criticism, it should be remembered that Lemkin defined genocide "as directed against the national group as an entity," not individuals in their individual capacity (*Axis Rule* 79). Lemkin therefore considered the repression of the Ukrainian peasantry and its cultural and social intuitions to be as genocidal as the destruction of the Ukrainian intelligentsia and the Ukrainian church as long as the destruction of these social institutions, including the arrests and deaths of hundreds of individuals, was intended to destroy the Ukrainian "family of mind." Consider the following passage from Lemkin's speech on the Ukrainian genocide:

> The third prong of the Soviet plan was aimed at the farmers, the large mass of independent peasants who are the repository of the tradition, folklore and music, the national language and literature, the national spirit, of Ukraine. The weapon used against this body is perhaps the most terrible of all—starvation. (Lemkin, "Soviet Genocide" 4-5)

Lemkin called the famine in Ukraine "the highpoint of Soviet cruelty" and took to task those who accepted unquestioningly "a Soviet economic policy connected with the collectivization of wheat lands" and thus dismissed the death of five million peasants ("Soviet Genocide" 5). He concluded by quoting Soviet government officials: "As a Soviet politician Kosior declared in *Izvestiia* on 2 December 1933, 'Ukrainian nationalism is our chief danger,' and it was to eliminate that nationalism, to establish the horrifying uniformity of the Soviet state that the Ukrainian peasantry was sacrificed" (Lemkin, "Soviet Genocide" 5).

For Lemkin, the interests involved were simple: the Soviet regime sought the "Russification" of the region in order to facilitate the rule of their state. The Ukrainian national identity, as distinct from a Russian identity, he argued, was a threat to the Soviet state and to the regime because the patterns of economic organization undertaken by people who held Ukrainian national identities were antithetical to the form of economic organization promoted by the state.[10] For Lemkin, the Soviet interest in, and intention to commit, genocide was clear. The Ukrainians, with their ethnic traditions that pre-disposed them to pre-capitalist forms of economic social organization, made them bad Soviet citizens who resisted integration into the "modern" socialist economy. But Lemkin was also clear that grand visions of economic reform were not the only motivators of this genocide; the genocide against Ukraine generated income for the Soviet state: "A famine was necessary for the Soviets and so they got one to order, by plan, through an unusually high grain allotment to the state as taxes," Lemkin wrote. "Much of this crop, so vital to the lives of the Ukrainian people, ended up as exports for the creation of credits abroad" (Lemkin, "Soviet Genocide" 5).

In Lemkin's assessment, these three "prongs" in the "systematic destruction of the Ukrainian nation, in its progressive absorption within the new Soviet nation" made the Soviet actions genocide (Lemkin, "Soviet Genocide" 6). While "there have been no attempts at complete annihilation, such as was the method of the German attack on the Jews," Lemkin wrote,

> if the Soviet programme succeeds completely, if the intelligentsia, the priests and the peasants can be eliminated, Ukraine will be as dead as if every Ukrainian were killed, for it will have lost that part of it which has kept and developed its culture, its beliefs, its common ideas, which have guided it and given it a soul, which, in short, made it a nation rather than a mass of people. ("Soviet Genocide" 6-7)

Emphasizing the social destruction wrought by the famine, as hunger shattered social institutions, Lemkin stated, "If for no other reason than this human suffering, we would have to condemn this road to unity as criminal. But there is more to it than that. This is not simply a case of mass murder. It is a case of genocide, of destruction, not of individuals only, but of a culture and a nation" ("Soviet Genocide" 8).

The "fourth prong" of the genocide, Lemkin wrote, was the "fragmentation of the Ukrainian people" when after the social destruction caused by the famine, non-Ukrainians were resettled into the Ukrainian republic ("Soviet Genocide" 8). By the end of his speech, he returned to the idea that the annihilation of the nation and the Soviet attempt to destroy Ukrainian national patterns caused an irreplaceable loss to world civilization:

---

[10] Lemkin appears to be conflating Soviet with Russian.

> If it were possible to do this even without suffering we would still be driven to condemn it, for the family of minds, the unity of ideas, of language and of customs that form what we call a nation that constitutes one of the most important of all our means of civilization and progress. It is true that nations blend together and form new nations—we have an example of this process in our own country—but this blending consists in the pooling of benefits of superiorities that each culture possesses. What then, apart from the very important question of human suffering and human rights that we find wrong with Soviet plans, is the criminal waste of civilization and of culture. For the Soviet national unity is being created, not by any union of ideas and of cultures, but by the complete destruction of all cultures and of all ideas save one—the Soviet. (Lemkin, "Soviet Genocide" 8)

Works Cited

Annus, Epp. "The Problem of Soviet Colonialism in the Baltics." *Journal of Baltic Studies*, vol. 43, no. 1, 2012, pp. 21-45. DOI: 10.1080/01629778.2011.628551

Bauer, Otto. *The Question of Nationalities and Social Democracy*. Edited by Ephraim J. Nimni, translated by Joseph O'Donnell, Minnesota UP, 2000.

Bronner, Stephen Eric. *The Bigot: Why Prejudice Persists*. Yale UP, 2014.

Corni, Gustavo. *Hitler's Ghettos: Voices from a Beleaguered Society 1939-1944*. Arnold, 2002.

Davies, Norman. *Rising '44: The Battle for Warsaw*. Viking, 2004.

Davies, R. W., and S. G. Wheatcroft. *The Industrialization of the Soviet State.* Vol. 5: *The Years of Hunger: Soviet Agriculture, 1931-1933*, Palgrave, 2004.

Davies, R. W., et al. "Stalin, Grain Stocks, and the Famine of 1932-1933." *Slavic Review*, vol. 54, no. 3, 1995, pp. 642-57. DOI: 10.2307/2501740

Feierstein, Daniel. *Genocide as Social Practice: Reorganizing Society under the Nazis and Argentina's Military Juntas*. Translated by Douglas Andrew Town, Rutgers UP, 2014.

Galtung, Johan. "Violence, Peace, and Peace Research." *Journal of Peace Research*, vol. 6, no. 3, 1969, pp. 167-91.

Goldberg, Amos. "The History of Jews in the Ghettos: A Cultural Perspective." *The Holocaust and Historical Methodology*, edited by Dan Stone, Berghahn Books, 2012, pp. 79-100.

Gutman, Israel. *The Jews of Warsaw, 1939-1943: Ghetto, Underground, Revolt*. Indiana UP, 1982.

Irvin-Erickson, Douglas. "Genocide Discourses: American and Russian Strategic Narratives of Conflict in Iraq and Ukraine." *Politics and*

Governance, vol. 5, no. 3, 2017, pp. 130-45. DOI: 10.17645/pag.v5i3.1015.

---. "Genocide, the 'Family of Mind' and the Romantic Signature of Raphael Lemkin." *Journal of Genocide Research*, vol. 15, no. 3, 2013, pp. 273-96. DOI: 10.1080/14623528.2013.821222.

---. *Raphaël Lemkin and the Concept of Genocide*. Pennsylvania UP, 2017.

Jiménez de Asúa, Luis, et al., editors. *Actes de la Vème Conférence Internationale pour l'Unification du Droit Pénal (Madrid 14-20 Octobre 1933)*. A. Pedone, 1935.

Jones, Adam. *Genocide: A Comprehensive Introduction*. Routledge, 2006.

Korey, William. *An Epitaph for Raphael Lemkin*. Jacob Blaustein Institute for the Advancement of Human Rights, 2001.

Kornat, Marek. "Polish Interpretations of Bolshevism and Totalitarian Systems (1918-1939)." *Totalitarian and Authoritarian Regimes in Europe: Legacies and Lessons from the Twentieth Century*, edited by Jerzy W. Borejsza et al., Berghahn Books, 2006, pp. 80-105.

Korostelina, Karina. "Crimean Tatars From Mass Deportation to Hardship in Occupied Crimea." *Genocide Studies and Prevention*, vol. 9, no. 1, 2015, pp. 33-47. DOI: 10.5038/1911-9933.9.1.1319

Kraft, Claudia. "Nationalisierende Transnationalisierung: (Inter)nationale Strafrechtswissenschaft in der Zwischenkriegszeit." *Leipziger Zugänge zur Rechtlichen, Politischen und Kulturellen Verflechtungsgeschichte Ostmitteleuropas*, edited by Dietmar Müller and Adamantios Skordos, Leipziger Universitätsverlag, 2015, pp. 15-26.

Lemkin, Raphael (Raphaël Lemkin). "Akte der Barbarei und des Vandalismus als Delicta Juris Gentium." *Anwaltsblatt Internationales*, vol. 19, 1933, pp. 117-19.

---. *Autobiography*. Raphael Lemkin Papers, Manuscript Collection 1730, Manuscript and Archives Division, New York Public Library, Reel 2, Box 1, Folder 36, "Introduction."

---. *Axis Rule in Occupied Europe: Laws of Occupation, Analysis of Government, Proposals for Redress*. Carnegie Endowment for International Peace, 1944.

---. "Les Actes Constituant un Danger General (interétatique) Considerés Comme Delits du Droit des Gens." *Actes de la Vème Conférence Internationale pour l'Unification du Droit Pénal (Madrid 14-20 Octobre 1933)*, edited by Jimenez de Asua, et al., A. Pedone, 1935, pp. 48-56.

---. "Soviet Genocide in the Ukraine." New York Public Library, Reel 3, Box 2, Folder 16, pp. 1-8.

---. *Soviet Genocide in the Ukraine*. Edited by L. Y. Luciuk, Kashtan Press, 2014.

---. *Totally Unofficial: The Autobiography of Raphael Lemkin*. Edited by Donna-Lee Frieze, Yale UP, 2013.

Lemkin, Rafał (Raphaël Lemkin). "Dzieje i charakter reform karnego we Włoszech." *Kodeks karny faszystowski Włochy*, Nakladem Ksiegarni F. Hoesicka, 1929, pp. 7-89.

---. *Kodeks karny Rosji Sowieckiej 1927*. Sklad Glowny w Ksiegarni F. Hoesicka, 1928.

---, and Tadeusz Kochanowicz. *Kodeks karny republik sowieckich*. Wyd. Sem. Prawa kar., 1926.

---. "Ustawodawstwo karne Rosji Sowieckiej, Kodeks karny, procedura karna." *Encyklopedja podręczna prawa karnego*, edited by Wacław Makowski, vol. 25, 1938, pp. 1581-87.

Lewis, Mark. *The Birth of the New Justice: The Internationalization of Crime and Punishment, 1919-1950*. Oxford UP, 2014.

Luciuk, Lubomyr Y. *Holodomor: Reflections on the Great Famine of 1932-1933 in Soviet Ukraine*. Kashtan Press, 2008.

Müller, Dietmar. "Zu den Anfägen des Völkerstrafrechts: Vespasian Pella und Raphael Lemkin." *Leipziger Zugänge zur Rechtlichen, Politischen und Kulturellen Verflechtungsgeschichte Ostmitteleuropas*, edited by Dietmar Müller and Adamantios Skordos, Leipziger Universitätsverlag, 2015, pp. 27-40.

Naimark, Norman. *Stalin's Genocides*. Princeton UP, 2010.

Nimni, Ephraim. *Marxism and Nationalism: Theoretical Origins of a Political Crisis*. Pluto Press, 1989.

Power, Samantha. *A Problem from Hell: America and the Age of Genocide*. Basic Books, 2002.

Rabinbach, Anson. "The Challenge of the Unprecedented—Raphael Lemkin and the Concept of Genocide." *Jahrbuch des Simon-Dubnow-Instituts*, vol. 4, 2005, pp. 397-420.

Renner, Karl. "State and Nation." *National Cultural Autonomy and Its Contemporary Critics*, edited by Ephraim Nimni, Routledge, 2005, pp. 15-47.

Segesser, Marc Daniel, and Myriam Gessler. "Raphael Lemkin and the International Debate on the Punishment of War Crimes (1919-1948)." *Journal of Genocide Research*, vol. 7, no. 4, 2005, pp. 453-68. DOI: 10.1080/14623520500349902

Serbyn, Roman. "Lemkin on Genocide of Nations." *Journal of International Criminal Justice*, vol. 7, no. 1, 2009, pp. 123-30. DOI: 10.1093/jicj/mqp002

---. "The Ukrainian Famine of 1932-1933 as Genocide in the Light of the UN Convention of 1948." *The Ukrainian Quarterly*, vol. 62, no. 2, 2006, pp. 181-94.

Szawłowski, Ryszard. "Raphael Lemkin's Life Journey: From Creative Legal Scholar and Well-to-Do Lawyer in Warsaw until 1939 to Pinnacle of International Achievements during the 1940s in the States, Ending Penniless Crusader in New York in the 1950s." *Rafał Lemkin: A Hero of Humankind*, edited by Agnieszka Bieńczyk-Missala and Sławomir Dębski, The Polish Institute of International Affairs, 2010, pp. 31-58.

Troebst, Stefan. "Lemkin and Lauterpacht in Lemberg and Later: Pre- and Post-Holocaust Careers of Two East European International Lawyers." *Institut für die Wissenschaften vom Menschen*, 2013, http://www.iwm.at/read-listen-watch/transit-online/lemkin-and-lauterpacht-in-lemberg-and-later-pre-and-post-holocaust-careers-of-two-east-european-international-lawyers/#_ftnref27. Accessed 6 Nov. 2020.

Trunk, Isaiah. *Judenrat: The Jewish Councils in Eastern Europe under Nazi Occupation*. Stein and Day, 1977.

United Nations Convention on the Prevention and Punishment of the Crime of Genocide. *United Nations*, 9 Dec. 1948, https://www.un.org/en/genocideprevention/documents/atrocity-crimes/Doc.1_Convention%20on%20the%20Prevention%20and%20Punishment%20of%20the%20Crime%20of%20Genocide.pdf. Accessed 5 Nov. 2020.

von Hagen, Mark. "From Imperial Russia to Colonial Ukraine." *The Shadow of Colonialism on Europe's Modern Past*, edited by R. Healy and E. D. Lago, Palgrave, 2014, pp. 173-93. Cambridge Imperial and Post-Colonial Studies Series.

Vyshinskii, A. Ia. "Predislovie." *Ugolovnaia interventsiia. Dvizhenie po unifikatsii ugolovnogo zakonodatel'stva kapitalisticheskikh stran*, by A. N. Trainin, Gosudarstvennoe Izdatel'stvo Sovetskoe Zakonodatel'stvo OGIZ, 1935, pp. 3-6.

Weiss-Wendt, Anton. *The Soviet Union and the Gutting of the UN Genocide Convention*. Wisconsin UP, 2017.

Index